It's Not F

CW00407384

Rick Brindle

Rick Brindle was born in Dorset, England, to an Army family. He was educated in Germany, then returned to the UK, working mainly in pubs before joining the RAF Regiment for three years. Afterwards, he trained as a nurse. He is currently working on his next novel.

Also by Rick Brindle:

Cold Steel on the Rocks

We Are Cold Steel

Cold Steel and the Underground Boneyard

It's Not For Everyone

For Linda
Because nothing else matters

Glossary

2iC – Second in charge. The deputy commanding officer of a squadron, usually a flight lieutenant.

66mm – Sometimes referred to as a LAW, Light anti-Armour Weapon. A single-use rocket launcher. By 1989 it was no good against armour but was an excellent infantry weapon against trenches and bunkers.

4001 Flight – Also known as Training Support Flight, a loose collection of gunners that supported the instructors.

AC – Aircraftman. A recruit's rank on joining the RAF, rising to LAC, leading aircraftman, on successful completion of trade training.

ACSK – Anti Camel Spider Knife.

Adjutant – An officer based on HQ Flight. I was never sure what an adjutant actually did, but every squadron had one.

AGM – Air-to-ground missile.

Basha – A basic tent made from stretching bungees between two tree trunks, then throwing an issue poncho over the bungees.

Beasting – Subjecting someone to a particularly harsh regime of physical endurance, such as a very long run in full kit, multiple river crossing or sleep deprivation. A beasting is considered to be over and above what one would normally expect in a given situation.

Bergen – A military rucksack. There are many different types and designs. In the late '80s and early '90s the American ALICE pack and British Berghaus Cyclops Roc were the most widely known and used.

3

Best blues/No. 1 dress – Uniform worn for ceremonial duties and any disciplinary procedures. A lot of guys also got married in their best blues.

BFA – Blank Firing Attachment. A metal tool that was usually painted yellow and fitted over the end of a rifle barrel. It allows for weapon functionality when using blank rounds.

BFG – British Forces Germany.

Blatting – Firing, shooting.

Blue on blue – Taking casualties from friendly fire.

Cadre – A small group of instructors and trainees.

Cambrian Patrol – A super-hard patrolling competition in Wales, held every year.

CEFO – Complete Equipment Fighting Order: Webbing and personal weapon.

CEMO – Complete Equipment Marching Order: Webbing, Bergen or large pack and personal weapon.

CFT – Combat Fitness Test. 10km timed run with webbing and weapon, then a 100m man-carry with two weapons.

Chiefy A – Flight sergeant, A Flight.

CO – Commanding officer.

CS – Also known as tear gas, and more recently, mace. Used as crowd control and also to simulate a chemical attack. Every recruit will breathe in CS during Basic Training.

CTA – Catterick Training Area.

CVR(T) – Combat Vehicle Reconnaissance (Tracked), including the Scorpion light tank and Spartan Armoured Personnel Carrier. For a few years, they were used by the RAF Regiment's field squadrons.

DP – Disruptive Pattern, or camouflage. The British pattern of camouflage at the time was called Disruptive Pattern Material, commonly referred to DPM. The RAF Regiment shortened it to DP.

D by P – Discharge by Purchase. If you wanted to leave the RAF while still a recruit, you had to pay about a week's wages, and you were a civilian within days.

Dragunov – A Russian-made sniper rifle.

DZ patch – 'Drop Zone'. A square badge, measuring about 10cm across, with an identifying symbol, either unit colours or an emblem. The RAF Regiment's DZ patches predominantly showed a squadron crest.

Endex – Officially, the end of the exercise, but adopted throughout the forces as the end of any given situation. The end of the deployment, the end of your service, the end of the night out. The end, game over.

Eng Flight – Engineering Flight. A flight of mechanics and technicians, non-Regiment trained, but assigned to each squadron to maintain and repair the equipment.

FIBUA – Fighting in Built-Up Areas.

Flight – A body of airmen or women, anything from twenty- to fifty-strong.

Four tonner – A Bedford truck with off-road ability and a four-tonne cargo capacity. It could also be fitted with benches for troop transport.

FRV – Final Rendezvous, the last checkpoint on a patrol before returning back to your base position.

Gash – Useless, no good.

GDT – Ground Defence Training, taught to all recruits at Swinderby.

GPMG – General Purpose Machine Gun. Universally known as the Gimpy. A 7.62mm belt-fed British-made version of the FN-MAG. A very highly regarded weapon within the Regiment.

Grouping – Gunners tended to fire five round groups when on the range, and the diameter of each group on the target was measured left to right and up and down. For example, you may have scored a two-inch grouping, dead centre, if you were really good. The idea was to get the smallest grouping, and also in the right place.

Gunner – Trade name for airmen in the RAF Regiment.

'Guin – Shortened, more common term of Penguin.

Hercules – C-130 Hercules, the RAF's transport plane in the '90s.

Jankers – A military punishment, usually but not limited to being confined to barracks, performing tedious and often pointless tasks, and being subjected to frequent uniform inspections.

Jaguar – An Anglo-French strike aircraft. Primarily used by the RAF and French Air Force, but also successfully exported.

LAC – Leading aircraftman, the first rank on successful completion of trade training. LACs could typically expect to remain at that rank for the first calendar year of service. Roughly equivalent to a private in the army.

Loadie – Air loadmaster. Aircrew responsible for the aircraft's cargo, human or otherwise.

LSW – Light Support Weapon. A longer-barrelled version of the SA80, fitted with a bipod. It replaced the GPMG as a section weapon.

Lux – Really good.

Make ready – Pulling the working parts of a weapon to the rear by means of a bolt. Sometimes referred to as 'cocking' the weapon. Pull the trigger after you've made ready, and it'll fire. Making ready with live ammunition was extremely rare. Usually reserved for war, the rifle range, Northern Ireland, or a mistake.

Maverick – A very commonly used AGM, and in most wars, possibly by both sides.

MFT – Military Field Training, the final training exercise at Swinderby.

MP5 – Heckler and Koch Maschinenpistole 5, a lux small arm, used by many units around the world, including the SAS, Bahrain Police and Hans Gruber's Nakatomi Towers team.

MT – Motor transport.

NAAFI – Navy Army and Air Force Institutes. A government-run company that provides recreational facilities for forces' personnel and dependents, including bars, clubs, cafés, restaurants. NAAFI clubs and bars were out of bounds to officers.

NBC – Nuclear, Chemical and Biological. The nightmare scenario of modern warfare.

NFI – Not fucking interested.

NI Gloves – Northern Ireland gloves. They were black leather gloves, initially issued to soldiers on patrol in built-up areas. In 1989 they were state-of-the-art items of kit.

Nosebag – Food, meal.

7

OCA – Officer commanding A Flight, typically a flying officer, but could also be a pilot officer or a flight lieutenant.

OGs – Olive-green trousers, lightweight. They were called lightweights in the army. I'm not sure what the marines called them.

Operation Granby – Britain's military operations in the Gulf, 1990–1991.

Oppo – Opposite, or opposite number. A commonly used term for colleague, or member of the same team.

Passing out – Passing or finishing a training course, often accompanied by a parade. It's quite common for participants to faint if they've been on parade for a long time, which may be where the term came from.

Penguin – Slang term used by the RAF Regiment to describe non-Regiment members of the RAF.

Peri-track – Perimeter track. A road that circled the outermost boundary of most airfields, which in most cases was several miles.

Pre-para – A two-week selection course before being accepted onto 2 Squadron, the Regiment's airborne unit. It's considered to be equivalent to the army's P Company. Those who've actually got their wings are best placed to decide which selection course, if either, is tougher than the other.

Phys – An all-encompassing, non-descript term for physical exercise in any form.

Poncho – Old-style waterproof garment that went over the head and supposedly kept you dry. By 1989, you were told to seal up the hood with a cord and use it to make a basha.

PT – Physical training.

PTI – Physical training instructor.

PVR – Premature Voluntary Release. Buying yourself out of the military.

Queen's Colour Squadron (QCS) – An RAF Regiment ceremonial squadron that represents the RAF on official engagements. Their standards of drill are world class.

RAF Regiment – The RAF's own 'army'. Trained to defend air bases against enemy attack, and to capture enemy ones.

Rapier – A short-range surface-to-air missile system used by the RAF Regiment and Royal Artillery.

Respirator – Gas mask.

Rock/Rockape – Military slang for RAF Regiment.

RTS(B) – Regiment Training Squadron (Basics). The training block for Basic gunners. Signals training was also based there, for both recruits and also Command Post Signaller courses.

SA80 – A 5.56mm bullpup rifle used by the British military from the late '80s.

SAC – Senior aircraftman, the next rank up from LAC, usually achieved after one year's service. Still roughly equivalent to a private in the army, but maybe a senior one. The next rank is corporal, and most SACs in the Regiment would serve for several years before making corporal.

Scuffer – Slang term for RAF Police.

SHORAD – Short-Range Air Defence.

SLR – Self-Loading Rifle. A 7.62mm British-made version of the FN-FAL.

Spacey – Space cadet, slang term for air cadets. Like the army cadets, but an air force version.

Sprog – Someone either very new to the unit, very inexperienced, or both.

Stag, stagging – Sentry duty, usually in a harbour or defensive position.

Stim – Canned, non-alcoholic drink.

SUSAT – Sight Unit Small Arms Trilux. A 4x magnification optical sight used on small arms.

SWO – Squadron warrant officer. The senior of all senior NCOs on a squadron, and a man with the absolute power of God.

TA – Territorial Army. The army's part-time reserve troops. Civilians who trained with the army at weekends but became regular units in times of war.

Tab – Tactical Advance to Battle. The term is also used by the Parachute Regiment, while the Royal Marines prefer 'Yomp'.

TC – Tactical controller, stands next to the Rapier operator and controls the kit, tells the operator when to fire. Usually a corporal or a sergeant.

T's and A's – Tests and Adjustments, daily checks on the Rapier kit to make sure all the component parts are speaking to each other. T's and A's also ensured that the missile fired when you pushed the button and went where you wanted it to go. Similar to zeroing your rifle.

Thunderflash – It's called a flashbang in computer games. A handheld pyrotechnic that simulates a grenade with a really load bang.

U/S – Unserviceable.

Webbing – A set of pouches attached to a thick belt that carries equipment such as ammunition, rations, water, respirator. Usually attached to a yolk that goes over the shoulders and distributes the weight more evenly.

WO – Warrant officer.

WRAF – Women's Royal Air Force.

Prologue

In *Skyfall,* James Bond tells Eve Moneypenny that fieldwork isn't for everyone. And that's a rocking good example of art imitating life, because it's not just fieldwork at MI6: the RAF Regiment isn't for everyone, either.

It definitely wasn't for me.

And yes, plenty enough guys (and now girls) have made it their best-ever decision, and they've thrived. And massive respect to every single one of them.

But it didn't, and doesn't, work for everyone who joins. And if that happens, then watch out, because even the armed forces would admit they're not the best in the world at trying to put a square peg into a round hole.

That's when the trouble starts. I know because a square peg is exactly what I was.

It might seem obvious to most people, and it was said to me on many occasions, but personality plays a big part in a successful military career, and mine was one hundred per cent wrong. I was an individual, and the military isn't about individuals. It's also not about independent thought, questioning the way things are. It's about fitting in, complying and doing as you're told. I was way too much of a loner for it to have ever worked.

So why didn't I see it coming? Why did I join in the first place? Well, pull up a sandbag, swing that oil lamp, and I'll tell you.

It didn't matter that I wasn't compatible; it was still inevitable. My father, stepfather and grandfather all served their whole lives in the army, and until I was eighteen I'd lived most of my life as an army dependant in Germany. What else did I know? What else was I going to do? My entire world and upbringing had an armed forces stamp on it. Even where I lived. In Germany, whole estates were set aside to house British servicemen and their families, and inside all of the generic houses and flats were the same furniture, curtains, beds, chairs and carpets. Everything was the same, and everything was provided.

This realm of uniformity was mixed up with a lot of house moves, typically every two to three years. It was an entire population in transit, with people coming and going all the time.

And if you're the one who's serving, when it's your job, you kind of accept it. But when you're growing up in that system, there's all sorts of baggage. You land somewhere new, make friends, develop relationships, and just when you're settled and starting to put down roots, it's time to pack your bags and move somewhere else. At the time, everybody I knew lived like that, and I didn't know anything else. It was only in later years that I realised how damaging it was, at least for me. I was always shy, my social skills weren't good and it took me a long time to establish myself. But as soon as I did, my dad got his next posting, it was time to move home and I had to do the whole thing all over again.

The end result was that I was quite happy with my own company and didn't really do the group thing very well (military compatibility problem number one). Despite the close-knit community I lived in, I had a small circle of friends.

But it was also all I knew, and as well as not knowing any different, it was a very privileged, very sheltered lifestyle. Within this insulated world I grew up in, there was no unemployment and no risk of my dad losing his job. I lived in a solid, German-built house, which was very cheap to rent. A lot of the goods available at the NAAFI, especially alcohol and tobacco, were much cheaper than either UK or domestic German prices. The forces schools were well staffed and resourced, as were the British Military Hospitals, with medical and dental care easily available and absolutely, totally free. The endless, lurching crises within the NHS was just another news story to me, I was utterly unaffected by it.

The army communities in Germany also saw practically zero crime and no drug or gang problems. There were none of the social issues that happened in civvy street. I hardly ever saw old people, ill people, never saw homeless people, or poverty, and nobody I knew was ever going to get evicted. All the things that a normal, complete society has to deal with and live with, I never did. The Toxteth and Brixton riots, the miners' strike, the unemployment and social strife in the '80s. For me it was only ever on television.

It was also a very traditional, rules-based society that worshipped the monarchy, was all for the reintroduction of capital punishment and where discipline was even implicitly imposed on family members. Extra-marital affairs usually resulted in the

13

offending party being posted a long way away within twenty-four hours. If you were at school and got up to no good, it was your dad's commanding officer who got informed, who would then bollock your dad for being a bad parent and then it would roll down to you when he got home.

Such intimate control of my life was something I'd never questioned, never thought of as anything other than normal. But it also worked. There was a great sense of security and safety. Apart from the royal family, we were probably more protected, cosseted and isolated from reality than any other group in British society. Taken as a whole, it's no wonder I didn't want it to end.

And if that's the lifestyle you want, you have to join up to get it.

Plenty of my friends, who were ultimately much wiser than I was, had already told me that that wasn't a good enough reason to be a soldier. I should reconsider, they said, because if I did join up it would change me completely. My response was always the same. It wouldn't change me, I argued. As long as I do my job I'll just carry on being myself out of work, I reasoned. No one will mind, right?

How wrong was I?

Even as I matured and made real friends, I was still quiet and not very confident. I didn't have an aggressive bone in my body (military compatibility problem number two), and I regularly lost myself in the world of heavy metal music. A recurrent theme within metal, the individual at odds with the world, struck a real chord with me. Embracing the skinny-fit jeans look and growing my hair long didn't offend the norms of army society overmuch, being as I wasn't actually *in* the army, but it did nurture my individuality. Dressing the way I did was an expression of my personal choices, which, as it turned out, was something I craved a whole lot more than I thought I did.

Nothing wrong with any of that, but nothing that would sit too well with a forces career, either, no matter how many times I was told and no matter how much I wanted a sheltered, protected, community lifestyle. But who listens to anyone else when you're young and just starting to learn about yourself? I sure as hell didn't.

Then I turned eighteen, I left school, my stepfather was posted back to the UK, the real world kicked in and everything changed.

Suddenly I was lost. Civilian life was this scary, whole other world that I knew nothing about. It was an uncertain place, and all I wanted to do was keep hold of the protected, ordered life which was all I'd ever known. It reinforced in my mind that the only way for that to happen was to join up. The crucial difference, though, was that as a member of the armed forces as opposed to a dependent, I'd have to do a whole lot more to earn the considerable benefits that a forces lifestyle offered.

I didn't know that crucial point back then, but I was about to find out.

Because some things in life you don't get told about, and plenty of things about the military you definitely don't get told about at the recruiting office.

But I'll tell you about it.

So if you're thinking of joining up and if any of the above seems like you, then sit down, tune in and read the rest before you make your decision. Then you'll be able to make an informed choice based on reality, not just what the recruiters tell you.

Part 1

Good Times

'I'm a young man alone, facing the world,
My colours to the post, my flag unfurled.'
Cold Steel

1986 to 1989, ignored signs, wasted chances

In July 1986 I was kneecapped and knocked to the ground by three
of life's sledgehammers, and all at once. Aged eighteen, I left
school, left Germany and left the army community. Real-world
reality ripped away my sheltered view of life and forced me to
engage in tasks that were routine for everyone else but completely
new for me. Signing on, looking for a job, paying my own way
and, most shocking of all, encountering different points of view.
My God, there were people that actually didn't like Margaret
Thatcher? Unreal. I'd never known anything like it. Even on an
army estate in the UK, and definitely in Germany, everyone's
opinion was as uniform as a line of troops on parade. Arthur
Scargill and Neil Kinnock were universally despised, while
Margaret Thatcher was universally revered. And like many close-
knit communities, opinions soaked through the generations. My
parents believed it, everyone around me believed it, so I believed it
as well. And it wasn't just that I dismissed other points of view;
until 1986 I actively ignored them.

But after coming back to the UK, I had no choice but to hear
what other people said, as well as having my own glibly voiced
ideas hung out and pecked over. I saw with my own eyes
unemployment, redundancy, hospital waiting lists, struggling
pensioners, all for the first time and all for real, not just on
television. It was a reality smack in the face that I simply wasn't
prepared for.

And as well as facing diverse opinions and backgrounds for the
first time ever, I was also starting to learn about myself.

Correction. I wasn't learning; I was ignoring what I was being
taught.

By the time I left school I had vague ideas about joining the
army, but past that, nothing. No real idea of a trade or speciality. It
was all about the community, the lifestyle and yes, the privilege
and the protection from all the real-world things 'back home',
things that I'd never ever experienced first-hand.

As well as wanting to join up, I'd also had a fair bit of peer and
family pressure to try and become an officer. My father and
stepfather had both risen from the ranks to become officers, and

17

while I had the qualifications, there it stopped. If you had the academic ability, so the argument went, your personal qualities would be there as well. Right?

Wrong.

Even at my best, I had zero self-confidence, zero ability to order anyone around and no experience of it, either. I wasn't even a prefect at school, for God's sake. My personal qualities would never in a million years have seen me commissioned. Other jobs, fine, but an officer in the army? No way.

And with the height of Napoleon, the build of Montgomery and absolutely zero charisma, I couldn't even bluff it with sheer presence.

Blindside disappointment number one came along in July 1986. I fell flat on my face at the Royal Artillery's first recruitment hurdle. The interviewing officer barely even heard my mumbled, nervous answers to his questions. Just because the older generations in my family had thrived and succeeded in the army didn't give me the divine right to front up and expect the same. It was a hard lesson to learn, and I learned it that day. And while I kept going back, kept on trying, it wasn't determination that drove me on, it was simply that I couldn't conceive of doing anything else. I was like a salmon swimming upstream, only to die in the attempt. Again and again I tried and failed to be an officer, in the RAF, Royal Corps of Transport, Royal Signals and Ordnance Corps.

The feedback was as constant as it was brutal. No self-confidence, no assertive qualities, no leadership abilities, goodbye. When I was kicked back by the Royal Signals, I was told in my debrief that I was a nice guy, and they made it sound like a bad thing.

I clearly wasn't officer material, but was I getting the message? No. I *was* slowly learning to say what they wanted to hear, but that was just talking the talk. When I could have been in my final year at university, or more realistically, given my A level results, polytechnic, instead I was cleaning pans in a school kitchen. And I was there because I was convinced there was no point in me taking a job with prospects, because the next time I tried to join up I'd be successful.

So I kept telling myself.

Then, in May 1989 my persistence got me as far as the Officer and Aircrew Selection Centre at RAF Biggin Hill, with a view to being an officer in the RAF Regiment. At the same time as the first crack in the Iron Curtain appeared, with Hungary taking down the barbed wire fences on the frontier with Austria, I reached the final stage in the selection process. Lots of eagerness and knowledge about planes and the RAF Regiment got me through the interview, I managed the bare minimum in the group discussion on current affairs and then it was into the hangar for the command tasks. Once there, you took it in turns to get your small group of fellow interviewees over a gym horse with a plank and two lengths of rope, or across a notional chasm along with an empty oil drum. It was what I'd worked towards for three years, my one chance to prove that I was a leader, that I could take charge of a group of people, bend them to my will and get the job done.

The selection board said no.

They were always going to say no.

To give you an idea of how utterly unsuited I was to the military, especially an infantry-type unit like the RAF Regiment, have you seen the film *Fury*? It's a war film about a tank crew who get a replacement soldier called Norman. Norman was a clerk who hadn't fired a weapon since training, had no idea about fighting, didn't understand the aggressive culture of front-line soldiers and had big trouble killing the enemy. It was a world where Norman clearly didn't fit, and that was going to be me. The main difference was that Norman didn't have a choice. I did, and I was just about to make a really bad one.

And it wasn't that I didn't consider other options. In between trying and failing as an officer, I also made several half-hearted attempts to join up as a private, but something inside me told me that it didn't feel right, and I'd keep making up excuses for stopping the process. The reality, even though I was a long way from accepting it, was that I was never cut out to be a soldier. Whatever it was I thought I wanted from life, joining up wasn't the way to get it. It was really that simple, and every time I stepped into a recruiting office, alarm bells clanged around in my head, shouting out this wasn't for me. But I just wasn't listening.

I'd left school with one A level, just, and a year later I re-sat and got a second one, just. In 1987, after being kicked back by the

Royal Corps of Transport, I was offered a polytechnic course in Building Studies. I didn't even know what Building Studies meant, but it didn't stop the letters arriving for me. Complex documents about the grant process, applying to local authorities for housing, having to prove my student status. All of this before wondering for the first time in my life how the hell I was supposed to cook and where to buy food from. Normal things that most people would take in their stride, I had absolutely no idea.

So I kept on trying to join up, because for me it was the easier option.

And I kept on failing. Then, even though it was pretty clear that it wasn't the wisest thing to do, after I nose-dived at Biggin Hill, I resolved that time was getting on. I was twenty-one with no real career plan in place, and it had to change. If I couldn't get into the RAF Regiment as an officer, I'd join as an airman, serve a few years and somehow attain those elusive qualities of self-confidence and leadership. Then I'd apply for a commission from the ranks. It seemed like a plan. What could go wrong?

Basic Training, RAF Swinderby

First days

Basic Recruit Training at Swinderby lasted six weeks. It was the interface that turned civilians into airmen and airwomen. Fundamentals like not doing what you wanted and being told what to do, it all started there. When I turned up on 3rd October 1989, I was the only recruit with long hair and an earring, a definite warning sign that also broke a cardinal rule for survival in the armed forces: don't attract attention. I took my seat in a large room full of recruits, and I felt the stares. 'You'd better take that earring out, mate,' was whispered at me before I'd even sat down. 'Christ, don't let the Regiment see you with that.' The Regiment, the Regiment, the RAF Regiment. I hadn't even seen any of them yet, and for all I knew no one else had either, but everyone was terrified of them. It probably wasn't helped by the first thing I and everyone else was told as soon as we set foot in the Guard Room: 'Here's your name card, walk on the left, processing is in the first block straight ahead, and if anyone from the Regiment tells you to do something, do it straight away.'

It also didn't matter that I was one of about half of the intake destined to become gunners.

I wasn't one yet.

New recruits arrived from all over the country throughout the morning. After I'd reluctantly taken out my earring, I concentrated on completing the wodge of forms I'd been given, starting each one with my name and service number. Within an hour of arriving, I'd written my number out so many times I knew it by heart. It's the first thing you learn and the last thing you forget. I served just over three years, I left thirty years ago and I still know my service number.

Massive reality check number one came as I flicked one completed document to the back of the pile and looked at the next: Service Personnel and Wills. What the fuck? A will? I could die?

Who should be my beneficiary? *What's* a beneficiary? I twitched and looked up at the soft-faced and friendly WRAF corporal who periodically came into the room. 'Is that the will?' she asked, instantly clocking my far-eyed, open-mouth look of having never before considered mortality.

'Yes,' I mumbled, still twenty-four hours away from being bawled at for not addressing an NCO by rank.

'Just put your mum's name, lad.' She smiled. 'That's what I say to all my boys.'

I never once seriously considered what it would be like for my parents to get that call, that letter, that visit. It sort of registered in my mind, but at the same time it didn't. It'll happen to someone else, if it happens at all, was my way of dealing with that particular piece of potential reality.

Every now and then a Regiment instructor would walk past, pause in the doorway and just stare, and whenever they did the low-level chatter would stop. The silence was almost painful after the easy conversations of seconds before. The simple warning not to wind up these green-clad other-beings had already soaked into the collective consciousness. They were immediately identifiable by their olive-green trousers and jumpers, everything pristine, sharp-edged and efficient. One of them, anonymous in his perfectly turned-out uniform, glared wordlessly into the room, his all-seeing eyes beneath his shaped beret taking in every detail. For the first time, but definitely not the last, I wondered if I'd ever be anything like that immaculate soldier. Was I really capable of doing it?

One of our group was a sixteen-year-old called Davis. He was less than five feet tall and his voice had yet to break. 'He's definitely a virgin,' said one of the Regiment instructors, before giving us our first mission in the military. 'I want you lads to make sure Davis gets laid before he passes out.'

My soon-to-be-removed blond hair was noticed next. It was always going to be. 'Fucking hell, Goldilocks,' he said, laughing. 'The WRAFs don't arrive til next Monday.' Nervous communal laughter, and the first gentle example of the group isolating the individual. 'Aren't you here a little early? What trade are you? And I'm a corporal, by the way.'

'Gunner, Corporal.' Cue taken.

It was his turn to laugh, and like everything the Regiment did, it was done to the extreme. He roared to the rafters, gripped his sides and almost bent double. Small specks of water squeezed from the corners of his eyes. 'Really, Rapunzel?' He smiled, but his eyes held me in a cold, direct stare. 'Well, once you've had your fucking hair cut, we'll make a man out of you.'

The WRAF corporal came back and read out forty names, mine included. We were ordered outside and formed into three rows. I didn't know it straight away, but this was now the flight I'd been put into. Still unable to march, we were walked together to an adjacent hangar where the station barber was set up in one of the offices. We stood outside and I waited my turn.

'Time to get it cut, boys.' An admin corporal stepped up and down the uneven flight line. 'And that means you!' He pointed at me, every head in the flight spun around and again I heard the laughter. I smiled and joined in. It was all very unthreatening, just general banter. And I'd expected it, known this was going to happen. I could have got a haircut before arriving at Swinderby, and to be perfectly honest I should have, but I wanted to make some small statement of individuality. Waiting until the absolute last minute to get my hair cut seemed like a good way to do it. I quickly learned, though, that I wasn't too good at being the centre of attention, much less scrutiny. I couldn't come up with smart, fast answers, and I learned too late that it was always much better to be anonymous.

But it wasn't just me who had to face the barber. Everyone had to have a haircut, even if you didn't need one, and the reason soon became clear: it was to make you look stupid. All recruits were to have a haircut on day one, all recruits were to have a bad haircut on day one.

I put myself at the end of the queue and waited until everyone else had theirs done before my turn came. I sat in the barber's chair and looked mournfully out of the window. The rest of the flight gleefully pressed their faces against the glass, desperate to see me losing my long hair. It was over in seconds to the tune of electric hair clippers. A big part of my identity was now strewn across the barber's shop floor in blond clumps. The lads looking in from outside had another memory of their first day, while I looked in the mirror and saw a stranger's reflection. It wasn't so bad, I thought.

At least he didn't take too much off the front, just an uneven shave along the back.

No one had been taught how to march yet, but we still had to travel as a formed body of men. Straight after our haircuts, the intake was split into three flights: 4, 5 and 11. I was part of 11 Flight, and that's what was important. It wasn't about me, or my haircut, or the guy next to me and his flash car. It was we. We suddenly had a group identity and we came together, and everything was seen through a them and us prism.

Taking charge of 11 Flight for the first few days was Corporal Vernon, a formidable WRAF drill instructor, solidly built and with a broad Manchester accent. Straight after the haircuts she walked 11 Flight as uniformly as possible to Stores for the first of many kit issues. I got in the queue and stood at one end of a huge storeroom, where a brand-new blue RAF holdall was thrust at me. Then, sliding it along the low counter like a tray at a café, I walked to the other end of Stores, by which time my holdall was chock-full of kit. One set of camouflage, loads of blues, a pair of shoes, a pair of boots and then, to make it real, and with the memory of my will still fresh in my mind, a brand-new S10 respirator. No time to dwell on the significance, I shoved my arms into my holdall's stiff canvas handles, and carrying it like a backpack re-joined the flight outside.

The introductions to military life now came along faster than a Tornado on reheat. The flight was herded across the road that separated the two halves of the station and we were taken to our barrack block. It was an old wartime H-shaped design, with four twelve-man rooms on the ground floor, communal showers and toilets, luggage room and drying room. The layout was duplicated on the first floor.

Each man had a bed, a small bedside locker and a wardrobe. And that's all there was in each room: twelve beds, twelve lockers, twelve wardrobes. 'Lock it away right now, lads.' Corporal Vernon prowled around the block and her thick accent scythed through the brickwork and steel. 'Back outside in ten minutes. I want you all wearing blue shirt, tie, jumper, civilian trousers, boots and beret. Move!'

Our berets had a coloured plastic disc behind the badge which marked us out as recruits, and the jeans and uniform mix marked us out as week one recruits.

At lunchtime Corporal Vernon marched us to the Airmen's Mess, where another gentle initiation awaited. Dressed in our jeans and blue jumpers, everyone knew we were the new boys, and everyone who'd been there even a week longer than us had made one step up in the pecking order. It was a term I was to become very familiar with: time served. As soon as we came into sight, every recruit in the huge dining hall hammered on the tables with their knives and forks. It was a deafening wave of sound, and it stopped after a few seconds. That was our ordeal every mealtime for the rest of the week, until the following week when the next lot arrived and we'd be able to do it to them.

But there was a reason behind it. There was a reason behind it all. The cutlery hammering on the tables wasn't telling *me* that *I* looked stupid, it was telling *us* that *we* looked stupid. But we all looked stupid together, we all went through it together and we bonded together. They weren't looking at me and laughing at me; they were laughing at us.

Us, and not me. And at Swinderby at least, it was done in a very gentle and very effective way.

And it really worked. I was an individual for sure, but I wanted safety and stability within a community. And to get something, I had to give something. Some individual thoughts and actions had to be sacrificed to be a part of a bigger group. And that applied to me as much as everyone else.

So to begin with, I kept my individual thoughts very much underneath my beret and my individual actions on hold.

The first night back at the block, we met our drill sergeant, Sergeant Gervill. He had typical air force slicked-back hair and was from Liverpool. And like Corporal Vernon, his uniform and bearing were both immaculate and pristine.

Until he spoke.

'Does anyone here have a problem with swearing?' he asked, in his oozing Scouse accent. He sat at a table in one of the rooms, and surrounded by the flight he explained to us how to iron and polish our kit. 'No?' he asked again. 'Well, that's just as fucking well.' It didn't take us long to catch on and start doing the same.

Recruits we may have been, but there was status for some. Senior and deputy senior men were appointed. Their jobs were to oversee the rest of the flight when the instructors weren't around, and to form us up in the mornings. These two guys were the luckiest in the whole flight because they had their own rooms. The rest of us had to share with eleven others. And as every instructor told us pretty much every day, 'It's absolutely essential that the senior man can have a wank in his own room.'

Each room also had a room leader. I was in room two, and our room leader was a six-foot-tall, gangly and bespectacled nineteen-year-old with Beach Boy blond hair, called Greg Oxford. He'd previously served in the Grenadier Guards and was now joining the RAF Regiment. On the face of it, we were very different people, but there was still some common ground. We were both joining the Regiment and we were both slightly older than most of the other recruits.

It was enough.

A quick word about the air force and nicknames. Everyone had one, and it was usually the most obvious thing about you. If you were from Liverpool you were called Scouse, red hair and you were called Ginge. If that didn't work, then your surname was either shortened or an 'ie', 'y' or something similar was added to the end. So Greg Oxford was called Ox, and I was called Brinders.

'Hey, Ox,' I said, nervously approaching him on the first day as we were stowing our kit. 'How was it in the Guards?'

'Fucking awful,' he replied, emptying his suitcase into his wardrobe at Olympic speed. He spoke with a slight Devon twang. 'A whole year of beastings and bullshit as a junior leader. And the drill, fucking hell, man, the drill. Why do you think I left?'

I chuckled. 'Do you think it'll be any better here?'

'They let a hippy bastard like you in, didn't they?' He smiled back at me. 'Can't be all bad.'

Ox was room leader because he'd served before, but he was a good room leader because he was exactly that, a leader. He knew when to chivvy everyone along, when to organise people to get their jobs done, but he never needed to raise his voice. He was always in control, and he spoke to everyone as though they were his mate. He did all of it effortlessly, and I quickly realised that leadership, you either had it or you didn't. Ox had it, I didn't, and less than a week in I was a lot less certain that I'd ever make officer, or that I'd even want to.

Ox and I clicked, and over the years we'd become good friends. He'd always joke about his military career starting in 1812, bringing up loads of Guards history, which I absolutely lapped up, and I made him laugh with my heavy metal talk, which was my way of keeping hold of my individuality once my hair had been cut. It didn't matter that twenty-four hours earlier we'd never seen each other before. From that point on we were in it together, going through it together.

'Bloody heavy metal,' joked Ox. 'Long-haired hippy drug music. What's it good for anyway?'

'Better than your house music, man,' I replied.

'Have you ever been to a house night?' asked Ox.

'As if!' I laughed.

'You don't know what you're missing,' he said. 'You spend an hour at a nightclub that plays house music, Brinders, and you'll forget about that daisy-chain peace shit you listen to.'

'No way, guy,' I said. 'If *you* went to a metal gig, you'd love it, you'd be rocking.'

'Are you asking me out on a date, nancy boy?'

'I'm making you a deal,' I said. 'You come to a metal gig with me, I'll go to a house night with you, and we'll see which one is best.'

'Sounds fair to me,' said Ox. He held out his hand and we shook on it.

It felt good. It was welcoming, we were all equals with a shared common goal, which was to get through training. And at that stage, and for the whole of Swinderby, it felt completely right. However strange my roomies might have thought I was, I fitted in. On the hierarchy of needs I had food, I had shelter, a career goal and friends, which, according to the psychologist Maslow, was the whole of the bottom level taken care of. For me, though, it was pretty much the entire pyramid. Maslow could have written a whole new textbook about my mind and retired.

So, parking my individuality, I got straight into the comradeship and team spirit, which started immediately. Even off duty, we had to work together, and to get us used to it we were introduced to the phrase 'bull night'. In the military, if something was bulled it was cleaned and polished to a mirror shine, and it invariably took a long time to achieve. A bull night meant the entire block had to be cleaned and polished from top to bottom. The flight was split into small groups, and we were then assigned areas of the block that we had to clean. I was one of four who were sent to the rear entrance hall every night. I was glad I wasn't given the ablutions and told to spend six weeks clearing away recruits' pubes. It was up to all of us to make sure the whole block was up to standard. Every single place where dust could collect was wiped, windows were cleaned, Brasso and Duraglit was liberally applied to anything that could, would or should be shiny. The linoleum floors were polished, either with an electric buffer or a handheld one that was swung laboriously from side to side at the end of a long pole. After that, no one walked on the floor wearing anything but socks. We couldn't stop the instructors from coming in, though, and leaving deep scuff marks around the place, just to give us a bit more work to do. I quickly learned about teamwork, how even getting down on my hands and knees and pulling dust from the corner of a stairwell was important. If my part of the block wasn't up to scratch, we were all marked down, and I didn't want that landing on my shoulders. It taught me about attention to detail and to follow orders straight away, even stupid ones. In a war, it was the kind of thing that might save my life, although cleaning a barrack block probably wouldn't.

Just as the first bull night started and I'd been given my part of the block to clean, I had a different priority that had nothing to do with the air force. I went looking for Corporal Vernon.

'Excuse me, Corporal.' There for less than a day, I didn't have to stand to attention, mainly because I didn't know how to. Corporal Vernon looked back at me as though I was a particularly rancid piece of dog crap she'd stood in.

'What do you want?' she sneered.

'On our last weekend here, Corporal, is there a chance we might be allowed off base?'

'You've only just got here, for fuck's sake. What do you want to leave for?'

'Just that night, Corporal,' I said. 'I've got tickets to see Aerosmith.'

Her expression suggested I'd said the dumbest thing in the world. She turned around, already disinterested. 'Sure,' she replied, barely audibly, leaving me thinking it was less than definite.

That first effort at a bull night was laughable, but looking back I doubt anything more was ever expected. One of the lads I worked alongside had a talent for literally eating dust balls. He'd pick up little bits of the stuff, roll it up and then swallow it, grinning all the while as I watched him with a mixture of surprise and laughter. And after not very long that first evening, it seemed as though we'd cleaned the place spotless. Bull nights weren't so bad, I thought, and I couldn't wait to impress Corporal Vernon the next day.

Morning inspections weren't like you see in the films. We didn't have an instructor screaming at us, or kit thrown around or anything like that. Well, not at Swinderby anyway. We were all very new into the forces, and if it was too extreme too soon, volunteers or not, we'd have just left. But our failings were still highlighted loud and clear. Lots of dirt I thought I'd cleaned away the night before was spotted by Corporal Vernon. She glared at me with a dusty finger held under my nose, and my previous night's optimism disintegrated. So much for my mate who claimed he'd eat it all. Nothing more had to be said, and the simple gesture told me all I needed to know about trying harder next time.

*

From day one I kept hold of my heavy metal persona, then I added a bit of hippy as well. Before joining up I never called anyone 'man', or 'guy', unless I was really, really drunk, but I did once I got to Swinderby. Almost without realising it, I found myself rebelling against the uniformity by putting my personality traits on steroids and magnifying them. The trouble was, being *too* much of an individual in the military can sometimes have its issues. At Swinderby though, absolutely no one cared about that and it didn't matter, so long as I stepped up every bull night, learned to march and obey orders.

But it became a big problem later on.

The first weekend at Swinderby was taken up with drill, and from that point on, the jeans and blue jumper set-up was ditched and we wore full uniform: DP, boots and beret.

Drill practice was done in an empty hangar under the watchful eye of Corporal Griffin, an immaculately turned-out instructor. He looked like he had his hair cut every day, although not by the station barber. The flight was sized off and then rearranged so that when we formed up, the tallest were in the outer corners and the smallest in the centre. And that's where you stayed. Slight of build and a mere five foot seven, I was anonymous within the flight's formation.

Ox's height and previous experience meant he was excellent at drill. His movements were fluid and he was totally on point with the changes. Corporal Griffin knew a natural when he saw one, and Ox was made flight marker. For the passing out parade he'd be the first onto the square, and the rest of the flight would march on and mark their dressing from him. But for those of us who hadn't been in the Guards, like all of the rest of us, we were a long way from being good enough for rifle drill, and for the next few days we had to shout out the timing. All around the station you'd hear 'ONE-TWO-ONE!', then a crash of boots as a very un-coordinated flight performed the required move.

From that point on, if you were in uniform, marching was the only way you were allowed to move around. Even if you were on your own. One lunchtime I was marching to the NAAFI with two other members of the flight. We trooped past a barrack block, probably out of step, when someone poked his head out of a window.

'Get in step.'

'Fuck off!' was my instant reply. Although I quickly learned to check before answering back.

Inspections

Pretty much every week night was a bull night. Each morning the block was inspected and then its occupants were. Standing by your bed, polished and ironed and everyone smelling of starch, while the instructor invariably found fault with some, if not all of your hard work. Apart from the blue scarf and plastic disc attached to your beret, another way to spot a recruit was by the stiff, ironed-to-death creases in your DP. Camouflage was never meant to be ironed. A straight edge in the field is just asking for a sniper to take you out, or so we were told. And while there was no danger of facing a Dragunov at Swinderby, drill instructors were everywhere.

But just like the bull nights and just like drill, morning inspections were designed to teach attention to detail, and to make sure that you did what you were told.

What everyone concentrated on most of all was footwear. The shoes that were worn with our best blues, collectively referred to as number ones, had to be immaculate. You wore your number ones for parades, punishments and weddings. The whole of the number one shoe had to be highly polished, but the toecaps had to be bulled. That meant at least an hour every night painstakingly rubbing polish into the toecap until a mirror-like sheen was achieved.

Shoes stood at the ends of beds on inspections. As I progressed through training, I had more and more kit to be cleaned and ironed, to the point where one of the inspections included my bed being covered with everything the air force had issued me. All of it polished, ironed and spotless, and laid out exactly the same on every bed. Wardrobes and lockers were never inspected unless they were left unlocked. But that was just asking for trouble.

One day as I stood by my bed and waited for Corporal Griffin to inspect the room, a couple of the lads were looking at a porn mag they'd bought that weekend which had pictures of hermaphrodites. It really wasn't the wisest thing to do just before an inspection, and they were fast running out of time to hide it away. Instead of doing the sensible thing, it was chucked from one giggling recruit to another, a kind of suicidal pass-the-parcel where

31

the loser would be caught holding it and then humiliated beyond belief. We could easily have averted disaster by sliding it under a mattress and we'd have been fine. What we actually did was hide it in an empty wardrobe by the room's one vacant bed-space. It was unlocked, but surely Corporal Griffin wouldn't look in there.

Looking back, an empty wardrobe was the one place where every recruit would put stuff he didn't want to throw away but also didn't want to confess to owning. Corporal Griffin walked into the room, went straight to the empty wardrobe and peered inside. He pulled out the magazine and silently looked through it while the rest of us cringed. Eventually he spoke.

'Jesus Christ, room two. Are you buying magazines containing pictures of women with tits and dicks? It's disgusting! Is this what you go looking for in Lincoln every weekend? Can't make up your minds what you prefer, so you want a bit of both? No wonder you all like living together, you bastards. I'm just glad you're with me, Senior Man, or I'd be too scared to even come in here.'

Corporal Griffin threw down the magazine and walked out, his perfectly polished shoes tapping on the linoleum floor. He'd probably seen it all before, but from then on our entire room was labelled as homosexual. 'You've got to become a team,' Corporal Griffin said to the whole flight one day. 'Look out for each other, share everything. Only don't take it as far as room two. That lot share each other's bottoms as well.'

It was an off-the-cuff, throwaway comment. It was said as a joke and it was taken as one. In 1989, it was perfectly legitimate and acceptable to use sexuality as a criticism, with the underlying message that anything other than full-on heterosexuality was a sign of weakness, of negativity. And as gays and lesbians were supposedly forbidden from joining the forces, it was an easy win. That was the culture, that's how it was. And up to a point, even civilian society was like that. The military just ramped it up even more, if only to reinforce that it wasn't allowed. Any term was acceptable: gay, queer, ponce, fudge-packer, always used as an insult, a term of derision. Shortly after I left the air force, I was asked if I thought gays and lesbians should be allowed to serve. My instant reply was why on earth would they want to? And not because they couldn't do the job, because I never believed that, but because they'd face absolute hate from day one. If you were gay and joined up on the same day as I did in 1989, and you were found out, I really believe it would be a flip of the coin to decide your fate. Heads, you were caught by the scuffers and booted out of the air force, or tails, caught by anyone else, beaten up to the point of hospital and *then* booted out.

That's just how it was.

And in (some) fairness, Britain wasn't the only military that banned gays and lesbians from serving. Most countries, but not all, did the same, although the history buffs among you will quite rightly point out that in the past this wasn't always the case.

As for me, I didn't know anyone who was gay. None of my friends were, none of my family were, I wasn't. As harsh as it sounds, it didn't really affect me, so it didn't bother me. I didn't think too much about whether it was intolerant, unequal, right or wrong. I never questioned it and I just went along with it.

That would change.

But make no mistake, in 1989, homophobia in the British armed forces was institutional, backed up by regulations, government and emphatically enforced by pretty much everyone.

Social

The RAF, like all branches of the military, is about group cohesion. It has to be, and a big part of that was developing a strong team dynamic, which meant lots of after-hours drinking. And this was where my misconceptions really kicked me in the arse. Did I mention that I was a loner, and that I thought if I did my job, I could do whatever I wanted in my own time? That I'd also be able to choose if I went out drinking or not?

That was all a mistake.

As an airman, the main social focus was the NAAFI, and you went there a lot. A NAAFI was a café, a shop and a bar. In the times before cashpoints were allowed on base, for a quid you could cash a cheque there, most of which you'd also spend in the NAAFI. They even had a video jukebox, and an enduring memory for me from Swinderby was sitting in the NAAFI with a pint, watching WASP's video single 'Forever Free' over and over again. That song just absolutely spoke to me, the soft acoustic start that grew into sweat-soaked, full-on heavy metal. And the video, leather-clad rockers riding into the sunset on their motorbikes, rugged individuals against the world. It was sheer essence music and imagery to me, and it prompted a lot more than one of my mates to ask me why the fuck I'd joined up in the first place if that was what I was all about.

But it was my mates doing the asking, and they liked me and I liked them. And I liked where I was, and apart from the short hair I was getting what I wanted from life. The contradictions weren't causing a problem. Yet.

So after each bull night, once I'd cleaned and polished my assigned part of the block, then my bed-space, then the room and then my kit, I went to the NAAFI, usually with Ox and a few other lads. It got tribal pretty quickly. Your mates, your room, your flight, we went there together, sat together, drank together, just like we would in trade training and beyond. Eventually you'd go out drinking with your unit, pretty much to the exclusion of everyone else. A few beers with your mates was seen as normal, and events like the weekly bop, and as I was soon to discover, squadron-organised events, were pretty much obligatory. There, if you didn't show up, the least you could expect was being pinned against the wall the next day and interrogated about where you'd been.

Perversely, I always thought I was a social animal when it came to nights out, but it turned out that big events at the NAAFI just weren't for me. 'Because it's Saturday night' or 'Because we're all going' felt to me like going out drinking because you had to, not because you wanted to. The NAAFI organised social stuff most weekends, either a band or a DJ, which I went along to but invariably left early.

I didn't realise it yet, but outside of work I actually didn't like being told what to do, and my rebellious nature was trying to find an outlet. I was fine going out for a drink with a few mates if I wanted to, but not if it felt like I had to. The signs of incompatibility were starting to show, but at Swinderby we were all there together, all mates together and no one really minded if there was an occasional oddball on the flight. But really, straight in from civvy street, we were all oddballs.

If only I'd known what was coming, because at Swinderby, probably through a mix of us still being civilians in transition, and for the most part aged sixteen to eighteen, just left home, immature and naive, it was all very gentle and friendly. The NAAFI at Swinderby was probably the only bar in the whole of the RAF where there were no fights, and it was also where we were encouraged to stay. Just before our first weekend off, Corporal Griffin gave us some fatherly advice about the local pubs in nearby Newark and Lincoln. We were told which ones to avoid, unless we wanted to get beaten up or worse, and because of the IRA we must never mention that we were in the air force.

Which was seriously wishful thinking. A bunch of young lads who'd just joined up, first weeks of Basic Training, stupid, short haircuts and a new vocabulary based around weird abbreviations and swearing, and they're not going to tell anyone, especially the girls, that they're in the air force? And the locals aren't going to work it out anyway? Even the blindest bat from a cave where the light never shone would have spotted us from a hundred paces. Any of us who went off base were clocked as recruits in less than a minute.

But Corporal Griffin's advice was well heeded, and the NAAFI was packed most nights. During the daytime on Saturdays, Ox, myself and a few others ventured out, and Lincoln's high street and shops were filled with plenty of off-duty recruits. It was there that I bought a pair of cowboy boots and a floor-length second-hand raincoat. I loved the look. No one else did, but I stuck with it. My individuality had found an outlet in the form of a seriously unpopular wardrobe.

Enter the Regiment

Basic Training at Swinderby was split into four main areas: General Service Knowledge (GSK), Ground Defence Training (GDT), weapons training and physical training.

A lot of the GSK was given in classrooms. It revolved around military discipline, rank structures, and what happened if or when you were charged, which was part of the disciplinary process. A commonly used term was that things that are legally acceptable in the rest of society are illegal within the forces. Like homosexuality. If it was discovered that you were gay, you'd be booted out there and then. And not just that, you'd be stripped of any medals you'd earned, never to wear them again. The reasoning was that it was bad for morale. How could you fight a war if the guy in your fire trench fancied you? When a lot of the accommodation was communal, would you want to have a shower or live in the barrack block with someone who might chat you up? These were the arguments that were used.

Flawed arguments.

Because you really didn't need to go as far back as Alexander, or even Frederick the Great, to evidence that sexuality had absolutely no impact on military effectiveness. And the fact that people had been found out, kicked out and stripped of medals kind of suggests they *were* more than capable of doing their jobs before they were outed. But that was the culture, and at the time I accepted it. If this was part of the life I'd signed up to, then so be it. It wasn't until years later that I realised just how much at odds the military community and its norms were with wider society. Well, when I say at odds, I mean at least thirty years behind the times.

GDT was taught by the Regiment instructors, and they made absolutely no bones about why they were there. 'We're here to train you to kill,' they growled. 'Because one day you might have to do that to stay alive.' It didn't come as any great surprise, but actually hearing someone say it brought it home with all the finesse of an incoming mortar round. And the Regiment instructors didn't just mention it once; they said it again and again. I don't

37

think it turned me into a steely-eyed killer overnight, but it got you into that headspace, it made you comfortable with the term and the concept, so that if or when it did happen, you'd deal with it. A term that I'd come across many times in the next three years was 'your training will take over'. Having said all that, I still made the definite distinction between being trained to do it and actually having to do it. Despite the Falklands, despite the Cold War, despite Northern Ireland and the fact that I actually wanted to go there, most servicemen and women at that time went their whole careers without having to pull the trigger for real. And if I'm being honest with myself, that's pretty much what I thought would happen with me.

The Regiment instructors, though, played to a different script, and they were terrifying. Even though the days of recruits being beaten up were long gone, I was still shit-scared of them. When they said 'jump', you jumped. As simple as it sounds, shouting and swearing at you from inside your personal space, while you stood to attention and couldn't move or answer back, instilled a lot of fear.

Like Corporal Entwhistle, who lived and breathed the RAF Regiment. His windproof smock had an RAF Regiment crossed rifles DZ patch stitched to one arm, and his leather banded beret clung to his shaved head. 'I'm RAF Reg all the way, lads,' he told us. 'When I'm asleep, I even dream about the Regiment. I'm a real military moron.' His main threat was to 'bin' us, which meant being put back to the next flight. Its official term was being re-coursed, and for a recruit it was the worst thing that could ever happen. It meant you had to leave one flight and join another, uprooting you from the friends you had just made and having to settle into another flight that had already got to know each other. As well as making you an instant outsider, it also put back the date you'd pass out, and you'd have to stay at Swinderby that much longer. I'd have done anything not to be re-coursed. 'I won't mess around, lads,' said Corporal Entwhistle. 'I'll just fucking bin you.'

I took him exactly at his word and always tried that little bit harder when he was around.

Because in every recruit's eyes, Corporal Entwhistle was the real deal. Whippet-thin and steel-wire hard, he moved fast, like a meerkat. The last person you wanted him to be looking at was you, with his cold blue eyes that seemed to stab into you like a bayonet. He told us a story about a group of off-duty airmen who had pulled up to the camp gates in a car and then poked a toy pistol at the gate guard. The armed sentry was on the point of making ready and shooting him when the 'joke' was spotted. The sentry wasn't Regiment, which probably saved the joker's life. 'If I'd been on duty that day,' said Corporal Entwhistle, speaking fast, like a machine gun, 'I'd have made ready and fired. I would *not* have missed, that fucker would have been dead, and I'd have made sergeant for doing it.'

Corporal Entwhistle's story also brought home just how seriously the terrorist threat was taken, although the steady drip of IRA murders made it impossible to think otherwise. Vigilance was drummed into everyone. Never wear uniform off base, always lock doors, always check under your car, and when you're on guard duty, you're live armed for a reason. It was taken on board a lot more than the threat of nuclear war, probably because it was so close to home and the casualties were real. No one went to bed shitting themselves about the Provos though. If you were careful and stayed alert, you'd do okay. The threat wasn't trivialised; it was constructed as a danger we could overcome.

But like the marching, it took a while to learn, and a collective fuck-up early on really rammed home the point. One night the barrack block door had been left unlocked and a lone, unchallenged instructor that I'd never seen before wandered up and down the corridors and into the rooms. It must have been pretty late. The bull night had finished, and I was sitting at the end of my bed reading the latest issue of *Kerrang!*. I looked up at the instructor and benignly waited for him to dish out his orders.

He went from silent to deafening in a microsecond.

'EVERYBODY OUT! NOW!'

I knew when to move fast. I jumped up and we all piled outside, some of us barefoot and most of us in nothing but underwear. It was night-time, it was cold and it was raining, but the instructor didn't give a shit about that. I stood outside the block on grass that was getting wetter by the second, and he called us all the stupid bastards under the sun for leaving the door open. He asked us if we had a death wish, did we want to get blown up or shot execution-style. Then he shook his head, called us all sick fuckers and let us back inside.

The next morning, I thought we'd all be bollocked sideways by Corporal Griffin. He never mentioned it, and none of us, not even the senior man, had the balls to tell him about it.

But we never left the block door unlocked again.

I also learned what to do if someone threw a grenade: lie down. It was another common greeting from the Regiment instructors. They'd walk up to the flight as we waited for our next training session, shout 'Grenade!', and heaven help the poor bastard who didn't hit the deck quickly enough.

While I didn't actually see any grenades at Swinderby, we were given a dramatic demonstration of just how powerful even supposedly harmless pyrotechnics were. One day a pair of Regiment instructors stuck a thunderflash into the ground, lit the fuse, then placed a gash Mk IV steel helmet over it. The thunderflash went off and the helmet flew a hundred metres straight up into the air. If that was what a non-lethal pyro could do, what was a grenade like?

*

Any World War Three scenario was reckoned to go nuclear very quickly, which meant I had to get used to firing a rifle with a respirator on. To do that I had to bend my neck back to the point of dislocation to be able to see through the sights. I was taught to put my respirator on quickly. As soon as I heard someone shout 'Gasgasgas!' I knew I had nine seconds. 'Mask in nine and you'll be in time' was the first military rhyme I learned, refined down to 'mask in five and you'll be alive'. My respirator was personal issue, remaining mine for my entire career.

I learned decontamination drills, how to eat and drink, how to administer first aid, all in a chemical environment. I learned how nerve agent killed its victims, what the symptoms were – pinpoint pupils, massive sweating, twitching, uncontrolled pissing and shitting, then dead. Death happened from anything between thirty seconds and five minutes. Nerve agent worked by blocking one nerve from passing messages to the next one, which caused the twitching. 'So if you're going to take a snort of nerve agent, lads,' said Corporal Entwhistle with a grin, 'make sure you're having a wank at the time, and the Sarin spasm means you'll go out having one last tug.'

Everything in a chemical environment was done in an NBC suit. The suit was made with layers of charcoal, and while it would save your life, it also made you very hot, very quickly. That was fine in the winter, but a nightmare any other time. The kit was designed for European climates, and it was inconceivable that there would be a need to wear it, for example, in a desert war…

But even in a British autumn I found out just how uncomfortable the suits were when the flight had to run from one side of the football pitch to the other, completely suited up. Then I had to do the same thing again while carrying someone in a fireman's lift, staring through the eyepieces of the respirator, feeling the sweat hose out of my skin, my vision blurring, heart pounding. I tried not to get my wildly pumping limbs tangled up with the guy I was carrying, desperate not to end up in a crumpled heap on the grass. Even after a few minutes of work, it was awful. Being carried while wearing the full kit was no picnic, either, and there was an even chance of yakking inside your mask. The instructors said that if you ever did, all the chunks and diced carrots would be filtered out and you wouldn't choke to death. Despite their chuckled assurance, I was glad I never had to test *that* theory out.

Much like being trained to shoot and kill people, and the rationalisation that it was at most an unlikely possibility, I don't think anyone thought that a nuclear or chemical war was really, really going to happen. I certainly didn't.

The final NBC test was the gas chamber. Long before I even joined up, I knew this was coming. I'd also had the shit scared out of me by flights that had already gone through it, and they exaggerated the story every time: I'd puke if I didn't mask up in time, I'd lose my sense of smell, the CS would soak into my uniform and I'd have symptoms for a week. The end result: I was one small part of a collectively terrified flight that was doubled over to the gas chamber, an isolated building on the far side of the runway. We trooped inside and the door clanged shut.

'Gasgasgas!'

I ripped open my respirator pouch and pulled on my mask. I could smell the rubber as I peered out of the eyepieces. My whole face seemed to be touching the mask, the moulded nosepiece and the drinking straw poked against my lips. I already felt the sweat building up against the seals. I wore the NBC suit over my camouflage, and inside the chamber it was hot and oppressive.

Corporal Entwhistle knelt down, pulled out four pellets and set them alight. White clouds of CS filled the chamber. Under his searchlight gaze I held my breath, took off my respirator, and with my eyes firmly shut I went through the drills. After a few seconds' scrubbing my face with the decontamination pad, I put my respirator back on, breathed out as hard as I could and slowly opened my eyes. My face was still stinging where the CS had wafted against my skin, but everything I was taught to do had worked.

I attached the drinking tube from my water bottle and then changed the air filter, repeating the process several times before it was on to the unavoidable final trial; a lungful of CS. Soon it was my turn. I took a deep breath and pulled off my respirator.

'D7619672', eyes shut, skin tingling, 'Brindle', coughing, 'Gunner', bent double, coughing and going blue, eyes streaming.

The door was hauled open and I was booted outside. I ran out and into the fresh air. It was a bright, clear November day, and I remember running along, chest tight and coughing my guts up, my eyes stinging like hell. After a few minutes of discomfort I could see once more. I stowed my respirator and returned to the chamber. One at a time the rest of the flight came out, then ran off into the distance until they too could see again.

Military Field Training (MFT)

In 1989, the long-serving 7.62mm Self-Loading Rifle, or SLR, was gradually being replaced. The RAF Regiment's Depot at Catterick already used the shorter and more modern 5.56mm SA80, while Swinderby still had the SLR. Compared to what was coming at Catterick, my time on the rifle range at Swinderby was short. I fired twenty rounds at a target from twenty- five metres, went through stoppage drills, was timed on how quickly I could charge a magazine, then I had to show that I could strip and reassemble the weapon. And that was it. Recruits at Swinderby weren't trusted with bayonets, but then again, they didn't need to be. If the shit ever hit the fan to the point of coming under direct attack, that's what the RAF Regiment was there for.

Then, in amongst all the talk of the Warsaw Pact and the Soviet tank divisions massing on the borders, on 9th November 1989, the Berlin Wall came down. I remember sitting on my bed in the block, bulling my shoes and listening to the radio as the news came in. I'd actually seen the wall for real when I lived in Germany, and it was something I felt would always be there: a solid symbol of what the West was up against. And despite Gorbachev's peaceful overtures over the past few years, it came as a complete surprise. I remember feeling elated, as though I'd been part of an amazing bloodless victory and the enemy were no more. But if they weren't the enemy, who were we going to fight? There was no overnight change in the military mindset, and for the purposes of Basic Training they were still the main threat. But I think the high command and probably the politicians as well were secretly a bit disappointed. After all, who could the nation focus on as the bad guys now?

I'd find out pretty soon.

*

But before all that, there was MFT to get through. MFT was a two-day exercise that took place at RAF North Luffenham. North Luffenham had stopped being a flying station in the '50s, and since then had become a kind of military scrapyard. It was covered with wrecked, abandoned aircraft and disused buildings and looked a bit like an air force version of *Mad Max*.

Set against this post-apocalyptic backdrop, MFT was the culmination and ultimate test of our GDT skills. We were taken there by bus, and the first stop was a hangar, inside which were the tents we'd be sleeping in. That seemed really strange, but with it being November, I wasn't complaining. I unrolled my sleeping bag onto a camp bed, which was inside the tent, which was inside the hangar.

'Lap it up, lads,' said Ox. 'Catterick'll be a lot harder than this.'

'But this is a beautiful hangar,' I said, doing my best imitation of Oddball, the slightly weird tank commander from *Kelly's Heroes*. 'Let's squat down outside the tent and make the most of it.'

'You mad fucking hippy,' Ox said, chuckling.

'Aww, mate,' I said. 'Give us your mug, I'll get you a brew.'

I picked up three mugs and came back with a mixed selection of tea and coffee. Ox and I sat down outside the tent in the weirdest campfire-without-a-campfire scene ever. Another lad, Robert Chapel, known to everyone as Vicar, also sat down and picked up a mug. I liked Vicar. He was still seventeen and one of the youngest gunners on the intake. He was always smiling, showing off a gap-toothed grin, and permanently cheerful. He was as unlikely a gunner as I was, but in a different way. He wasn't fit, wasn't even remotely ripped or toned, and he was utterly accident-prone, always walking into doors, tripping over the smallest obstacles. Perpetually scruffy, he'd try like hell to get himself, his unruly, light brown hair and his uniforms well turned out, but somehow he'd never get it right. While he didn't look tough, and some said he wouldn't even make it through Swinderby, let alone Catterick, his outward appearance was utterly deceiving. He was tougher than a hobnailed ammunition boot, and I never knew anyone who could break him.

'Hey, Vicar,' I said. 'Squat down with me and Ox, we'll have a cosmic triangle.' As a civilian five weeks earlier, I *never* spouted crap like that.

'Will it protect us from the gods of cold weather?' asked Vicar, grinning and playing along.

'You bet, man,' I replied. 'Tonight we'll sleep like we're in the tropics.'

'And tomorrow?'

'That's another story,' I said. 'I think it'll be cold and wet in the morning.'

'No shit,' said Ox, laughing. 'If it's not raining, it's not training. I don't need a bloody psychic psycho like you to tell me that.'

'You needed me for the coffee though, right?'

'Right.'

Ox was right about the weather. It rained every day, and I got my first, but definitely not my last, experience of being outside and piss-wet through. Everything on MFT happened in the rain. Moving across country, rain. Fire and manoeuvre, soaked. Guard and sentries, torrential. NBC, it was all done under grey skies, hosing rain and soaking wet uniform. I had waterproofs in my kidney pouch as part of the kit issue, but I never wore them. They were pretty good, double-skin items, and why I didn't even try to put them on, I'll never know. It might have been something as simple as no one else did, or no one told me to. More likely, though, there was always the more than even chance that if I'd so much as reached for them, a Regiment instructor would have appeared out of nowhere and screamed at me to leave them where they were.

Not entirely unwelcome, a lot of time on MFT was spent in NBC kit. The NBC suits weren't waterproof, but they sure were warm. Whatever activity was going on though, it was only ever for a few hours, then it was back to the hangar for a hot meal and a partial dry-out.

At the end of each day, the whole intake was doubled back in one massive, soaking wet, rained-on formation, all wearing ill-fitting steel helmets and squelchy boots. Our wet belts and ammunition pouches were as stiff as cardboard, our NBC suits soaked through and heavy.

The instructors kept the formation tight, and the hangar got closer and closer.

'Right wheel.' Just when I thought they'd let us inside, we were turned back the way we came, then around again and then back again. It felt like an endless fuck-around. Sometimes they'd let us shout encouragement, other times they'd bawl at us to shut up.

The CS gas also made a comeback as the exercise drew to its end. We were lined up along the peri-track in NBC suits. A few paces away, the Regiment instructors had gathered. One of them pulled out a CS tube and began to prime it. They were all wearing their respirators, and as I stood there wondering when they'd let us put ours on the decision was made by a recruit.

'Gasgasgas!'

I didn't need to be told twice and I yanked my respirator on as the CS wafted towards me. The instructors were furious but they couldn't do anything about it. They went straight to the recruit who'd made the call, held the gas tube right in front of him and told him to decontaminate.

Then the instructors prowled up and down our line while the gas tubes spewed out the CS. I continually masked and unmasked and blotted my face with Fullers Earth. One instructor stopped in front of me and put the CS under my chin. I'd just put my mask back on and there was no way I was taking it off again with the gas that close. He glared at me through his respirator eyepieces and I glared right back at him through mine, in a weird kind of NBC Mexican stand-off. I waited for him to yell at me to start decontaminating, but then the guy next to me got a lungful of gas and started coughing his ring up. I was promptly ignored as the instructors descended on him like a camouflaged plague until he got his mask back on.

It was the last ordeal of the exercise. As the CS slowly dissipated into the cold November air, MFT drew to a close.

Drill practice

With MFT done, it was more and more drill lessons, but now it was with rifles in preparation for the passing out parade. For the last week we practised and practised, slowly getting better, smarter, sharper. Even *my* drill movements, which were never good, became half-decent.

After Swinderby it was trade training, which for me, Ox, Vicar and half of 11 Flight meant Catterick and the Regiment. I should have been looking forward to it, we all should have because it was what we'd joined up to do, but there had been scary stories since day one about what was waiting for us there, and one in particular was more persistent than airburst VX.

Our senior man's elder brother had joined up a few weeks before, also Regiment. Apparently he'd phoned through and said that as soon as he'd got off the bus at Catterick, the whole intake were told to pick up all of their luggage and issued kit and then run twice round the peri-track.

Ox believed it, and if it was good enough for him, it was good enough for me. Even before MFT, several of us, myself included, tried to work out how we could sling our luggage and kit around our bodies, and still be able to run without dropping it or losing it in the dark or the rain. Suitcase, RAF holdall, best blues, civilian suit. It just couldn't be done. It was like an RAF Regiment version of *Star Trek*'s deliberately impossible Kobayashi Maru training exercise. Both were equally un-doable.

On the last weekend before the passing out parade, Corporal Vernon was as good as her word. I practically danced to Newark train station on my way to Birmingham to see Aerosmith at the NEC. There was nothing to beat live music, especially when it came in the shape of Aerosmith, archetypal American rock gods, who could strut and pout like world champions. At Birmingham train station I met my brother and an old friend from my Germany days, and I rubbed shoulders with thousands of rockers once more. The connection was still there, no matter how short my hair now was, but I was also still buzzing from Basic Training. With less than a week to go before passing out, it hadn't been the nightmare as portrayed in the Vietnam film, *Full Metal Jacket*. I'd made new friends, and sure, I didn't talk or dress like most of the recruits, but no one around me saw it as a problem. So I rocked up in Birmingham with the two big parts of my life, the RAF and heavy metal, seeming to compliment, not contradict, each other.

It wouldn't last, but that was still to come. That night at the NEC, new Brit band Thunder played support, and their gritty rock with a commercial shine received polite applause. They were a good intro for Aerosmith who were touring the UK for the first time in years. Then the interval ended, the lights went out and the stage was illuminated, outlines blurred by a thin, film curtain. Suddenly it dropped and Aerosmith exploded onto the stage, shooting toxic riffs around the arena, while the crowd went nuts. 'Birmingham,' screamed Stephen Tyler. 'How is your fine ass?' With a large wodge of tracks from their two most recent albums, *Permanent Vacation* and *Pump*, there was still room for their older classics like 'Walk This Way' and 'Mama Kin'. They owned the night, and like everyone else there I was on a feel-good high that you can only get after a concert. The hours-long train ride afterwards did absolutely nothing to dampen my spirits, and I went back to Swinderby with an armful of requested T-shirts and programmes to take back to the block.

Passing out

The 22nd November 1989 was my passing out parade, and the whole intake had to be off base straight afterwards. Everybody's uniform and personal kit were already packed away, but we still had to march to the armoury to collect our rifles. Because we weren't expected to get them in our best blues and crease them before the parade, we were dressed in civilian clothing. I wore my usual jeans, tour T-shirt, cowboy boots and floor-length raincoat. I'd seen five other intakes get to this point, and it felt good to be a part of the final tradition at Swinderby. I drew my rifle from the armoury, this time with a sheathed bayonet.

'11 Flight,' shouted Sergeant Gervill. 'Shoulder arms!'

'ONE-TWO-ONE!' The whole flight roared out the timings as though we were back in the first week of training.

'Move to the right, riiiiiiiiiiiight turn!'

'ONE-TWO-ONE!' As the last 'one' was shouted out, we stamped our feet down in unison.

'Fucking noisy bastards,' said Sergeant Gervill, with a grin. 'Do you want to go back to week one? I can still send you there.'

But he wouldn't, and we all knew he wouldn't. It was a mark of how far we'd come since we'd got there. Even me, and I was shite at drill. I'd never make QCS but I could handle a passing out parade. The flight was marched back to the block, where we parked our rifles on bare beds and got into our best blues.

'Oh, wow, guys.' I did my last bit of hippy at Swinderby. 'We've got knives on our guns.'

Standing behind me as I made the comment, Corporal Griffin performed a despairing facepalm gesture. In the military, rifles were never called guns, and bayonets were definitely not called knives.

Back outside, 11 Flight formed up alongside 4, 5 and A (WRAF) Flights. Ox wasn't there. He was one of the four flight markers who were already on the otherwise deserted parade ground. We marched over the road one last time and rounded the corner towards the parade square. The band were playing and Sergeant Gervill effortlessly guided us towards Ox. The band were behind us, the families watching, and the final flypast of four Chipmunk training aircraft sent a rush of feel-good shooting through my body. I didn't feel the biting November wind, or the discomfort of my tightly tailored uniform jacket.

Watching me pass out, my mum and stepfather did the usual proud parent thing and found it hard to fathom my apprehension as I faced Catterick. They hadn't heard the luggage run around the peri-track rumours.

It's not for everyone, and that's true. It wasn't for me, and that's also true, but it wasn't really apparent at Swinderby. I hadn't been conscripted, I wanted to be there, I was determined to give it my best shot and at Swinderby I'd bonded with the whole flight. I'd enjoyed the training, and apart from being told at times that I was a bit weird, which, quite frankly, had happened to me all my life, I wasn't picking up any warning signs, and nor was anyone telling me. With the benefit of hindsight, sure, I'd see it differently, but right there and then, I was nervous about Catterick, but so was everyone else, including Ox, and I wouldn't have walked away, even if you'd paid me.

RAF Regiment Basic Gunner Training, 22nd November 1989 to 14th March 1990

Straight after lunch in the recruits' mess with our families, a coach waited to take us to the Regiment's Depot at Catterick. The coach was about half full and I don't remember anyone even talking for the whole of the two-hour journey up to North Yorkshire. Each of us was lost in his own world of self-doubt, and I was no different. I'd wanted to join up for what seemed like all of my life, and however much I'd enjoyed Swinderby, I was wondering if I'd done the right thing, if I really could do this. Actually becoming a gunner seemed more and more unbelievable. How could I ever be anything like the Regiment instructors with their impossibly high standards? I remember thinking to myself that as long as I got more than halfway through my training, even that would be an achievement.

By the time we arrived at the camp, it was dark and raining. I wondered if the Regiment could even control the weather and make it optimally dismal.

The coach stopped just inside the camp gates and we got out. Waiting for us wasn't a ferocious sergeant, but some recruits who'd passed out from Swinderby the week before and were waiting for us to join them. They took us to the barrack block and as we dropped off our kit, they told us how great it was to be at Catterick and that they couldn't wait for the course to start. After the self-demoralising silence of the bus trip, where we'd all tortured ourselves with what we thought the place would be like, I felt my morale start to climb.

More importantly, we didn't have to run around the peri-track in the rain.

'Our flight at Swinderby was told that as well,' said one of the escorting recruits. 'What a load of bollocks.' He laughed, and I felt the tension drain away from me like an upended beer.

We went from the block to the Airmen's Mess and then to the main training building for airmen recruits, called RTS(B), Regiment Training Squadron (Basics). The drab, breeze-block structure backed onto the disused runway and from there into the training area, a large expanse of wilderness. But in the biting November darkness I saw none of that.

We filed into a room and for the first time I met our lead instructor, Sergeant 'Brummie' May, his Midlands accent rolling out from underneath his regulation moustache. His windproof smock was stretched taut over a beer-barrel chest, and I quickly learned that most sergeants at Catterick looked exactly the same, like they'd been cloned. Same build, same windproof smock, same moustache, just different accents.

'Relax, lads,' he said. 'And you can forget all that shite they told you at Swinderby. We're not going to kill you, we're not going to rip your arms off, we're not going to eat you for breakfast. What we *are* going to do is train you all to be soldiers, and that's exactly what you joined up for, right?' We all nodded frantically. 'There's four flights here,' he said. 'Each one's named after one of the Regiment's battle honours, and you lads are in El Alamein Flight.' This was known to everyone as El Al. 'Don't let that name down, lads, don't let the flight down and don't let yourselves down.'

I quickly felt pride in this small, shadowy unit that no one else seemed to have heard of. I no longer wanted to get through part of Basics; I wanted to pass out the other end. Determination then became belonging after a short, sharp address from the flight commander, Flying Officer Johnny Edge. He walked into the room after Sergeant May had spoken. His quick eyes looked at us. 'Every one of you men can pass this Basic Gunner course if you want to,' he said. I believed him. 'The final obstacle you'll face is Exercise Omega, and you can *all* pass it if you want to. If you want 2 Squadron after that, you can *all* pass the pre-para. If you want to.' His intense gaze traversed the room while my eyes fixed onto the para wings sewn on the arm of his smock. 'All you've got to do is want it.' I believed him, I believed him because him and Sergeant May believed in me, believed in all of us. Flying Officer Edge grinned a shit-eating smile beneath a pencil moustache, then sand-stormed back out of the room.

Bloody hell, he called us men.

Just like at Swinderby, a senior man was appointed for El Al, a squat, heavy-jawed recruit called Tony Chan. 'You'll do.' Sergeant

May grinned. 'You look like just the kind of bastard who actually wants to be in charge. Get them outside, senior man.'

Sections, ranges and winter

In the daylight, Catterick was poles apart from Swinderby. There were a lot less recruits, everyone was either in green or DP and there were two Regiment squadrons, 51 and 58, as well as the Light Armour Training School (LATS), which was the first stop for anyone posted to a CVR(T) squadron. The two squadrons added a real diversity to the place. It wasn't just recruits and instructors. Gunners of all ranks were everywhere, and in the Airmen's Mess I looked with awe at their Regiment shoulder slides, wondering how it must feel to earn them and wear them with such easy familiarity.

Swinderby suddenly felt like a youth club, while Catterick was for the grown-ups.

El Al Flight was split into sections of eight, and each section was assigned a room in the recruits' block, plus the usual single rooms for the senior man and his deputy. On the noticeboard in each room was a photograph, showing a wardrobe with all the issued kit either folded on a shelf or hanging, perfectly ironed in a specific order. 'Study that layout,' growled Sergeant May. 'I expect your kit to be set up exactly the same.'

The block had plenty of hot water for showering and washing, but the heating was permanently switched off. 'Must have just happened, lads.' Sergeant May uttered his first lie. 'Don't worry, it'll be fixed next week.' Which was lie number two, because just like tomorrow, next week never came.

We remained instantly recognisable as recruits. On the range and training area we wore DP, but on the station it was green overalls and DP jacket. We had plastic discs behind our beret badges, and we definitely didn't wear the RAF Regiment shoulder slides on our epaulettes. At mealtimes, we'd queue up in the Airmen's Mess smoking room on the way into the dining hall. There were usually blokes from 51 and 58 relaxing with a cigarette, and they passed comments on us as we slowly walked past them. 'He'll pass, he'll fail, he'll get binned, he won't get through Omega. Fucking hell, that one won't get through breakfast.'

Each section was under a corporal instructor, and the first part of our training covered weapons and section battle drills. Six of us carried the SA80, while one man from each half-section, known as a fire team, had the LSW. Unlike Swinderby, where you marched, at Catterick, recruits doubled everywhere in webbing.

Every soldier can tell you their own, personal story about their webbing. It's a set of pouches attached to a belt, then connected to straps that fit over the shoulders to spread the weight. As a minimum, you'd use it to carry ammunition, water, rations, respirator, but you hardly ever just carried the minimum. The '58 Pattern webbing that was dished out to us on day one at Catterick was a one-time issue and stayed with us throughout our careers. It was made of thick canvas, so it was really strong, but when it rained it doubled in weight and took on the flexibility of plywood. By 1989 it was an old design and we spent the first night customising it to get the best fit. During Basics you could add to it, but you couldn't remove anything. Over the next few weeks I bought extra pouches, and I saw how our instructors did theirs, how 51 and 58 did theirs, and in my mind I planned the perfect webbing set-up.

Every Saturday, almost everyone went to HM Supplies, a military shop on the garrison a few miles up the road and a place where I spent huge wodges of cash. Range cards, fingerless gloves, extra bungees, cam cream, all the essentials I simply had to have, and egged on by the section corporals, who were always suggesting helpful ways for us to empty our bank accounts. 'I'm not *telling* you to buy this piece of kit, lads, but…' I'm sure they were getting backhanders from that shop.

We went to the Catterick Training Area (CTA) most days, either to go through section battle drills or to use the ranges. With winter closing in, the weather quickly went south. I'd been issued with everything to keep me warm, if not dry, but once it was folded and set up for inspection, no way was I actually going to wear it. No one was specifically told to, but everyone knew that's what happened.

By strange coincidence, the whole flight was then strongly encouraged to buy one or more Norwegian Army shirts from Sergeant May, who also did a roaring trade getting his wife to sew creases into our OGs for two quid a pair. The Norwegian shirt was used by so many British soldiers that it's now issued to them when they join up, but in 1989 you had to buy them, usually from your instructors.

I bought two, and I've still got them.

Unfortunately, we weren't allowed to wear them on the ranges.

Which was a shame, especially when one day out on the firing point, the weather was absolutely shite, with a driving wind and sleet that was coming in almost horizontally. The first things to go numb were our hands. The standard issue gloves at the time were black leather ones called NI gloves, but they weren't dished out to recruits until the end of Basics. They're hopelessly out of date now, but in 1989 they were totally lux. Even when they were soaking wet they kept your hands reasonably warm, and unlike woollen gloves, your hands never slipped when you were wearing them. My pristine, issue, woollen gloves were nicely laid out in my wardrobe, and I wasn't moving them for anything. I just knew if I'd taken them to the range, got them dirty, then had to clean them, they'd shrink down to Barbie size after one wash.

'Take care of your hands, lads.' Corporal Andrews spread his arms wide and showed off his lived-in NI gloves. 'A warm hand is a happy hand. And a happy hand is a happy gunner.'

Fucking well issue us with decent gloves, then, I thought miserably to myself.

I looked through my weather-blurred SUSAT, couldn't see a thing, didn't care either and just blatted away. The windward side of my face was completely numb, and I'd long since lost all feeling in my hands. I didn't give a toss about getting a good grouping. All I wanted to do was fire off my rounds and get back to Catterick. I stood in the pre-fab fire trench, almost sobbing with the cold as I vaguely pointed my rifle at the target and fired. Sergeant May stalked up and down the firing point and growled at us to be men. 'This is nothing,' he bawled. 'This is fuck all. There's a bus to take you back for a hot meal after this and you're fucking crying? Jesus Christ, if you bastards want to be gunners, you'd better get used to this!'

The shoot finally finished and the flight doubled back to the bus. I wondered once again if I really had what it took to be a soldier. Even Ox looked shell-shocked as he sat on the bus. I drew some comfort from that, but not much.

Back at Basics, Sergeant May bollocked seven shades of shit out of us. 'You useless bastards,' he snarled. 'What did I tell you about not letting anyone down, you wankers? The weather's nothing, lads, nothing. At worst it's an occupational hazard which you'd best learn to ignore. Don't any of you ever let it stop you from doing your jobs. Do that and you'll get yourselves and everyone around you killed. If you can't handle the cold, then you need to think long and hard about staying here. Who wants to go sick?' Nobody answered. 'Who wants to D by P?' Nobody answered, but I know I was tempted and I wasn't the only one. I'd done badly, I'd let myself down, but I was determined to stay. I froze my nuts off every night in a supposedly warm block, I couldn't wear any warm clothing because it was folded up on inspection layout, and I still had a stupid haircut. But Basic Training hadn't killed me yet, and I wouldn't let it beat me. If they wanted me out they'd have to kick me out.

In the block that night, I sought out Ox's advice. 'Could we have done any better, man?' I asked him.

He shrugged. 'Yes and no, mate. Sergeant May was right, we do have to ignore the weather, even if it *was* fucking cold out there.'

'*They* didn't think so,' I moped.

'Sure they did, lads.' Vicar came in and sat at the room's small table.

'No way, man,' I said. 'Not them, they must have anti-freeze for blood.'

'That's not what they said at Basics.' Vicar grinned wide, showing off his missing tooth. 'When we got off the bus today they dicked me to take their Bergens back into the office.' He preened slightly as he spoke. 'I must have bloody good cam skills because they utterly ignored me when I was there. They all said how fucking cold it was on the range and they were glad to get back for a brew.'

'Bullshit,' I said.

'It's true, mate. Would I lie?'

It was the first and only time I realised that the instructors were actually human, but it didn't make getting through Basics any easier.

Bull nights, compare and contrast

Bull nights at Catterick had some similarities to Swinderby. The linoleum floor had to be polished, the ablutions had to be spotless and every single surface had to be dust-free.

There were also some differences.

We learned that if we put a blanket on the floor, then walked on the blanket, we could move around without leaving any footprints. Then we started sledging around the room on blankets. Then we realised that if one of us sat on the blanket and someone else spun you around in a circle, you could clean the floor and have a great laugh at the same time.

We probably should have seen it coming.

I was the lightest, so I sat on one corner of a blanket while Ox grabbed the other end and started spinning. It was hilarious, even when I felt my dinner burbling up my oesophagus and threatening to reappear. Suddenly, Ox accidentally let go and I went sliding across the floor and crashed head first into a bed frame. I felt a flash of pain, saw a bright light, then felt dizzy and sick at the same time. The section's first aid training kicked in, I was hauled to my feet, frog-marched across the room and then told to sit on a chair.

'Are you all right?'

'Fine, man,' I mumbled.

'How many fingers am I holding up?' I focussed on a hand in front of me, the predictable middle finger exposed.

'One, man, and fuck you too. Next time, keep hold of the blanket.'

'There won't be a next time,' said Ox. 'There shouldn't have been a this time. Someone give him a brew and, Brinders, sit there for an hour.'

It was the easiest bull night of my life.

Another difference was the massive lack of basic supplies. Deliberate or not, and I never knew which, but none of the sinks had plugs, and if you found one you'd steal it and hide it in your washbag. It was the same with toilet paper.

So a lot of our spare time was spent scavenging, and sometimes the searches didn't end well.

One evening after the bull night, I was on my usual quest for toilet roll. There were none in El Al's ablutions, so I crept upstairs to see what I could nab from Capitals Flight. Jackpot! I grabbed one and scuttled downstairs before anyone clocked me. I hid my booty in my wardrobe and then turned around as a wide-chested bloke in civvies and handlebar moustache walked up to me.

'Are you the senior man?' he barked in a thick Welsh accent.

'Not me, mate,' I replied, perfectly friendly. 'Who are you?'

'I—' He suddenly looked at me. 'Are you wearing an earring?'

'Sure I am, man.' I grinned. 'Why?'

'Take it out, now.'

'Oh, okay, if it makes you feel better.' *He's a bit gobby for a recruit,* I thought.

'AND I'M A CORPORAL!'

Holy shit! I stood to attention and shat myself at the same time. The corporal from upstairs lunged forward so close I could count his nose hairs. He showered abuse over me with a voice like an exploding claymore. He called me a poof and a bender and demanded to know what the fuck I looked like. He had a point. Standing to attention in faded, years-old tracksuit trousers, tour T-shirt, bandana and slippers, I must have looked a little strange. He got angrier the louder he shouted, and the more he shouted the angrier he got. He walked around me in tight circles, like a lion eyeing his prey. A lion who swore constantly. 'Do I look like a fucking recruit?' he bawled.

'No, Corporal,' I replied. He was in the recruits' block and wearing civvies. Why *wouldn't* I think he was a recruit? But I wasn't dumb enough to say it.

He stomped back out of the room, then turned around to fire his departing shot. 'If I see you wearing that thing again I'll rip your fucking ear off.'

He left my line of sight, I breathed a sigh of relief as he went back upstairs, and everyone else in the room pissed themselves laughing. They'd all seen him as he walked in, and even stood behind him making two-fingered corporal signs on their shoulders to warn me, but I'd missed it all and sailed closer to oblivion than I ever wanted to again.

'Well, fucking hell, lads,' I said, trembling. 'What's a corporal doing here on a bull night?'

My question was never answered, but at least I got a bog roll out of it.

*

The block was inspected each morning after breakfast. We made our beds and did our last-minute cleaning as the radio played 'Downtown Train' by Rod Stewart. All wardrobes had to be opened and the instructors inspected everything, including civvies. Military kit had to be laid out exactly as it was in the photo on the noticeboard. Sometimes there were bollockings, but even when there were, it was never really serious. How could it be when just out of the instructor's eyesight was a recruit pulling faces, trying to make you laugh and then quickly jumping back to attention as soon as the instructor turned around. New additions to our vocabularies were 'minging' and 'howfing'. Both meant dirty or unclean. If our kit wasn't spotless clean it was minging and you were a minger. Howfing was even worse than minging.

One time, Corporal Faith pulled apart my civilian locker. 'Fucking hell, Brindle.' The same size as Ox, he towered over me and threw my underpants on the floor. 'What kind of minger are you, eh? Don't you iron your commandos?'

'No, Corporal,' I said, and I didn't know anyone else who did, either.

'Fucking weirdo.' He stomped past me.

'Did you starch this sleeve?' Sergeant May bawled at the guy in the bed-space next to mine.

'Yes, Sergeant.'

'What with, spit?' he roared, showering the poor bastard with sergeant saliva.

And so it went. Some days the inspections went well, some days they didn't. And there didn't seem to be any pattern to it. If I thought we'd done a good job we'd still be pulled up, and sometimes, even when the layouts were shit, we sailed through. Looking back, it seemed that maybe even the bollockings were timed into the syllabus as much as the ranges and mealtimes were.

One morning, not long after the corporal from Capitals chewed me out over my earring, we were standing outside the block, waiting to be doubled over to start the day's training. From upstairs I heard the same dreaded voice screaming at his recruits, then the

60

scrape of beds and furniture being shoved around the rooms. I breathed a sigh of relief that I wasn't on Capitals.

At least on El Al the furniture stayed where it was.

Christmas

I've often thought that if the Warsaw Pact ever did decide to come for us, then Christmas would have been an ideal time to do it because with the exception of Northern Ireland and maybe the Falklands, the entire British war machine shut down and got shit-faced for ten days.

Which included the whole of RAF Catterick. On the last working day, which was a Friday, a lot of people would be driving home, so the party started the day before with Christmas dinner in the Airmen's Mess. The sliding doors were pulled back and the dining hall doubled in size. It was the only day of the year that officers were allowed in, and on that day they traditionally served the airmen their meals. It was your typical Christmas roast and there was loads of it. It was loud, festive and most of 51 and 58 were already pissed. Food fights started almost straight away, and the officers tried to make sure most of the food stayed on people's plates. It worked with the recruits, but not the squadrons. I think they threw more than they ate.

The two squadrons based at Catterick, 51 and 58, also had their own bar. It was separate from the NAAFI, and we'd been told that on that night only we could go there for a drink. Sergeant May read us the Riot Act before we went over. 'No fighting, because they'll win, no drinking contests, because they'll win and no spandex pants or tassled fucking leather jackets,' he growled, looking straight at me, 'because you really don't want to piss them off.'

But other than my uniform and civilian suit, my options were really limited. So I went there in my usual: jeans, tour T-shirt, cowboy boots, bandana and raincoat. Despite Sergeant May's warning, I didn't give it much thought. None of the lads on El Al had a problem with the way I looked, where my weirdness was accepted. Among El Al, I had friends, I was getting what I wanted from life, and I really believed I was going to be part of something much bigger than me. And besides, we were training to be Rocks, and we were going out for a pint with some Rocks. Surely we'd all be mates, right?

If only. Walking into the squadron bar was like walking into The Slaughtered Lamb. Groups of blokes stood together facing inwards, already excluding us with their body language. Our arrival was greeted with hostile glares, as though it wasn't even their choice we'd been allowed there. Looking back, maybe it wasn't. A couple of us, very few, seemed to fit in, buying a pint and starting a conversation. Most others were picked off one at a time, singled out, pinned against a wall and terrorised.

'What are you doing here?' they'd growl, nose to nose and flanked by their mates. 'Get the fuck out of my bar.'

No one was actually hurt, but the underlying atmosphere was definitely not friendly. To a bunch of beered-up SACs, we were easy entertainment. 'All right, lads.' I beamed cheerfully at a small group of blokes as I tried to make contact.

'Who's this cunt?' They glared poison at me. 'Want a bit of 2 Squadron when you pass out, do you? You look like it.'

'No, mate,' I said guilelessly. 'I want to go to 3 Squadron.'

'Fuck off.'

Suddenly my leg felt wet as a passing admirer chucked a pint over me. And so it went. I looked around and didn't see any friends, just groups of Rocks who I didn't know and who didn't like me. I was picking up threatening looks from right across the room, was being jostled by strangers and heard 'Fuck off' whispered at me as people walked past. I sensed trouble everywhere I looked. It was time to go. I walked away and headed back to the block, wondering what it was I'd done so wrong. I didn't think I'd done anything wrong. Christ, all I'd done was turn up for a pint, like I'd been told to. What *reason* was there to be such wankers to the new boys? I didn't know, but my sense of injustice was transitory. I was encroaching on their territory, I rationalised, I was a recruit who shouldn't have been there, and that was all. I clung to something, anything other than the possibility that I wasn't a good fit, because at that time I was sure I still was. Well, among everyone on El Al I was, and as the night went on most of the rest of the flight came back to the block in ones and twos as well.

If I'd had any kind of foresight I'd have realised that social events were pretty much the same on all squadrons, although I was very far from being the only one who got shat on that night. I should have realised that if I didn't fit in at a squadron bar in Catterick, I'd be unlikely to fit in at a squadron bar anywhere.

The next day, just before we knocked off for Christmas, we were on parade outside RTS(B). Sergeant May came out of the building and screamed across the empty car park. 'Brindle, front and centre!'

Being front and centred meant you were about to be bollocked in front of the whole flight for some serious shit. I had no idea what I'd done wrong. I stepped out and doubled to the front. Sergeant May walked up to me and chuckled. He put a brawny arm around my shoulders and I wondered what was going on.

'This is Rick,' he sniggered to the whole flight. 'And Rick's daddy is an officer in the army.' He looked at me with a pseudo-benevolent smile. 'Kept that quiet, didn't you, Brindle?'

'Yes, Sergeant.'

'Yes, Sergeant,' he mimicked me. 'Mummy and Daddy coming to collect you tonight, are they? Taking you home for Christmas?' He was laughing his head off, and the corporals joined in with the mirth.

'Yes, Sergeant,' I repeated.

'Not straight away though,' chortled Sergeant May. 'Daddy's just phoned,' he said. 'Seems that Mummy has to get her hair done, so would you mind awfully waiting an hour for them?'

I was writhing with embarrassment while everyone around me pissed themselves laughing, and they never let me live it down. For the rest of the course, the instructors never used my surname and just called me Rick. Twenty-four hours after having beer chucked over me, I was back to laughing and joking with both the instructors and my mates. It said it all about the RAF Regiment's Jekyll and Hyde nature. And only in the RAF Regiment could being called by your first name be used as an insult.

Bayonet training

After Christmas leave, January 1990 started with a shock. For no apparent reason, Tony Chan was fired as senior man and the job was given to Ox. Until then, Ox had been section leader, and he was the ideal choice. But he couldn't have both jobs so it was given to me instead, and they went from the best person to lead the section to the absolute worst. Ox gave everyone advice about bulling their kit, what items to add to their webbing, and he got the whole section where it had to be.

Typically very modest, during a camouflage and concealment lesson Ox pulled out a cam stick and offered it round the whole section.

'Hey, man,' I said. 'How come you added that to your stash and we didn't?'

'Because I'm switched on,' he replied.

And he was.

Only to be replaced by me. My life experience and advice-giving ability were absolute zero, and with my hippy mellow image and timid personality, I was the last person to bark orders and get people into line. The once upon a time when I wanted to be an officer was long gone. At least I'd worked *that* out.

Tony Chan was a good senior man, and I liked him. But for me, Ox did a better job.

Unlike me.

I was a shite section leader. I didn't have the looks, the build or the voice. And I definitely didn't have the presence. The times I was told to fuck off suddenly multiplied by ten. 'Don't worry, Brinders,' said Ox. 'They said that to me as well.' He smiled. 'Just shout and swear back at them even worse.'

I tried it at the end of that day's training. 'Stride.' I picked out one of the section at random. 'Check the windows are secure on this floor.'

'Fuck off.'

'Don't tell me to fuck off, you lazy cunt. I'm telling you to do it, so fucking well do it, man.'

'Fuck off.'

I seriously doubt that any military is as wedded to the bayonet as the British. The order to fix bayonets is steeped in history, from the Falklands to the trenches of World War One and right back to the Peninsular War. The bayonet that came with the SA80 was used for wire cutting, sawing through wood, and the scabbard even had a bottle opener.

But it was still used for killing.

'What's the bayonet for?' screamed Corporal Andrews. His rugby-player build and permanent scowl was already intimidating, and on that day he was terrifying as he fired looks of pure evil at everyone.

'To kill!' we roared back, all of us grouped on a patch of open ground.

'Who are you going to kill?'

'The enemy!'

'That's right, you bastards. Now run over there and run back even faster.'

In between being beasted and shouting out that we were going to kill the enemy, everyone's aggression levels, even mine, soared. And that was exactly what they wanted.

I looked at four overall-clad dummies, each one hanging from a wooden frame that looked a lot like a gallows. Four of us held our rifles with bayonets fixed, while behind us stood another recruit, sticking close by and constantly screaming, 'Kill, kill, kill! Kill him before he kills you.' Everyone else stood behind the dummies and hurled abuse at us, calling us poofs, wankers, telling us they were going to shag our girlfriend, sister, mother, anything to wind us up.

'You useless fucking hippy weirdo,' I heard Ox screaming at me. 'Where's your peace-loving shit now?'

I felt my heart racing, and my skin tingled. I gripped my rifle and fire-stared murderous hatred at the dummy that had done me no harm.

'Advance!' bawled Corporal Andrews.

I approached the dummy to my front and shouted out a challenge, 'On guaaaaaard!' Then, screaming at the top of my voice I charged, rammed the bayonet into the hilt, kicked the dummy, spat on it for good measure, then pulled out my rifle, screamed, 'On guaaaaaard!' again and moved forward. With my enemy suitably dead, I got on the ground, crawled forward with bayonet in hand and stabbed another dummy that was lying down. All the while being verbally abused and having someone shout 'Kill!' over and over again in my ear.

After I'd taken my turn with the bayonet, I swapped round and screamed at an oppo to kill and then it was all change and I took a turn at yelling mass abuse at the four with their bayonets. At every changeover Corporal Andrews roared out once more, 'What's the bayonet for?'

'To kill!'

'Who are you going to kill?'

'The enemy!'

'Fucking right you will. Now run over there and back again.'

By the end of it, everyone, including me, was seeing everything through a red haze murder-mist of testosterone. For the first time in my life I felt the rush of aggression, the trembling, quick nervous movements, the short temper, the instant Robert De Niro 'Are you talking to me' persecution complex. It didn't stay with me for long and I calmed down pretty quickly afterwards, but quite a few from the flight, including Ox, remained keyed up for the whole day, glaring at everyone around them, snarling and clenching their fists. If there was ever going to be a mass fight among recruits, it would have been straight after bayonet training. It was easily and without a doubt the most visceral, aggressive point of my training. Ever.

But I never actually thought that it was a person I was bayoneting, or that I'd ever actually have to kill anyone. It was a strange kind of paradox. Yes, I joined up to be soldier, with, I thought, my eyes wide open. I accepted that I was being trained to kill, and being in the RAF Regiment, I might be among the first to do so if it ever came to it. But the thought that it would actually happen, even with Northern Ireland, even with the Falklands less than a decade earlier? That I might have to pull the trigger or plunge that bayonet into flesh? It wasn't something that was ever seriously spoken about, much less thought about. I probably wasn't the only one who just thought that when the time came, if the time came, my training would, as I was always being told, take over.

Even for a heavy metal oddball like me, the training would take over.

Fieldcraft

The week after bayonets I pulled on my Norwegian shirt for the training exercise, Fieldcraft. It was five days of putting everything we'd learned so far into practice. The new word of the week was CEMO, Complete Equipment Marching Order, which meant tabbing with webbing, rifle and large pack. The large pack was the precursor to the Bergen, and it didn't have shoulder straps. It hooked onto your webbing yoke and in doing so pulled the whole thing down at the back and up at the front.

Wearing a large pack was terminally uncomfortable. It also wasn't designed for all the kit that was issued in 1989. That meant you had to jump on it from a great height in order to get it closed once you'd packed spare DP, boots, field towel, poncho, waterproofs, NBC kit and all the extra chocolate bars you'd bought at the NAAFI. Sleeping bag and bed roll were strapped to the outside, with the sleeping bag sitting on the top, the end result being that it skylined higher than your helmet.

We double-dosed on breakfast, and the four tonners took us out to the CTA. Ups, downs and turns later they stopped, and we jumped out and went into all-round defence, rifles outwards and boots overlapping. We were supposed to scan out to the distant horizon for enemy activity, but the shortcomings of large pack CEMO quickly became apparent. As I lay down, my sleeping bag, which was strapped to my large pack, pushed against the back of my helmet, which meant the front of my helmet was jammed into the ground and all I could get a good look at was the CTA mud an inch in front of my eyeballs. I reckon I was doing something wrong and it was a good job I wasn't on point. At least the overlapping boots told me when it was time to get up and move out.

We tabbed towards a field near a place called Gandale Farmhouse, where tents had been set up. Fieldcraft was two nights in tents and two nights in harbour. It was a North Yorkshire January and I was glad I'd spent most of my wages at HM Supplies. And not just me either. A good half of us were wearing green fleeces under our DP, and a few had also bought Gore-Tex boot liners. The two lux pieces of kit we weren't allowed but really could have done with were Bergens and NI gloves.

For the next week, the instructors trampled and dragged us through everything in the infantry manual: moving across country, camouflage and concealment, night noises. We did ambushes, anti-ambushes and lots and lots of section battle drills. Every training area always has hundreds of streams running through it, and every drill involved walking through one, kneeling in one or falling into one and trying to climb out of it while staying tactically quiet.

Even without the streams to help with our approach routes and awareness, the CTA in January was never dry. If it wasn't snowing it was raining, and if it wasn't doing either of those the wind howled across the moors like an invisible werewolf. The ground never really dried out, which I quickly discovered as I spent a lot of time in a prone fire position, feeling the ice-cold moisture seeping through my DP.

The instructors also did their best to make sure we didn't avoid the best that the winter had to offer. One time I went to ground in a pretty dry area and scanned ahead, only to feel my ankles being grabbed as Corporal Andrews dragged me backwards into a mud patch. 'Much better concealment there,' he said. A few minutes later I heard him shouting at Vicar. 'Chapel, what's that?'

'A puddle, Corporal.'

'No, it's not, it's a fire position. Get in it.'

One of our attacks went in with blank ammunition to make it as real as possible. Delta fire team, a four-man half-section, took cover on a low crest and put down suppressing fire, while I took Charlie team in along the stream. I dropped off a rifleman and the second LSW as intimate fire support and then two of us snaked forward up a gentle slope. The last part of the attack was coming. Simulated fire was going in from two angles. Corporal Bevan followed us in, encouraging us, moving us along. He was getting pretty carried away and excited himself. I signalled the intimate support to fire a pretend 66mm, and I lobbed a thunderflash into the enemy position. As soon as it went off, my oppo went in and fired into the trench and then it was my turn. 'Go on, Brindle.' Corporal Bevan was shouting himself hoarse. 'Get in there and take the position.' I rushed forward, screaming at the top of my voice. I held my rifle at my hip and pulled the trigger, but the magazine was empty. I reached into my ammo pouch for a fresh magazine, but there were none. I had no idea what to do next so I stopped dead in my tracks, and hippy mode took over. I shrugged and looked behind me. 'I've run out of bullets, Corporal,' I said, massively pleased that I hadn't called him 'man'.

The first two mornings at Gandale Farmhouse included a site inspection, as though the place was a barrack block, and it was a no-win situation. It was a field in Yorkshire, it was January, it was shit weather. There was no way it wouldn't be minging. It was howfing, even. And wherever a recruit was, anywhere in the world, the instructors could always spot a telegraph pole or lone tree to make you run to.

'What the fuck, lads,' shouted Corporal Roberts. 'You bull the block til it's fucking gleaming, and you come out here and live like pigs on a bender. And so help me, it looks like you *want* to.' He stalked towards Vicar. 'Chapel,' he shouted, nose to nose with Vicar. 'Did you polish your boots this morning?'

'Yes, Corporal.'

'Fucking liar. Run to that lone tree and back.'

Straight-backed in his DP, Corporal Roberts marched left and then quivered like a planted sword in front of Ox. 'Oxford,' he bawled. 'Did you bother to clean your bed-space in that minging tent?'

'Yes, Corporal.'

'You bullshitting wanker. Run to that telegraph pole and back. And Brindle.' He looked at me and shook his head in mock disapproval. 'Have you bothered your arse—'

'No, Corporal.'

'Fucking right you haven't, you lazy cunt. Run to that lone tree and make sure you're back before those other two wasters.'

The third night should have seen us sleeping in the woods under ponchos, but instead it was spent actually inside Gandale Farmhouse, as weather conditions ran foul of Health and Safety. We were all cramped into one tiny room around a paraffin heater, but I definitely wasn't complaining.

On the Thursday morning, we were up before dawn, kit stowed and cooking our rations outside in the drizzling rain. I poured my carefully boiled water into my sachet of rolled oats, added the drinking chocolate and the entire sugar ration. Seconds after my first mouthful of super-sweet field breakfast, the sugar rush hit me and I felt warm, dry and utterly invincible. A ration pack and hot water was instant morale, even on a freezing cold Yorkshire morning in January.

That night, things returned to normal and the flight bivvied up in a harbour. Turfed out early the next morning while it was still dark, Corporal Bevan roared at me to get my section in order. 'Brindle,' he shouted, loud enough to wake the whole CTA. 'Brindle, where the fuck are you, and where the fucking hell is your section?' Right then I had no idea where my section was. Instead I was frantically trying to untangle bungees and roll up my sleeping bag, before desperately figuring out how the hell I was going to get my large pack strapped shut again, all in the dark. At the same time I was also supposed to be managing the section. The recruit-level shambles and instructor-level bollockings continued until well into daylight.

Heavy rain on the final day welcomed us to the CTA's FIBUA set-up, where we hunkered down in a derelict house, munched through a cold ration-pack lunch and were briefed on urban warfare. The exercise-ending attack was put in that afternoon. We scrambled over windowsills, thundered up and down stairs, lobbed thunderflashes into rooms and absolutely blatted off every single one of our remaining blanks.

Fieldcraft was one of the major obstacles on Basics, and one of the usual characteristics of a Basic Gunner course was dwindling numbers as people either left or were binned. For El Al though, everyone got through Fieldcraft. Sergeant May was a real flip-flop character when it came to failing a recruit. The threat of being re-coursed was made practically every day, but at the same time, Sergeant May also went on about how he wanted El Al's passing out parade to have more gunners in it than the band, which was something that had never happened before. I'd expected more people to have either left or gotten kicked out by that point. I was still mildly surprised that I hadn't been binned, although if I had, my world would have imploded. By the time Fieldcraft happened, being a gunner was all I wanted to be. The nightmare of not liking it, regretting my decision or not fitting in hadn't materialised, and I was desperate to prove to everyone, friends and family, to say nothing of the instructors, that I had what it took to be in the RAF Regiment.

Too scared to pass out and be posted

In 1989 and into 1990, the days of recruits being slapped, kicked, punched or physically abused in any way had long since stopped. The instructors said it used to go on, but then again, they also said the heating would be fixed *and* that a freezing cold range shoot was nothing, the lying, bullshitting, just-as-human-as-us bastards.

But while they couldn't/wouldn't give us a kicking any time they wanted, they were still experts at psychological warfare.

'You're all crap,' sniped Sergeant May as the flight formed up outside the block. 'The last El Al Flight beat the shit out of you lot. Fucking hell, every flight we've had was better than you. I'd love to bin you all right now but I can't. We need the men. That's why Basics is so fucking easy these days.'

Then, as the end of the course came within reach and I started to think I might actually pass, even that was stopped from becoming the life-changing achievement I wanted. 'You think you're in the Regiment just because you passed Basics?' Corporal Faith sneered at me one day on the range. 'Sure,' he said, shrugging his shoulders. 'You'll be an LAC, you'll get posted to a squadron, but you won't be in the Regiment. Not really. Not until you're an SAC. So don't start getting ideas above your station just because you've been asked how many family you've got coming to the passing out parade.'

All pretty standard so far, but then they scared the shit out of all of us. 'Jesus Christ,' Sergeant May shouted across the parade square. 'What the fuck have I done to get such a bunch of useless cunts like you? Pathetic, soft bastards, every fucking one of you. I'd like nothing more than to take you out back and kick the shit out of you.' His half-closed eyes blazed pure hatred. 'We can't do that here any more, but they sure as shit can on the squadrons.' Evil glare turned into evil smile. 'And we know people on every squadron, lads. I think it's time me and Corporal Faith made a few phone calls and arranged a nice little welcome for you fuckers wherever you get posted to.'

As far as I know, they didn't make those calls, but by Christ I was terrified as my contradictions crashed down around me. I wasn't tough and I wasn't aggressive, and here I was wanting to be in the RAF Regiment. And even though I was told almost daily that I was shit, I was still on the course. I survived on El Al because it was enjoyable and challenging, because we were all friends, all equals, all in it together. But then I thought back to the pre-Christmas drink in the squadron bar, I thought about Sergeant May's threats, and the opposites just kept on hitting into each other. Surely he didn't mean me? He was the one who laughed and called me Rick as a joke. Then why did the squadron guys hate me? I rationalised that they hated all of us, and I shrugged. It was too late to back out now, and I was determined to make a success of it. Just like Cleavon Little said in *Blazing Saddles*, once you establish yourself, they've got to accept you.

Nights out in Darlington

Most weekends, I'd head into Darlington with Ox, Vicar, whoever wanted to make the trip. We'd go to the garrison first, spend an absolute fortune at HM Supplies and then it was off to Darlington. Usually it was utterly uneventful. Lunch at McDonald's, then the cinema. Popular with most recruits at the time was the Vietnam film *Casualties of War*, starring Michael J Fox. It was like playing spot the squaddie in the cinema before the lights went down. After that, all you could hear were anonymous audience members saying stuff like 'shit spacing', 'gash fuckers' and the ever popular 'fasten your chinstrap, you wanker'. After watching a film, we'd maybe have a few pints and then head back to Catterick.

The weekend before Range Week, a taxi-full of us decided on a late night in Darlington. A few beers, unwind, no trouble, no problems.

Then, walking back to the taxi rank at the end of the night, a lone local lad was singing a football song.

Ox replied with a Torquay United chant.

Not the wisest thing in the world, but not exactly trying to take over the Suez Canal either. Except that the local guy kept following us, ballsy bastard that he was. And even when one of ours, John Brand, started saying, 'Lads, lads, we can take him. Let's do him,' he carried on tailing us. John Brand was usually a quiet bloke, mellow and slightly older than most of the lads on El Al. He was the last one I'd have thought would start anything, but he suddenly swung at this guy. The rest of us rushed back, pulled him off and carried on walking to the taxi rank, a bit quicker this time. The cold weather and sudden violence started to sober me up. I stepped out and did the meerkat head-spin, while out of nowhere, more locals suddenly appeared and before we knew it, *we* were the ones outnumbered and being herded along.

I was never in a million years going to start swinging my fists, but apart from John, nor were the rest of us, either. I'd never even *been* in a fight before, and if I wasn't still half-pissed, it would have felt even more unreal than it already did. John kept piling into one or the other of the locals and we kept pulling him away. 'Go on,' the local lad started sneering. 'You're good lads, why don't you just run?' My gaze shifted, we were a long way from home and no one was going to help us. 'Why don't you run?' they chanted.

I don't know which one of us went first, or maybe we all did, but suddenly we went from walking to running and being chased through Darlington's empty night-time streets. I found myself sprinting across an almost deserted market square, my cowboy boots loud on the cobblestones. Two blokes were walking towards me. I ran past them and one of them swung a fist. He chinned me and I dropped to the floor. As I hit the deck I heard his mate say, 'That's not him.' I didn't stick around to tell him he'd got the wrong person. I was straight up and running like a jackrabbit before the people who actually *were* chasing me caught up with me.

It was a good job we had Ox with us, even if he did sing football songs at the totally wrong time. Our pursuers gradually dwindled away into the night. 'Re-org!' shouted Ox. 'Re-org!' We coalesced around him.

'Where's John?' asked Ox.

I looked at Ox. 'There's something different about you. Are you OK?'

'I lost my glasses when we pulled John away from them locals.'

'Shit, Ox. Can you see all right?'

'Never mind that,' snapped Ox. He took a deep breath. 'Where's John?' he asked, louder this time.

'I don't know, man,' I replied. 'We were all split up way back there.' I flung out a haphazard arm. 'What if they've got him?'

'Then we go back and we find out.'

'Are you sure about that? There was an awful lot of them.'

'So we get a taxi to Catterick, wake up the lads and we come back and we get him.'

Hardly Operation Nimrod, but then again, it *was* still Basics.

Back at Catterick, we piled out of the taxi and walked nonchalantly past the Guard Room, making damn sure we didn't tell them what had happened. Once we got round the corner we sprinted along deserted footpaths to the block, woke up the rest of the flight, piled into cars and headed back to Darlington, like a Basic gunner version of a night-time revenge/rescue squad.

We drove around for over an hour but there was no sign of John, so we headed back to Catterick, again. As we slowed down at the barrier, we were told to park the cars and head into the Guard Room. The night had just got a lot worse. Someone had told the guard commander what had happened, and now we were in some serious shit.

I walked into the Guard Room and stood in a pristine polished corridor at some stupid time of the night, any residual alcohol in my system long gone. One of us, a huge, massively shouldered, overhang-forehead bloke nicknamed Ogre, couldn't believe the injustice. He'd been fast asleep in the block, then woken up and had half a dozen lads pile into his car and demand he drive them to Darlington. It was nothing to do with him, but he was in just as much crap as everyone else.

'Look, lads,' he said, in his gravelly cockney accent. 'I haven't done anything. You'll back me up, right?'

'Sure,' replied Ox. 'Right, lads?'

We all agreed. Those of us who'd been out since the start of the night nodded.

'Go and tell the corporal,' said Ox. 'We're with you.'

It sounded pretty reasonable, although never in my entire military career of a few months had I ever seen a recruit cross a corporal. They were the ultimate power in our lives. Completely uncharacteristically, Ogre crept timidly around the corner, while the rest of us stood still and stared at the whitewashed brick walls.

'Excuse me, Corporal,' Ogre murmured, his soft words barely audible. 'This is nothing to do with me. I just—'

'Get outside, you fucking wanker!' screamed the corporal. 'I thought I told you cunts to stand in the fucking corridor, and that includes YOU! You'll move when I fucking well tell you to move!'

Ogre sprinted back to his spot in the corridor and stood next to me, while I quivered like a jelly and shat myself. The corporal thundered around the corner and glared at the rest of us.

'What flight are you?' He fired the question like a magnum double-tap.

'El Al, Corporal,' said Ox, always the senior man, always the spokesman, even when we were in a world of shit, even when we'd just had our arses handed to us in Darlington.

77

'So…' he jeered. '*You* lot are El Al? I've heard all about you useless pricks.' He paced up and down the corridor, and I trembled as he passed. 'You people are the worst fucking troops we've ever had here, and now I know why.' Without him even realising it – or did he? – he'd said the worst thing possible, instantly reinforcing what the instructors had been saying for weeks. All I'd ever wanted was to be told I was worth it, that I was doing all right, and now a corporal I'd never even seen before had heard how useless we all were. The dreaded thought burned through my mind: *we must be really shit if everyone's saying it.* My morale dropped another notch and the corporal's tirade continued. 'What the fucking hell were you wankers playing at? Got into a fight, left a man behind and now you come back here like a bunch of whipped pussies. Jesus H Christ, we'll be the laughing stock of Catterick if this gets out, and you cunts are the reason why. And thank you for ruining the rest of my night while I decide what to do with you bastards.' He looked at his watch. 'Get back here at six o'clock.'

None of us moved.

'Move, you wankers!'

Having an order barked at us was much more familiar territory, and we shot out of the Guard Room as though we'd had a mortar tube shoved up our arses. Once we were out of sight we stopped doubling and walked back to the block. It was three o'clock in the morning and in three hours we'd have to be awake again to learn our fate. Jesus, Sergeant May was going to kill us when he found out about this on Monday.

Just before six, we were up again and this time we marched back to the Guard Room in our civvies, only to be screamed at for not being in uniform. The corporal wasn't any happier than he'd been at three o'clock, and whatever squadron he was on, not that we dared ask him, we sure as hell hoped we weren't posted there. He shouted at us some more, then sent us back to the block.

What could, and should, have been a mellow Sunday, chilling before Range Week started, was instead spent shitting ourselves and wondering what our instructors were going to do to us when they found out.

Multiply that by a thousand if John Brand didn't get back in one piece.

Thankfully, John rolled back to camp later that day. A few cuts and bruises, but no worse otherwise. He'd been lucky, but it didn't take away the effort everyone had made to find him, or that it was Ox who'd driven it, even at the expense of losing his glasses. By lights out the whole flight had pitched in to buy him a replacement pair.

The next morning, expecting the worst bollocking ever, the instructors pissed themselves laughing. Ogre blushed as a chuckling Corporal Roberts stood eyeball to chest and looked up at him. 'I don't care if you were just the driver,' he said. 'I'd have been disappointed as fuck if you hadn't been there.'

Then, 'What the fuck, Brindle? *You* were in a fight?'

'Yes, Corporal.'

'Fucking hell, lad, on whose side?'

'Ours, Corporal.'

'Our side,' snorted Corporal Roberts. 'Fuck me, Brindle, one look at you and they probably thought they were fighting Neil from *The Young Ones*. No wonder you fuckers lost.'

Re-coursed

When I was being chased through Darlington like the steely-eyed killer I was and after I got twatted by mistake by a stranger, I'd collapsed backwards, twisted my leg and pulled a muscle. I was too shit-scared to notice at the time, but after a day the swelling started, the bruising came out all along my thigh and I was limping badly. Worse than that were the sudden chills, high temperature, and diarrhoea so bad I was practically pissing out of my arse.

It was a crucial week in training. Range Week involved practising a lot of what we'd learned, but with live ammunition. On the grenade range and shrouded by damp clouds of mist and shite weather, I pulled the pin out with shaking hands. Corporal Roberts looked at me with an evil grin, just aching for me to drop it in the pit so that he could grab me and chuck me over the lip to safety, which was also apparently the quickest way to get promoted to sergeant. I just about lobbed the grenade over the lip, Corporal Roberts called me a faggot, and without waiting yanked me to the ground, shouting 'Grenade' a whole lot louder than I had. Then he pulled me to my feet, booted me out of the pit and I shuffled round to the troop shelter. 'Next!' he screamed.

'Are you bastards cold?' Sergeant May stormed into the troop shelter. We were huddled in there while the instructors sat in the four-tonner cab with the heating on. 'Cold? Cold? Fucking cold, are you? Like that day on the range, you poofs? Well, you won't get warm sitting in the troop shelter. Run round the fucker right now. Go!'

We took off around the troop shelter in a mass of damp DP misery. Normally I'd have made a good fist of running. It was definitely my strongest point physically, but my aching leg and jumping-bean squits wiped me out, and I immediately started trailing the flight.

'Look at that limp dick,' crowed Flight Lieutenant Anderson, an officer I'd never even seen before. 'He's not even bloody trying.'

'He's fit as fuck, Sir.' Ox peeled off from the flight and faced the officer. 'If he was on his game he'd be right at the front. He's not well.' Ox about-turned as smartly as you can in mud-clogged

80

boots and DP and went back to the flight. As shit as I felt right then, I thought my heart would burst when I heard Ox speak. He'd pushed the power gradient as far as he could while staying within the rules, and he did it for me. How many recruits do *you* know that would face off an officer for their mate? Ox did, but would it make a difference?

'Brindle!' bellowed Sergeant May. 'Get over here now.' I tottered over. 'What's your major malfunction today, *Rick*?'

'I don't know, Sergeant.'

'I don't know, Sergeant,' he minced back at me with a sneer. 'Of course you don't know, you useless prick. If you did, you'd be a fucking doctor. Symptoms, you bastard, and now, before I die of old age.'

'I've got a swollen leg and the shits, Sergeant.'

'Fucking wimp. Get a brew, get in the troop shelter. Excused range duties today, report sick in the morning.' I pulled my mug from my webbing and trudged towards the four tonner and the tea urn. 'Brindle,' snapped Sergeant May.

'Yes, Sergeant.'

'Make sure you wash your hands after you've wiped your arse and stay the fuck away from me until you're shitting solids.'

'Yes, Sergeant.'

The following morning I was prescribed a truckload of Dioralyte and bedded down for the day. From the Wednesday onwards I was back out with the flight, but I wasn't taking part in the ranges. The next week was Exercise Omega and then Basics would be done. I was so close to the end, but it wasn't going to happen with El Al. I hadn't completed Range Week, and I still had to.

Basics being Basics, and the instructors being instructors, they didn't tell me straight away, the bastards. As the week drew to a close, and even over the weekend, I was still part of El Al, and along with the rest of the flight I got ready for Omega. My large pack was crammed with everything I'd need. I checked, checked, checked my webbing again, readjusted the straps, got everything just right. On the Monday morning El Al paraded outside RTS(B) in full DP and CEMO. We were told to empty out our packs to make sure we hadn't left any kit behind and then I was called into the office.

'Brindle,' barked Sergeant May, level-eyed and his voice devoid of all emotion. 'You can't pass Basics if you haven't done Range Week. You're being re-coursed to Meiktila.'

And just like that I was off El Al. I was no longer on BG15/89 El Al, I was now BG16/89 Meiktila. Was Sergeant May glad to see the back of me, or disappointed to see me go? I never knew.

But there was no mistaking the feeling. It was like I'd been kicked in the balls, kneed in the face and trampled on by an entire rugby squad. It was the worst thing ever. Re-coursed. Binned. I wouldn't be passing out with the guys I'd gone through eleven weeks of training together with. It didn't sound like much, but we'd all been through the same things at the same time and we'd bonded. Now I'd have to fit in with a whole new bunch of lads who I didn't know, and they didn't know me. It was terrifying.

I trudged back outside and asked Ox for the block key.

'Fucking hell, Brindle,' he moaned. 'Really? What have you forgotten now?' He shook his head and spat on the ground. 'You people are really pissing me off.'

'I've been re-coursed,' I replied.

Ox's mouth dropped open and he froze. He stood still for five seconds and the silence compounded my despair. He didn't say anything. Ox *always* said something, and he always said the right thing. It was what he was best at, and he was also my friend. Without a word, he handed over the keys. I picked up my webbing and large pack and went back to the block, utterly alone and totally pissed off. I'd come so close to passing out with El Al. Shit, I'd come so close to passing out full stop, and now it was like I was starting all over again.

I was allocated a bed-space in Meiktila's section of the block, then changed into OGs and joined my new flight on their first week of signals training. I quickly struck up a good friendship with a Sri Lankan recruit called Hendricks, who'd been nicknamed Jimmy since day one. Like me, he was well into his heavy metal and rock music, and he also wore a floor-length raincoat. That made both of us outcasts. We got on straight away.

I was still a recruit among recruits, all equals, no seniority, no pecking order. Despite my initial fears, I got on with the lads on Meiktila. Sure, I'd have loved to finish the course with El Al, but I couldn't, and I couldn't change that. There were no issues from

Meiktila with me being dumped onto the flight, and it actually reinforced to me that I could fit in, that I could get on with people around me.

What was I worried about?

My case of the raging shits as well as my temporary limp had me on light duties for the week. It would have been good to do the same stuff as Meiktila to bond with them, but as I'd already done my signals training I was put into the Airmen's Mess to work. There was always lots of cleaning to be done in a kitchen, and after months of bull nights I was used to it. All I wanted to do was get back to fitness and finish the course.

Meiktila Flight finished their signals training, completed their CFT and then we were all back to the same place I'd been at before it all went sideways. It was the weekend before Range Week and I made damn sure I didn't go out on the piss in Darlington. A trip to HM Supplies was as far as I went. Jimmy and I then tabbed around the peri-track in our webbing and fine-tuned the fittings on our newly purchased pouches, ready for the week ahead.

Range Week

All I managed to do on El Al's Range Week was the grenade throw, but there was so much more I hadn't done. First, there were Close Quarter Battle ranges where you had to advance to contact, go to ground and then fire at targets that popped up. You had to fire from cover, move up and down the range with an instructor on your shoulder watching your moves, checking your fieldcraft. First you did it as a single-man shoot, then in pairs.

I did my first single CQB with Corporal Haynes hovering at my shoulder like a malevolent spectre with small man syndrome. 'That was fucking shite, Brindle,' he snarled at me once I'd finished. 'I've never seen anything so gash in my life. Standing in exposed window frames, no crawling out of position and that last engagement, you simply stood up and smiled like a fucking pansy. What the fucking hell did they teach you on El Al? Get some more ammo and do it again, you wanker.'

My confidence collapsed. Already binned once and I felt like I was on a downward spiral, never making the cut, then getting binned, binned, binned again until I was booted out. I walked back to the ammunition point and refilled my magazines. 'Double, you bastard,' bawled Corporal Haynes. He was barely five feet tall but had a voice like a mining town baritone. 'I haven't got all fucking day.'

I doubled back to the point and my stubborn streak solidified. I'd had enough of being doubted, no one believing in me and everyone, even my friends from school, telling me I shouldn't be there, that I'd made the wrong choices in life. How could I be so wrong if it still felt so right? Well, I wasn't doing this for any of them, I was doing it for me. My 'if they want me out they'll have to kick me out' mantra was getting pretty damn close to happening, and it was only me who could stop it from coming true. I had to impress the instructors a lot better than I was doing so far. It was that simple.

My stance firmed up as I stood at the point. I clenched my jaw and took a real chance by looking Corporal Haynes direct in the eye. Was it just my imagination or did he nod ever so slightly? 'Load!' he barked.

My second shoot wasn't brilliant, but it was better than the first and it was good enough for Corporal Haynes.

The week ended with an uphill section attack, and it had been five full-on, exhausting days, each one ending with a cold and wet climb back into the four tonner. During the down time and on journeys back to Catterick, Jimmy and I compared notes on what tapes we'd loaded into our Walkmans and were they better off stored in webbing or pocket? Our shared taste in music and dress sense cemented our friendship.

Now there was only Omega to get through.

Only Omega.

Only Omega

The Greek symbol Omega is the last letter in their alphabet, and it symbolised the end, the final, the last thing, ever since. For the RAF Regiment, Exercise Omega was the final hurdle. Pass Omega, and you pass the course and you're in the Regiment. It started with a deployment on Monday morning and you came back on Thursday afternoon, and in between those days you did absolutely everything in the training book except sleep.

After I'd been binned onto Meiktila, El Al returned from their Omega, and Sergeant May's plan to have the entire starting line-up pass out had taken a real beating: five failed and were re-coursed, which meant that the new Number Three Section on Meiktila was a six-man squad, all bin boys from El Al. Meiktila's instructors didn't want to dilute the teams they'd built over eleven weeks with re-treads, so they put us all into one section and I didn't blame them. I'd have done the same.

The good news was that Meiktila was the first flight allowed to do Omega with Bergen rucksacks instead of the worse than useless large packs, which were probably pointless even in 1958 when they came out. We had to buy our Bergens, of course, but by then the principle was firmly in place. Off to HM Supplies we went, where there were plenty to choose from. Most people believed the best military Bergen in 1990 was the Berghaus Cyclops Roc, with detachable side pouches for patrol/day use. If I'd had any sense I'd have got one, but as I didn't, I bought a Karrimor Condor instead. The Condor was a great piece of kit, but it was also huge, unlike me, and the bigger the pack the more you put in it. And the more you put in it, the heavier it gets. And the heavier it gets, well, you do the maths.

So, I'd made it to Omega. Christ, how many didn't get this far and how many got binned straight afterwards? The other lads in Three Section were feeling the pressure. You only had two chances at Omega. Get binned once and you've got one more shot. In a way I had to admire them for even trying, because you really only ever wanted to do Omega once. Doing it twice took some ballsy determination.

I did it once, and I'm damned if I'd ever do it twice.

As with Fieldcraft, on the Monday morning, everyone went back for seconds at breakfast. Then we had our kit checked before climbing aboard the four tonners, which dropped us off in the CTA. We tabbed away from the drop-off point and the first time we went to ground I slowly lowered myself to prone, webbing and loaded Bergen making me wonder if I'd ever stand up again. I rested my LSW's bipod on a tree stump and the prongs twanged apart.

Bollocks.

I picked up the now useless bits of metal and stuffed them into my hip pocket. Not a good start.

On the high ground either side of a small, grassed valley, we laid up among the trees. The corporals set out the trench positions with a curt, two-word order.

'Dig in.'

And that's the next twenty-four hours spoken for.

Who'd have thought a fire trench could take so long to dig? If you've never dug one before, you're probably wondering what I'm talking about, and if you have dug one before, you'll know exactly what I'm talking about. It's a lot more than just digging a hole, which, believe me, is hard enough. To begin with you've got to de-turf, peel and roll back the top two inches of turf all round to give you your spoil tip, which you then roll the turf back over once you've dug the trench. But before you even think of doing that, you've got to dig six feet down, six feet along and two feet front to back.

Most of the ground on the CTA was thick clay and it sucked at my digging ability like quicksand. That was without the tree roots and stones that jarred up my whole arm every time my pickaxe found them. I collected blisters and sores on my hands within the first hour as I dug into the ground, and after two hours, the blisters started to burst, I couldn't straighten my fingers and my hands began to feel like claws.

Three Section was split into two fire teams, with three of us to each trench. Each trench had one man on sentry in front of the position, which left two to dig until another one of your number was dicked to go on patrol. So a lot of the time there was just one left to work on the trench.

87

When you're digging in, that's all you do until it's dug, which means you don't sleep until it's finished. And finished meant finished to your instructor's satisfaction, which tended to mean never.

Right through the night it was dig, sentry, patrol, then dig some more. Our rations were eaten cold as we crouched in the slowly, very slowly, deepening trench. As Tuesday morning dawned, tedium, boredom, exhaustion and back-breaking work began to wear us down. Progress slowed as we tried, tried and tried to get the damn thing dug so that we could sleep. At one point we were 'attacked' by one of the gunners from 4001 Flight. He blatted a few blanks at us and we blazed away right back at him. A bit later a load of dogs and fox hunters went right through our positions. Then a low-flying Phantom screamed overhead, and the instructors boiled out of the admin tent, threw smoke grenades and screamed, 'Gasgasgas!' For the next hour we were digging in with respirators and NBC kit.

On Tuesday night it was my turn to go on patrol. It was a recce patrol, but by that point I was so knackered I wouldn't have known if I was going on a snow patrol. We headed off into the wilderness, supposedly to watch a specific point for enemy activity. Going into my second sleepless night, I was absolutely bollocksed. At the FRV we went to ground and I had the struggle of my life trying to stay awake, while Corporal Williams and another recruit went off to spy on the enemy. It was March in North Yorkshire and it wasn't warm, but my head was still nodding, and all I gave a shit about as I took up my fire position was how much I wanted to go to sleep.

One of the more commonly told stories about Omega was the hallucinations that came with not sleeping, and they were spot on. As I rubber-necked over my SUSAT and paid not the slightest attention to what was going on around me, I started seeing cardboard cut-out zoo animals prancing all over the CTA. I shook my head, blinked and looked again. They were still there, only this time they were covered in chocolate.

I lost all track of time, but however long I lay there waiting for the recce team to return to the FRV, my world had descended into a cosmic torment of absolute fatigue, creeping cold and hallucination. At the same time I tried but utterly failed to keep alert and look out for a sign of enemy activity. Finally, eventually, thankfully, the rest of the patrol came back and we moved out, back to our positions and even more trench digging.

Wednesday's dawn slowly crept over the CTA's barren, pre-spring horizon, and the fire trench was getting good, really good. All three of us in the fire team were sure it was deep enough, and we looked forward to starting trench routine and getting some sleep. Sleep. We were craving it more than anything else, but it was up to the corporals to let it happen, and they weren't giving up their power over us just yet.

'Almost there, lads.' Corporal Williams looked down at us, while I stood in the trench and peered over the edge. Well, I *would* have peered over the edge if we hadn't dug the damn thing so bloody deep that even on tiptoes I was still staring at the trench wall. My LSW was perched on the spoil tip, leaving me precariously holding the pistol grip one-handed with an outstretched arm. I couldn't see over the top, and to fire at anyone I'd have had to randomly point it in front and pull the trigger. Maybe if I'd jumped up and down as I fired I might have seen where the rounds went. But combine that with no bipod and if I'd had live ammo, I'd have been so far off the mark that any incoming enemy wouldn't even have gone to ground. And the trench *still* wasn't deep enough, even though I was standing in water.

'Another half foot and you'll be done,' said Corporal Williams. 'Keep going, lads.'

So we did, but even when it was deep enough, there was the spoil to be flattened, turf to roll back, arc markers and comms lines to put out. Anything, everything, always something that needed to be done.

Finally, eventually, as the third night started to fall, I stared longingly at my sleeping bag. In the gathering dusk, it quickly turned into a hallucination, monster-sized, green witchetty grub. Corporal Williams ghosted into my vision from nowhere. 'Right, lads,' he snapped. 'We're leaving. Prepare to move.'

My heart dropped to the absolute bottom of the newly dug trench. I'd been literally dreaming of getting some sleep, and now I had to get my shit together and move out.

It was fully dark by the time the whole flight was formed up. And it was here that my choice of huge Bergen really kicked me in the nuts. Having too many adjustment choices also helped me not at all. The Condor had these groovy rails on the back frame which let you have the whole pack sit higher or lower on your back according to preference. And for some weird reason I was obsessed with having the whole thing on top of my kidney pouches, which gave me a silhouette about a foot higher than my helmet. It also made the Bergen push down on my webbing even worse than a large pack ever did. So not only did I have an utterly un-tactical silhouette, but I also had to pull the shoulder straps uber-tight for it to stay there. It was uncomfortable as hell, crammed full of kit and weighed a ton. After a while, the very poor set-up began to cut off my circulation, and pretty soon after that my fingers started to go numb. To make it even worse, it was my turn to carry the radio.

Carrying all your kit on your back was never easy, never comfortable. But it could be done, and sometimes it had to be done. The Falklands War showed every British infantryman what was possible, and they achieved it in 1982 with some seriously outdated kit, which, coming from the British forces, was really saying something. And as soldiers came in all shapes and sizes, it was very much up to the individual to get their kit properly set up so that they could cover long distances, if not comfortably, at least competently.

Unfortunately for me, I'd parked my competence back at the barrack block, and I'd fucked up in a big way by not thinking properly about my kit. I'd just piled it on my back, and now I was suffering. The radio straps were cutting into my arms almost as bad as my Bergen was. I couldn't feel my fingers and after a while couldn't keep hold of my LSW. I was forced to give the radio to someone else in the section, but not before an almighty and utterly deserved bollocking from the flight commander. And the solution was so simple. The other lad just took the radio off its frame, slung it in his Bergen and carried on. I'd have felt better if I'd been told to do that myself, and I reckoned that was my chance gone and I'd be binned.

We tabbed into a wooded area and set up a triangular harbour with a section to each side. We were told that once we'd dug shell scrapes, we could set up trench routine and then, finally, finally, sleep. Sometime on Wednesday night going into Thursday morning, I crammed some rations down my neck, cleaned my weapon and washed. Three of us sat on the edge of our newly dug shell scrape, and extreme fatigue fudged my addled senses. 'I guess we'll need to take it in turns on stag,' I whispered, keeping my voice low and trying to be tactical.

'Where's your sentry?' Corporal Haynes' voice hammered into my ears. I turned around and he was right behind us. 'What are you three wasters doing, apart from nothing?' he shouted. 'Having a fucking orgy in your shell scrape, while the enemy gets through and skewers us, you slack bastards.'

'We were just about to sort it out,' I muttered, speaking before thinking.

'We were just about to sort it out, CORPORAL! And don't question my instructions, you little shit. Get yourself on stag, Brindle. NOW!'

I crawled to the treeline and peered outwards over my SUSAT. It was daytime by now, and lying prone on stag, trying desperately to stay awake, the hallucinations didn't go away. The trees and bushes in the distance suddenly morphed into a whole regiment of cammed-up Land Rovers coming to get me. After an hour of staring ahead, of seeing everything but noticing nothing, my stag was over and I could sleep.

It sounds utterly unbelievable, but when I actually got under my poncho and slithered into my sleeping bag, I *didn't* go to sleep. Well, not straight away anyway. I was completely exhausted, my whole body ached and my hands felt like they'd had the skin flayed off by the endless digging. I was cold, damp and filthy and my mind was utterly fried, but it just wouldn't switch off. I stared up at my poncho and wondered why on earth I remained awake. It was nuts. The second you're put on stag and get into your fire position, it's impossible to stay alert, but as soon as you get into your basha you can't sleep. What's that all about? At some point I must have dropped off because I was suddenly woken up by the sound of a thunderflash being thrown into the shell scrape.

'Fighting patrol,' said Corporal Williams. 'Get your kit stowed, re-plen your ammunition. The enemy have taken our old positions, and we're going to mount a flight attack. Any enemy formations we meet on the way, we'll destroy. Prepare to move.'

We tabbed back the way we came and just before the jump-off point, a four tonner appeared and we were told to ditch our Bergens. We then peeled off by sections and headed for our old trenches. The shooting started and I went to ground, scanned for the trench I'd spent nearly three days digging, sighted a TSF 'enemy' and opened fire. I'd gone through the drills for weeks, I could almost do them in my sleep and very nearly did. The flank attack went through the woods and I stumbled over tree roots and fallen branches.

'Move, Brindle!'

I bounced between close-set tree trunks like a camouflaged pinball.

'Put down some fire, you bastard.'

My LSW was all over the place without the bipod. I had about three rounds left and I fired them off.

'The fuckers are dead, take back what's yours.'

And then we were back in our trenches with a few lads from TSF playing dead. I stood in the trench once more and I still couldn't see over the top.

Compared to Range Week, the attack had been short and anti-climactic, but the running and crawling kicked my body reserves into gear. Crushing fatigue had been replaced by a grating weariness. My mouth was dry, my fingers tingled and I felt light-headed.

'Well done, lads,' said Corporal Williams. 'Now get this trench filled in. The four tonners will be here in an hour.'

It was Thursday and the end was in sight. I didn't know if I'd passed or failed, but at least I could say I'd done Omega. Three of us shovelled the earth back into the trench that we'd hardly ever used, then rolled the grass over the top, making a slight mound. All around us were lumpy reminders of trenches that had been dug in the past. The four tonners pulled up and we piled inside. I sat down on the metal bench, pulled out the remains of my last ration pack and chomped on a packet of dry crackers. There was only one thing left to do, and it would start at Gandale Farmhouse.

Gandale Farmhouse, last seen during Fieldcraft, and always the setting for the final part of Omega: the Gandale Gallop. I'd be reunited with my bastard Bergen and have to do a tab in full kit from there back to Catterick, about six miles. How well I performed on that tab would say a lot about whether I passed Omega or not. Some of the lads on El Al hadn't done the whole thing and still passed, but if you'd dropped a bollock earlier on, like I had with the radio, this was your last chance to redeem yourself.

The four tonners stopped and I was part of a haphazard pile-out that had absolutely nothing to do with military precision. We harboured up in a wood and then it was the same battle with exhaustion. As soon as I hit prone position and stared over my sights, my eyes weighed ten tonnes and I just needed to sleep. I simply wasn't functioning any more, and the instructors walked around the harbour kicking rifle barrels. If the kick didn't wake you up they'd try to pull your weapon away. Never lose your weapon, and definitely don't let it get taken from you when you're supposed to be awake. Sleep, sleep, the word and the thought were almost painful.

I looked around through bleary, grainy eyes. I couldn't see the farmhouse, but really, one part of the CTA looked just like any other: barren and empty and miles from civilisation, with every clump of woodland playing host to a group of poor knackered bastards trying to stay awake. Somewhere nearby I heard helicopters landing. Two Pumas, but that was nothing to do with us, was it? Surely not. We were still recruits, not even proper soldiers yet.

The corporals lined us out of the woods in sections. We were given a very quick briefing and told to hold our weapons at both ends, then ushered into a waiting Puma. My first thought was, helicopter ride, cool. My next thought was, Christ, how far are we from Gandale and how much further will we have to walk?

The answer was not very far. It was a couple of minutes in the air, then a put down on the air side at Catterick. Omega was over and I'd been spared the Gandale Gallop.

But had I passed?

We were marched to the training block, and inside a large room we started cleaning our weapons. I was filthy, damp, residually still cold and despite being absolutely, utterly knackered, I was grating and on edge. It was judgement time and we all knew what was coming. Stay in the room and you've passed. Get your name called and your future hangs by a thread. The whole of Three Section and Jimmy Hendricks were called out, ordered downstairs and stood to attention outside the flight commander's office. Waiting to see the flight commander meant you were either going to get bollocked or binned. Right then, everyone else upstairs were being told they'd passed, while I had to agonise as I waited to be told my fate. Bollocked or binned, bollocked or binned? What was it to be? One by one we were called inside. Jimmy was fine. The corporals had just sent him down to the office as a joke, the bastards. The rest of us were there for real. Christ, would I be binned again? Would I have to do Omega again? *Could* I do Omega again? I was called in, halted, saluted and stood to attention in front of Flying Officer McCrae. Himself still in DP and unwashed, but at least he was sitting down at a desk, while I stood to attention and felt myself swaying, my eyelids dropping. After a minute of painful, life-deciding silence, he looked up from the desk.

'Corporal Haynes tells me you have a problem with discipline, Brindle.'

'Sir?'

'When a corporal asks you why you haven't posted a sentry, even if it is for the minor reason of keeping the harbour safe and your mates alive, the last thing you should be doing is answering back.'

'Yes, Sir.'

'Yes, Sir?'

'Sorry, Sir. I meant no, Sir.'

'You don't know what you bloody mean, do you, Brindle? And most of the instructors don't know why the hell you're even here. But that's not my problem.' He sighed and leaned back in his chair. 'You're a long way from being the best recruit we've ever had, Brindle, and so was the rest of your section. But I'm told you were keen and cheerful right through Omega, and apart from your colossal fuck-up with the radio, you gave it loads of effort. Anyway, you've passed the course, so well done. A word of advice, though, the next time you want to argue with an NCO, keep a hold of your tongue. They don't take too kindly to that kind of thing on the squadrons.'

94

I couldn't move, I couldn't think, I couldn't speak. I certainly couldn't take it in.

'What are you still standing here for?' he barked. 'Fuck off out of my office.'

I saluted, about-turned and marched out, my mind numb with the enormity of my achievement. I'd done it, I'd passed. I might have only just done it, but I didn't care about that. I'd passed Basics and I was going to be a gunner in the RAF Regiment.

Two others from Three Section weren't so lucky. Binned at their second attempt, they had no more chances and they were out.

Passing out

Omega finished on the Thursday, and the passing out parade was the following Wednesday. It didn't leave much time for practice.

It also took a while to sink in that I'd actually done it. After dinner on Thursday and then a serious, scalding hot skin-scrub shower, followed by a death-like sleep, I was still dazed and goggle-eyed the following morning when we were doubled over to Basics for our final kit issue, which included Gore-Tex waterproofs, NI gloves and RAF Regiment shoulder slides.

The instructors shook hands with every one of us as we were given our slides. Twenty-four hours earlier they hated my guts, now they were smiling and telling me how well I'd done. My head spun with the sudden change. It was intense and real and unreal all at the same time. It also took the whole of the weekend before I recovered from four days of no sleep.

Despite passing Omega, despite the handshake from Corporal Williams, despite the shoulder slides I'd earned and the champagne-fizz of unsaid jubilation, I still had to keep telling myself I'd done it.

The day of the passing out parade came round and it still felt completely dreamlike. We formed up at the training block as the cars with our families arrived. I caught a glimpse of my parents and grandparents, and we all craned our necks to see who had the best-looking sister.

'Eyes front,' snapped Corporal Haynes, a thickset concentration of hostility, dressed in his best blues. 'You think any woman on this planet is seriously going to look at you scrotes?' He chuckled to himself. 'You're LACs in the RAF Regiment now, lads, so I can call you scrotes and not get charged.' I couldn't remember a single day since the previous October when I hadn't been insulted by an instructor. Being called a scrote was kind of mild, but I still faced front.

There followed a less than serious inspection. Corporal Haynes found a speck of dirt on my hat-band. 'What's that, Brindle?' He smirked. 'Looks like a bogey. Get it cleaned, you fucking minger.' He chucked a stiff-bristle clothes brush at me and I got to work.

Corporal Williams walked up and down the flight and pretended to cut our ties with a Stanley knife, then laughed at our varied reactions. Once I'd cleaned the non-existent bogies from my hat-band the flight was marched to the armoury to collect rifles, with bayonets fixed. The mid-March weather was typical for Yorkshire, so the parade was held inside the LATS hangar. We were brought to a halt just outside, I watched the band march past us and then Sergeant Jeffries took us in.

The band weren't playing heavy metal, but the RAF March Past was ideal for the event. The drums and big brass instruments kept the timing. Sergeant Jeffries called out the orders and Meiktila Flight stamped into the hangar, bulled shoes crashing into the concrete flooring. I looked for my family out of the corner of my eye and clocked them looking at me. I didn't believe the stories of how your chest filled with pride at that moment, but they were all true. I felt all the fatigue and doubts wash away from me. Even if I was the shittiest recruit on the worst flight that had ever gone through Basics, I'd still got through, and that was what mattered. Whatever standard had been set, and it wasn't down to me what that was, I'd met it and earned the right. I wasn't a recruit any more. None of us were. We weren't marching into that hangar as recruits; we were LACs in the RAF Regiment, and on that day there was no one prouder. Even when our back row marched out of step, made shockingly obvious by our white gloves, we recovered, got back into step, and still I felt unbeatable. It must have looked utterly gash to those watching, and having seen the video years later I can tell you it did. But that didn't matter, and after we'd been marched back to the armoury to hand in our rifles, we were then allowed to walk as individuals to the NAAFI to meet our families. It was the first time that any of us were allowed to go anywhere in uniform without marching or doubling, and it's hard to explain just how big a change that small thing really was.

And while I might have been leaving Basics, a part of me would, and maybe still does, remain. Mounted on RTS(B)'s canteen walls was a mass of eighteen-inch, flat-board squares. On almost every BG course there was someone who could draw cartoons, and every flight was allowed to decorate their square any way they wanted. The BG number took precedence and then there was a small cartoon character of each recruit who passed, along with their initial posting. By then I was known for my cowboy boots and bandana, and that's how my image looked. I was labelled LAC 'Rawhide' Brindle. I guess it would be called an avatar now.

So Basics was over and I'd passed, I'd earned the right. And whatever it was I'd joined up for, the security, the safety, insulation from the civilian world and all its complications, it was all now within reach. I didn't have to worry about paying the bills, where I was going to live, where the next meal was coming from, or if I'd lose my job. I'd got what I wanted, or so I thought.

And it was easy to see why.

I'd joined as an individual, and despite the total institution I'd willingly entered, I remained an individual. Usually, that was something that got ironed out at Catterick, and if not completely, a bit more than happened with me. That was going to cause some problems later on, but right there and then, who knew? Not me, that's for sure. Because in training, as a recruit, whether that was Swinderby, El Al or Meiktila, everybody was an equal. Whatever it was about you, it didn't matter as long as you pulled your weight. And because we were all equals, all sharing every experience, we were all there for each other, like the way Ox spoke up for everyone when he was senior man, or stuck up for me on Range Week when I was ill. And again when the whole flight whipped round to get Ox a new pair of glasses after the failed rescue mission to Darlington. Even the ones who weren't involved chipped in.

And really, what wasn't to like about Basic Training? Sure, there were the odd moments, like at the squadron bar and being re-coursed, but that was offset against everything else. Sometimes it was hard and lots of times it was funny, but it was also a completely unique experience. I hadn't lost my individuality and I'd been accepted in spite of it. I'd bonded and made friends, sometimes for years, sometimes for life. There was no pecking order or 'old sweat' seniority, there was no brutality, no singling out of individuals. I hadn't gone through it, *we* had, and we'd all gone through it together. As far as I was concerned I'd made the right choices and had a great career to look forward to. I was at the start of an exciting journey and I couldn't wait to get posted.

Part 2

Bad Times

'You think I came this far just to give up now?
You never really knew me, anyhow.
So hit me with the best you've got, give me your worst.
You'll never see me broken, beaten or coerced.'
Cold Steel

4001 Flight

Ninety per cent of the RAF buy a car straight after trade training, and I was no exception. Well, when I say buy, I mean get a bank loan to buy a car and start the lifelong debt journey. On my week-long post-Basics leave I got the standard 3k loan and went car hunting, settling on a Skoda Estelle. And not just any Estelle. It had a vinyl roof, sun window, spoiler and alloy wheels. The glove box was crammed with cassette tapes, and the stereo played heavy metal and nothing else. Its official Skoda colour was Rowan Red, but it actually looked orange. In a homage to the Stephen King horror film, I called the car Christine, my four-wheeled flame chariot from Hell, and it was the absolute nuts. Its engine was in the back and for the next two years, every time I opened the boot, which was at the front, I always said the same thing: 'Bloody hell, someone's stolen the engine. Never mind, I've got a spare in the back.'

It was just a shame the damn thing was so utterly unreliable, with a habit of overheating thanks to poorly fitted pipes and a not very good thermostat. I quickly learned to keep a gallon of water in the boot at all times to deal with any unexpected engine-melts. Back then, Skodas were the pariah cars of everywhere, and as well as picking up jokes about it every day, it cemented my weirdo image, along with my dress sense and musical tastes.

A bit strange that your choice of car could make such a difference, but in the laddish, excessively masculine arena of the RAF Regiment, if it wasn't fuel-injected with lots of mods and wide tyres, your ride was shite, and so were you.

After my annual leave, with the exception of Jimmy Hendricks who was posted to 48 Squadron, the rest of Meiktila were back at Catterick, where we joined El Al on 4001 Flight until the postings came through. We were mostly used for guard duty, and we made ourselves really unpopular when we were ordered to check car tax discs as well as IDs before opening the gates. The guard commander was an instructor. 'You're not in Basics any more, lads,' he greeted us at guard briefing. 'So if there's no officers around you can call me Andy.'

Along with being able to walk around the base instead of doubling, it was another small but concrete gesture, and very strange to see these all-powerful demi-gods from a few short weeks ago as just people.

All of the new LACs were moved into an older barrack block near the back of the station, and thank God, the heating was also working. Luckily for me, I'd been given a single room. I set about hippifying it straight away, putting an Indian rug down, buying in copious amounts of joss sticks, and getting shedloads of postcards with pictures of metal bands. It wasn't your normal Rockape décor, with not a single military or aircraft print in sight, but in my mind what did it matter, it was my room, right?

17 Squadron, Knettishall, 9th April 1990 to 17th December 1992

April to May 1990

I was lucky, my posting came through after two weeks, and in early April, myself and four others were posted to 17 Squadron at Knettishall.

I've always had an unashamedly optimistic outlook on life. I've always sought to be happy and tried to put myself in places where that would happen. And as I headed to Fersfield, a small satellite station a few miles from Knettishall, I really thought I'd done it. I really thought I'd been proved right by my experience of Basic Training.

At Swinderby it was like a production line, diverse trades all together, there wasn't time for the instructors to really know you. Everyone brought their individuality and civilian mindsets into the military, and as long as you stepped up with the teamwork, accepted the new rules you lived under, that was all you needed. At Catterick, a lot more time was invested in the recruits, you were there a lot longer, and with the dividing down into sections, each corporal really got to know their recruits. But even with my weird clothes, music tastes and outlook on life, I was treated mostly with bemusement, but no hostility. I got on with my fellow recruits, and they accepted me. And if I could be accepted on Basics, I'd be accepted on a squadron, right?

So when I parked my car at Fersfield for a night in transit accommodation at the Guard Room, I thought I'd cracked it. I'd passed Basics and earned the right to be in the Regiment. I hadn't changed as a person, and I could look forward to my safe, sheltered life within the military. It was the start of a whole new adventure.

At least, that was the plan.

17 Squadron was part of 8 Wing, a mixture of field and air defence squadrons permanently tasked to defend the Jaguars, and the whole shooting match was based at Knettishall and set up to deploy anywhere in the world. 17 Squadron had eight Rapier kits,

102

four each on A and B Flight, and if the Jaguar Force ever had to deploy, so too did 8 Wing.

That Monday morning, myself and four other new LACs fronted up to B Hangar at Knettishall. Squadron Warrant Officer Lipp met us at the front door and marched us upstairs to see the CO. Five LACs close-ordered tighter than sardines, we marched in like we were squeezed out of a toothpaste tube.

'Leftrightleftrightleftrightleftrightleftrightleftrightleftwheelmarkti me, haaaaaaaaaaaalt! Ateaseattenshunateaseattenshun! Five new LACs for the squadron, Saaah!'

Squadron Leader Dillon sat back at his desk and looked at us. He wasn't the smartest officer I'd seen. His green jumper was creased, boots unpolished and his unkempt sandy hair was shot through with grey, but his eyes were like sniper scope lasers, and when he looked at me I felt like he was staring right into me and reading my soul.

'Welcome to 17 Squadron,' he said. He had no real accent, a gravelly voice and none of the landed tones that most officers, even air force ones, affected. 'This is a good squadron, and you're going to do your bit to keep it that way. Work hard and obey orders, and you'll get to play hard. But not too hard.' He stood up, planted his fists on the desk and leaned over it. If I wasn't under orders to stand to attention I'd have stepped back. 'So listen in,' the CO growled. 'The station commander has just spent a fucking fortune on the NAAFI, and it's a good place, great for a night out. It's even somewhere you could take your bird.' His eyes narrowed and his voice dropped a notch. 'But I don't want any of you thinking it's somewhere you can cause trouble. Right now, you're the juniors here, but in a few weeks, or a few months, someone else will be. Don't for one second think you can play the bully when that time comes. And if someone, *anyone* gives you any trouble, Warrant Officer Lipp and I will be only too pleased to deal with them. So I don't want you having any fears about that. Questions?'

Bloody hell, I was six feet away from a squadron leader and he wanted me to actually speak to him? By the time I'd have thought of anything to say, he'd have retired. He smiled. 'Introduce them to their crews, Mister Lipp.'

'Saaah! Airmen on parade, move to the right, right turn! By the front, quick march! Leftrightleftrightleftrightleftrightleftright.'

Each Rapier kit was worked by an eight-man crew, and I became part of A2: A Flight, crew and kit number 2. Every crew had a wire-fence caged area with a table and chairs and storage space. I hung up my DP jacket and my first job was to get my room sorted at the block, then get my webbing and Bergen into A2's Cage.

17 Squadron had its own barrack block. Officially called Block 6, unofficially, it was simply the Rock Block. It had single rooms with wash basins and was newly decorated with modern fittings for the time. I didn't get a room there straight away, not because I was a new boy, it was simply an availability issue. Until a room came up, myself and the other four were put in Block 3, otherwise known as the Javelin Suite, because right outside it stood an obsessively polished Gloster Javelin, Knettishall's gate-guard aircraft.

At the end of my first day on the squadron I went to collect my DP jacket and found that my Regiment slides had been stolen. Brothers in arms perhaps, but also light-fingered brothers, so always lock your kit away was lesson number one.

Lesson number two was that even if I wasn't an LAC, I was still utterly superfluous because I wasn't yet Rapier trained. That meant I couldn't touch the kits.

So I couldn't actually do anything.

Which inevitably led to myself and the rest of the new arrivals getting all of the shit jobs: stocking up the squadron canteen, sweeping the hangar floor, emptying the bins, cleaning the toilets. Generally not far removed from being recruits.

Although a few short weeks ago, that's exactly what we were.

But that didn't stop the social induction. And with Easter just around the corner, the TA centre's bar in Bury St Edmunds had been booked that Thursday night. The whole of 17 Squadron was going out on the piss.

And that meant everyone.

There was no choice. Seriously, no choice. It wasn't, 'Are you going to the Easter party?', it was, 'You *are* going to the Easter party.'

I wasn't the only one who was utterly terrified at the prospect. So were the other four LACs. We all remembered the instructors telling us how shit we were, how they wished they could have booted us off the course, never mind that some people actually had been. I especially remembered them saying they'd phone people on whatever squadron we were sent to and ensure we got a special 'welcome'. All of that trundled around my fear-addled mind and coalesced into one thought: *What the fuck are they going to do to us on Thursday night?*

Thursday evening came around. Dressed in our suits, myself and the other four LACs walked to the Guard Room, and as we waited for the bus, I felt like we were condemned men. The rest of the squadron were there. Everyone around us was laughing and joking and generally being mates on a night out, apart from us. We didn't even talk to each other and no one spoke to us. The bus arrived, I stepped aboard, sat at the front, stared at the driver's back and quietly shat myself as the bus drove to Bury St Edmunds.

At the TA centre we climbed the stairs to the first floor, stood at one end of the bar and didn't move. The whole squadron was there from the CO down, along with a liberal helping of wives and girlfriends. There were about two hundred and fifty people in total.

It was the SACs who deigned to speak to us. Some of them had been LACs themselves only a few months before. Some of them were younger than me, but that didn't matter. They'd been in the Regiment longer than I had, even if it was just weeks or months, and that *did* matter. It was all about time served. Most of the conversations went along the lines of what we thought of Basics, who our instructors were, how their training course was so much harder than ours because they'd had to use the SLR/Gimpy, or that their Omega was a day longer. Anything to really hammer home that they'd earned the right but we hadn't. It didn't take long for me to feel completely inadequate, as though everything I'd been through at Catterick didn't mean a thing. Nobody was impressed, and the conversations always ended with 'Now buy me a drink'.

The night progressed, and apart from being randomly fleeced for drinks, the SACs came and went and we found ourselves being left alone. I dared to hope. By about ten o'clock I started to think to myself that maybe we were safe.

And then one of the SACs came back. 'Right, lads,' he said. 'You'd better get some drinks down your necks. You're stripping at eleven.'

I looked at the SAC whose nickname was Geordie. His black hair was permed and gelled into tight ringlets, and his '70s porn-star moustache was thick and bushy. I guessed he had something to do with Newcastle although he didn't have an accent. I looked at him with a blank expression. I must have misheard him.

'Did you say strip?' I asked him.

'Fucking right I did.' Geordie squared his shoulders, and his moustache spiked outwards. 'Look, lads, I don't want a debate about it. One hour, on the dance floor, all five of you fucking naked.'

Suddenly he was backed by half a dozen others, all of them with the same 'don't fuck with us' expression, all dressed in early '90s finery, all with a pint or bottle of lager. I looked at him, then them, then us. Five LACs, surrounded, outgunned, outnumbered and definitely unloved.

There was no choice whatsoever.

So we started drinking.

I felt a kind of helpless acceptance. It didn't feel right, but what could I do about it? I was in effect being given an order by my seniors, so refusing wasn't even considered. A few hours earlier I thought I might have been beaten up for entertainment, so perhaps just having to take my clothes off wasn't as bad as it could have been. I'd have felt a lot more worried if it had been in the barrack block with no oversight, but the CO and the officers were there, the sergeants were there. Jesus Christ, their wives were there. With that kind of spectator base, how bad could it be?

One of the LACs, Steve Lake, had just turned eighteen, so the SACs clubbed together and bought him a pint of top-shelf: one measure of every spirit behind the bar was poured into a pint glass. And hats off to him, he downed it in one. So that was him pissed, and the rest of us followed at our best speed.

'We can't get out of this,' I said.

'No point even trying,' said Dave Wilkins. He was a huge Manchester United fan, which, along with his surname, earned him the nickname Butch. We'd been on the same section on El Al. 'Look, lads,' he said. 'They're testing us tonight, to see if we've got the balls to do this. If we go through with it, if we do it right and make a real show of it, they'll respect us tomorrow.'

'Well,' I said. 'If we've got to strip for these fuckers, no matter what, why don't we try and do it like real strippers?'

'Good idea, Brinders, mate. Let's get pissed and do it.'

I'd never actually even *seen* a stripper, but when you're pissed, when you've got absolutely no choice, it seemed like the thing to do. Eleven o'clock finally arrived and we were shoved through to the dance floor in the main function room. While the DJ played the usual stripper's theme – he must have worked for 17 Squadron before – we started to take our clothes off, starting with our ties. Had we been in any way attractive, or sober, it might have been more of a tease, but who were we kidding? We were five drunk Rocks who could barely stand, stripping for a whole roomful of drunk Rocks and their wives. It must have looked awful. I wonder what the bar staff thought.

I've never been able to hold my beer and I was totally legless by this point. All I can remember is slowly getting more and more undressed, trying and completely failing to appear seductive, while surrounding me was a boiling, sweating group of pissed-up Rockapes, all of them screaming, 'Off! Off! Off!' at the top of their drunken voices.

How long it all lasted I have no idea, but eventually we were all five of us mother-naked. The gleeful audience grabbed our clothes, chucked them out of the window, then booted us down the stairs and out of the building. Then they hung out of the open windows and cheered us on as we lurched around in the unlit car park and tried to find our clothes. As I was pulling on my underpants with slow, drunken determination, I saw that Steve Lake's face was bleeding. At the same time, a flat-top haircut and tattooed SAC called Pete Jones came down and walked up to him. 'I'm not a hard man,' I heard Jones say. Later on I discovered that he'd head-butted Steve for no reason.

Occasional random violence was all part of my new life. All of my optimism from Basics, the feeling of being accepted, welcomed into something bigger, was suddenly and brutally ripped away.

How do you feel when you're forced to strip for an audience? Was it somehow acceptable because I volunteered, because I joined up, signed on the dotted line? Should I have seen this coming even though no one had told me? Sure, as I progressed through Catterick, I'd been expecting something to happen once I got posted, but expecting it and the reality of it happening were two different things. And having now experienced ritual humiliation, I felt numb, still trying to process the events. In a moment of cataclysmically over-estimated optimism, I thought to myself, that's my initiation over, now I can be mates with everyone.

I was hopelessly naive.

Inside the hangar the following morning, Chiefy A came up to me, smiling as though I was his long-lost son. 'All right, Brinders,' he said. 'Good night last night?'

'Yes, Flight.' I stuck to the script. The thought of reporting such events, or any form of official complaint, was utterly inconceivable. And what would be the point? Everyone saw it anyway.

'Good lad.' Chiefy A grinned, and that was that.

You'll remember the CO telling us on day one that he'd stamp down hard on bullying. Despite that, along with the rest of the squadron, he'd seen five LACs get railroaded into stripping butt-naked with no choice, after which one of them also got assaulted. But that's not what the night before was. In the eyes of everyone there, it was initiation, a rite of passage that every LAC had to go through if 17 was ever their first posting. And so it was. Usually it happened at the regular Thursday night bop at the NAAFI. But me and my four mates were unlucky enough to have arrived a few days before the Easter piss-up, where everyone from the CO down saw it, knew about it, tolerated it.

And there was an unwritten, but definitely not unspoken, expectation that once it happened to you, you joined in when it came to doing it to the next poor bastard who was posted in. It was how it became a cultural norm, how it tied you in to the shared compliance, culpability even. It was also one of the ways you were both accepted into the squadron and how you slowly climbed the intricate pecking order.

But your status didn't change overnight. It took a lot more than being kicked bollock-naked out into a car park to scrabble around for your clothes to become one of the lads. Some of the SACs, the self-styled old sweats, took a positive and unholy delight in tormenting the LACs for a whole lot longer. It didn't take long to spot the sweats, or senior SACs as they liked to call themselves. Most of them wore a combination of arm brassard with a squadron DZ patch, chains laced to the inner hem of their OGs and a KD (Khaki Drill) shirt as opposed to the standard olive-green one.

It also took less than a few days to learn one of 17 Squadron's more unique slang terms: Freddie. The first few days in the hangar, I heard almost everyone refer to something, anything, as a Freddie. It was a Freddie, he's having a Freddie, this whole place is a Freddie. I asked Tommy Harpen, the half-Irish, half-Argentinian SAC on A2 what it meant. Wire-thin but still freakishly strong, Harpen spoke with a soft, upwardly inflected Irish accent. His cleft lip, partially covered by a thin, ginger moustache, gave him a slight lisp.

'Freddie,' he said. 'It's like Freddy Krueger. If you're having a Freddie, you're having a nightmare. Have you got any fags?'

And for the next two and a half years, Freddie was perhaps one of the most commonly spoken words I heard uttered.

*

A few days later, the squadron went on exercise to Spadeadam. The new LACs couldn't go as we were still waiting for our Rapier course, and along with a small rear party of light duties and injured, we stayed behind.

Our main job during this time was to polish, clean and generally make the hangar look perfect, as a big inspection was coming up. Quite where I'd got the idea that once you finished Basics you wouldn't have to clean anything or have a bull night ever again, I don't know. As I was put to work washing air pipes that were fifteen feet in the air, and dusting the tops of equipment cages that hadn't even been looked at since the last time an LAC was sent up there to clean them, I quickly realised how wrong I'd been.

Inspections and bull nights didn't end just because your training had. They were a permanent fixture of military life.

Sometimes there was painting to be done as well. All of the hangers were green, a throwback to their World War Two construction and the need for camouflage. There were always parts of it that needed to be repainted, as did the red and white parking stripes on the hangar floor.

And there were a lot of them.

If it moved, clean it. If it didn't, paint it. And if you weren't sure, nail it down and do both.

It was around this time that I ventured into Knettishall's NAAFI for the first time. I was really nervous. After the horror stories I'd been fed by the instructors, after having beer chucked over me at Catterick, after the stripping and seeing the results of Steve Lake being head-butted, I was under no illusions that an LAC on 17 Squadron had no friends and no protection. I was just glad that most of them were away and I could establish myself quietly.

Being a loner didn't help. Being shy and quiet didn't help, and not being aggressive definitely didn't help. What I had to do to be accepted was to take the shit, laugh it up and then put on some kind of bluff, alpha-male front and do the exact same thing to the next poor bastard who was posted in.

All of which I kind of had a problem with.

I could see that this was going to cause a few issues further down the line, because it just wasn't what I was about. *The Lords of Discipline* had been a defining film for me in my teenage years. It was set in a military academy and centred around a bunch of students called The Ten who terrorised other students who they felt shouldn't be there. I massively identified with the central character who stood against them and ultimately defeated them. But it was other little things that really could have, should have and eventually did, set the alarm bells ringing.

Like my off-duty wardrobe.

With Vulcan-sized butterflies skittering around inside me, I walked into the NAAFI wearing what I always wore: my long, black raincoat over a heavy metal tour T-shirt, tight jeans, cowboy boots, and a bandana loosely tied around my neck. As I'd already discovered at Catterick, my earring was a really big issue and seriously frowned on. But what the hell, I'd already had my hair cut, for God's sake, there was no way I was giving up the rest of the look. I'd always dressed like that, and anyway, what did it matter what you wore when you weren't at work, right? I mean, every day at five o'clock you're told exactly what's planned for the next day and what to wear. So if you're told what to wear, literally for every working day of your life, why the hell *can't* you exercise a little freedom and be yourself in your down time?

110

A good point, but actually, no.

And the relatively predictable counter-argument was that it was all about building the team, the identity, the brotherhood and all that stuff. Which meant work together, drink together, and to promote the identity, all wear the same clothes. Even in civvies there was a strict dress code, and what I usually wore definitely wasn't it.

'So.' Gary Hayward glared at me over his pint. He'd recently been posted in from the soon-to-be-disbanded 501 Squadron. His albino-white hair and moustache were trimmed to regulation length. 'Have you got yourself a pair of desert boots yet?' Gary was a corporal, and definitely the first one I'd shared a drink with. I had no idea whether to call him Corporal or Gary, but I was pretty damn sure that 'mate' was out. Whatever I chose, though, I knew I'd be pulled up for it, so I picked neither and waited to be told.

'No,' I replied.

'Why not?'

'I don't like them.' I shrugged.

Such a wrong answer.

Gary swooped in, grabbed my bandana and pulled me nose to nose. I looked down and out of the corner of my eye saw him sporting a pair of well-worn desert boots. It turned out that at any one time, at least half of all off-duty Rocks wore a Regiment T-shirt/polo shirt/rugby top, blue Ronhill Tracksters, and desert boots, usually referred to as dezzies.

Which meant that my clothing choice got people's backs up before I'd even said a word. But I was stubborn as hell and no way was I changing my wardrobe just to keep the sweats happy. And even if I did, I'd still get a shitload of abuse for something else until some sprogs who were even bigger sprogs than me arrived.

Sometimes, stubborn was good. But sometimes, stubborn didn't help.

It was starting to dawn on me that I was a square peg trying to fit into a round hole, and unless I rounded my edges it wasn't going to take. I was fit, I was keen, but that wasn't enough. It had to be a twenty-four-seven commitment, body and soul, in all thoughts and actions, including what I wore.

Big things to think about as I left the NAAFI early and headed back to the Javelin Suite. It wasn't the single pint I'd drunk that was making my head spin.

*

In my first month on 17 Squadron, I clung to my freshly trained LAC eagerness, just hoping for a small segment of acceptance. Having committed another social faux pas by simply sitting where there was an empty space, I quickly learned that even in the Airmen's Mess, 17 Squadron sat at certain tables. Mingling with the 'Guins was utterly frowned on. Not that I was particularly viewed as mingle-material by the Rocks either. It was isolating, and the only real conversations and bonding was with the other four LACs I'd been posted in with. My room at the block was my retreat, which for me was thankfully a long way from the sweats who were all in the Rock Block. I tortured myself with what might happen when I moved there, as I surely would when a vacant room came up. In my more optimistic moments I'd expected something like 'welcome to the squadron', or 'well done on getting through Basics, here's where we put all that into practice', or even 'what can you bring to the table?' I still believed that eventually I'd be accepted, eventually they'd get to know me, I'd settle in and make friends. The only positive feedback I got was after a flight run, where I finished first. 'You need to drink more beer,' wheezed Corporal Stewart. Skinny to the point of anorexic – even I had more meat on my bones than him – he straggled in a few minutes after me, spat on the ground and then lit up a cigarette. Everyone else just glowered at me as though it was my fault I ran faster than them.

What I needed was some small validation of myself, of my personality, and there was one place where I'd definitely get that.

At a concert.

On 4th May I went back to the NEC at Birmingham, this time to see Heart, and it was something I absolutely needed. Thanks to my Skoda, having to endure the four-hour Freddie of extortionate, middle-of-the-night train journeys back home were a thing of the past. Thunder were once again the support band, laying a solid foundation for their fan base as they played a similar set to the Aerosmith show. Heart were a revelation. Not the heaviest band I ever listened to, but Nancy Wilson could really play the guitar and

112

she was a draw all on her own. Heart didn't pretend to be anything other than what they were, which was an accessible American radio-rock band, with a bit of hippy thrown in. And they did it phenomenally well. Their latest album, *Brigade*, was getting good air play due to their single 'All I Wanna Do Is Make Love To You', and onstage they made it sound amazing, even though the band themselves hated the song and the message it sent out. I soaked up the experience like a sponge in a desert rainstorm and remembered what it was like to feel normal around other people, where no one gave a toss what I wore, where I wasn't on edge or being judged. Anonymous within the arena, I shared a common love of the music with the audience, all of them strangers, but still sharing a common goal. The two sides of my life, music and the RAF Regiment, were now two different worlds, and at times it felt like they were competing for my soul.

Rapier Training Course R2-45. 17th May to 28th June 1990

With the sheer number of vehicles on a Rapier squadron, everyone had to have a driving licence. If you couldn't drive you were dead weight, and if you couldn't drive when you got to a squadron, you'd be sent to RAF St Athan to learn. If you could drive, you went to West Raynham for six weeks' Rapier Training.

I already had my driving licence, so my next stop was Raynham.

Apart from one SAC from 2 Squadron, the para boys and one from 3 Squadron, Northern Ireland, everyone else on my Rapier course were LACs, either straight from, or very soon after, Basics. It was good to meet a lot of the other lads from El Al and Meiktila who'd been posted to other squadrons and a relief beyond words that there was no pecking order, none of this senior SAC, old sweat bullshit and definitely no ritual stripping. No one gave a crap how I dressed, or any of the other bollocks that seemed to characterise 17 Squadron. Once again, it was a collection of equals with a common goal of passing the course.

So, yeah, I enjoyed the six weeks at Raynham.

Under the watchful, benevolent eye of the balding and slightly overweight Sergeant Price, myself and the crew I was assigned to put the kits into action every day. We then went through Tests and Adjustments (T's and A's), the daily Rapier ritual when the kit was deployed. I learned aircraft recognition, how to use the kit, how it worked. There was always the rivalry between the Rapier and field squadrons, lots of talk about which was better, which was more soldierly, but even the two SACs who'd been on field squadrons both agreed that putting a Rapier kit into and out of action was a hell of a lot harder than anything they'd done before.

Socially, it was a world apart from the intimidating beer-frenzies at Knettishall. The biggest highlights during the week were either *Neighbours* or an early knock-off to watch some Italia '90 World Cup football, and I hardly ever went to the NAAFI. Big films at the Fakenham cinema included *Pretty Woman* and *Harlem Nights*.

Some nights though, I'd join a few blokes on a drive to King's Lynn. Nothing exciting, just a few drinks in the pub and then drive back. As a car owner, I was usually the designated sober driver. It was such a relief just to go out for a drink with my mates, my peers, in fact, anyone who didn't make an issue about what course I passed out with, anyone who wasn't looking for an excuse to humiliate some other poor bastard. No one telling me to buy them drinks, trying to strip me, pour drinks over me, none of that shit. Just regular conversations, a few drinks and for me, being occasionally sidetracked by the video jukebox playing Alannah Myles' 'Black Velvet'.

Even sober, even driving, it was good.

One night, I was taking a full car-load back to Raynham from King's Lynn. Apart from me, everyone had had a few beers and were clowning around, the usual pissed-up lad stuff. I looked left once and saw some guy's arse on eye-level display between the seats as he mooned at me and Tony Chan.

So my attention wasn't fully on the road, and suddenly in front of us, right in the headlight beam, was a whole family of rabbits, adults and babies. I had no time to do anything except scream and feel the bump on both sides as I drove over them. My car was full of beered-up young gunners, so they cheered their heads off while I was mortified. I reverted back to hippy mode and felt awful about what I'd done, which, perversely, made the other lads laugh even more. Me, with all my love and peace shit, doing a multiple roadkill on a bunch of harmless rabbits.

'Bloody hell, Brinders,' roared Tony Chan. 'That has made my course.'

We got back to Raynham and while I checked my car for any sign of the murderous destruction I'd just wrought, the other lads had formed up as though they were on parade and started marching in slow time towards the block, humming 'The Death March' as they went. Once they got to the door they halted in perfect unison, and shouted out, 'Ehhh, what's up, Doc?'

The next morning someone had stuck a hand-drawn picture to the outside of my room door, showing the back wheels of a car with bloodstained tyres and a teary-eyed rabbit. Above it was written 'baby killer'.

The news had gone around the whole course by breakfast, and I was the running joke for about a week. It was a rough and unpolished way of cheering me up. They were laughing with me, not at me.

It was also around this time that I started to form some long-term plans. I was signed into the air force for nine years, so what was I going to do when I got out? I didn't have any real idea, but I wanted to have the best chance I could, so while I was at Raynham I applied for an Open University degree course. It took six years of study to get an OU degree, and I was too late for a '91 start, but that was okay. If I began in '92, I could graduate in '97, ready to leave the air force in '98. Ideal. Gone were any starry-eyed visions of going back to Germany and the carefree dependent lifestyle, and my plans of one day becoming an officer were also lost in the wind. I'd tried that for three years before I joined up and even I finally got the message. A few people, including the course instructors, kept suggesting it, but I was adamant. I didn't have what it took and I knew it. I wasn't going for it.

It didn't stop Sergeant Price from nicknaming me Flight Lieutenant Rawhide. So one day I found some flight lieutenant bars and put them on my shoulder slides, then I wore my camo jacket over my shirt. Inside the classroom I took off my jacket and waited to see how long it would take before it was noticed. Sergeant Price clicked in about ten seconds and burst out laughing.

'Flight Lieutenant Rawhide,' he said, chuckling. 'Very funny. Now take them off, you wanker.'

It was a good course, it did what it said on the tin, and after six weeks I'd learned how to be a Rapier operator. Steve Lake, one of the LACs who'd passed out with El Al and joined 17 Squadron at the same time as me, won the top operator prize for the course.

Not long after the course started I went to Hammersmith Odeon to see Dio, my all-time favourite metal band. Ronnie James Dio was an absolute heavy metal legend, famed for playing alongside Ritchie Blackmore in Rainbow, then achieving what many would have thought impossible, replacing Ozzy Osbourne in Black Sabbath. By 1990 he was fronting his own band, and while I'd already seen them twice before, I'd never been to the Odeon, which, with its art deco and faded grandeur design, was itself a renowned venue. It was quite a long drive from Raynham and I missed most of the support band called Trouble, but Dio blew my socks off as well as my cowboy boots, dusting off 'Stargazer' from the Rainbow era, and 'Egypt' from the second Dio album. Neither song had been played for years, and they slotted right in alongside the other stuff, as well as five tracks from their latest album, *Lock up the Wolves*. There was even a guest appearance, a rare and utterly unique experience for the audience. During the encore, Nicko McBrain from Iron Maiden came onstage and played drums on 'Rainbow in the Dark'. Only one way to describe it: fucking amazing. *Kerrang!* might have rubbished the gig the following week, but what did they know? I loved it. This wasn't the affirming experience I craved and needed from the Heart concert, because, even if only temporarily, I was in a better place, but even so, I was never going to say no to a concert, especially Dio.

Then, for the last weekend of the course I went to Glastonbury. It did my image no end of good when the ticket arrived, liberally stamped with CND signs, and reminding me that by purchasing a ticket I was helping the nuclear disarmament cause. Everyone else laughed and said it was just like me to go somewhere like that. If I'd been at Knettishall when the news got out, I'd probably have been taken out back and stoved.

And despite the Berlin Wall coming down in '89, in '90 it was still the Cold War and, officially at least, the Warsaw Pact were still the enemy. So you had to give contact details if you went anywhere at the weekend, just in case there actually was a world war and you had to deploy. Typically, you had to give an address and phone number, but what do you do if you're at a free-wheeling music festival surrounded by thousands of peace-loving, drugged-up hippies? No street address, no phones, nothing. So when the weekend book came to me I just did my best. I wrote LAC Brindle, a field, Glastonbury.

On the Thursday I was hauled into the instructors' office and asked what the fuck I was playing at. I said I was going to Glastonbury, it was in a field and there were no phones. I'm not sure if any of the instructors had even heard of it. I got a few weird looks, and we negotiated a phone number for Glastonbury police station as my weekend address.

You really couldn't have made it up. Can you imagine, World War Three kicks off and LAC Brindle, not yet even a trained

Rapier operator, is so essential to the freedom of the western world that the Somerset police are mobilised to Glastonbury, where they ask every bloke in the field, 'Are you Rick Brindle?'

Although I joked about it at the time, the shit was just a few weeks away from getting real.

But no one saw that coming, and Glasto was a great weekend. I hooked up with my Aerosmith mate from Germany who was now a student. Headliners for me were The Cure. It was the festival's twentieth anniversary, and there was even a riot at the end, which I didn't see. I also didn't dare even *look* at the literally hundreds of drug peddlers who walked around the entire site saying 'hashspeedacid' and 'I got good e's'. Shit, I drove there and back so I didn't even have a beer.

Told all my mates I did, though.

*

Sports was, is and always will be, a big part of the military. And as much as I was already realising that I didn't quite fit in, I was pretty good at running, and that *did* fit in.

It also saved my arse.

The last day of my Rapier course coincided with the one-day sports event called the Rock Olympics, which was a sports event in which 8 Wing competed against each other.

Everybody plays to their strengths, and the last event of the day, a five-mile road race, was mine. I might have been shy, timid and utterly un-aggressive, and in the rest of 17 Squadron's eyes I was a wanker who didn't dress right, but I always knew I could bring home the bacon when it came to running. I was pretty sure I'd do okay, but bugger me, I actually won.

And that took loads of heat off me back at 17. I was a weirdly dressed Rock with an earring, but now I was a weirdly dressed Rock with an earring who brought the running glory to 17 Squadron.

And that made all the difference.

Well, some difference. I think. Maybe.

I was still treated like shit, but the threat of a sudden beating receded slightly.

Queening

I hadn't long been back from my Rapier course when there was a barbecue on the lawn outside the Rock Block. It was a social event and specifically arranged, so if you didn't go it would be noticed and commented on. The Block 3 LACs turned up as a group. There hadn't been any social advancement since the Easter do, so we quietly drank our beers, stayed the hell out of the way and didn't talk to anyone. And no one talked to us, either.

While the food was being cooked, for some inexplicable reason one of the SACs had a garden hose and was liberally watering the lawn. It wasn't long before Pete Jones shouted out, 'The LACs, get the LACs.'

Inevitable really. All it took was time and alcohol.

It was a warm night and there were worse things than being soaked by a garden hose, so with no choice in the matter we lined up, took our turn and got doused. By then the food was cooked and the focus shifted. For the next hour I stood quietly by in my damp clothes, on the periphery of every conversation, and did everything possible short of not being there to attract zero attention. The survival rules were simple: don't look at anyone, don't comment, don't laugh and only talk to another LAC.

At that time, a popular spectator sport among the squadron was sumo wrestling. Two evenly matched gunners would stand inside a small ring marked on the lawn, face each other off and slap their thighs. Then they'd stamp one foot after another into the ground and try to sumo wrestle the other one out of the circle. Blokes were paired off and took their turn. Dave Wilkins, my fellow strip-victim from a few months earlier, was matched against an SAC and lost. As soon as he was chucked out of the circle and sent sprawling to the ground, Pete Jones, who clearly couldn't shut up, ever, shouted out again, 'Queen him!'

Straight away, everyone else joined in and chanted, 'Queen him! Queen him!'

I looked nervously at the other LACs and then back at the SACs as the chanting got louder. 'Queen him! Queen him!' What the fuck was this? I'd never heard about queening, never seen

119

queening. I had no idea what was going to happen, but Dave Wilkins was at the centre of the storm and there was nothing I could do except watch in horrified silence as he was grabbed and held down. *Oh, fucking hell*, I thought. *What are they going to do now?*

One of the real, real old sweats, a guy called Spanner who'd come over to the RAF Regiment from the army, stood over Dave, feet either side of his head. All the other sweats were watching, cheering Spanner on with beered-up red faces, but cheering him on to do what? The chanting didn't stop.

'Queen him! Queen him! Queen him!' Fists clenched as they shouted Spanner on and pressed around him in a tight circle.

Spanner did a Steptoe squint at Dave, dropped his shorts and naked from the waist down, he slowly lowered himself til his naked arse was touching Dave's face. As soon as he made contact the cheering got even louder, Spanner showed off a deviant smile of exultation and then gave Dave Wilkins a liberal rubbing of SAC sphincter all over his face. I stood there, my half-drunk beer forgotten as I watched in utter, stunned, disgusted disbelief.

Dave Wilkins had just been queened.

I later learned that Spanner had brought queening over from his time in the army, where what has got to be the vilest practice on the planet was then gleefully accepted by 17 Squadron's sweats.

Alarm bells were now ringing in my head loud enough to deafen me, and given the number of high-decibel metal gigs I'd been to, that's saying something. In a little over two months I'd been stripped, used as an SAC beer fund, told on an almost daily basis that I was a stupidly dressed, useless weird sprog and soaked at a barbecue for a laugh. Then, I saw with my own incredulous eyes that the men I was supposed to go to war with liked nothing more than dropping their shanks and wiping their naked arses into the faces of other men who they expected to stand shoulder to shoulder with if it ever got real.

Jesus H Christ, if that was what passed for selfless team building by our own side, who the fuck would ever even *need* to go looking for enemies?

Dave, myself and the rest of the recently hosed LACs looked at each other. Fucking hell, what was Dave thinking right now? What would *anyone* think after something like that? Dave's whole body was tense, he twitched slightly and he gripped his empty beer bottle so tight it nearly smashed. None of us said anything, we just nodded and silently agreed: time for a sharp exit before something even worse happened. We drifted towards the edge of the crowd and stepped away.

'Where are *you* fuckers going?' asked Pete Jones.

'Getting some dry clothes,' I said.

'Oh, yeah.' He chuckled. 'Just make sure you come straight back.'

'Sure thing, mate.'

We didn't go back.

What developed, for me at least, was a pattern of going to squadron social events, suffering some form of ritual humiliation and leaving early. Having beer chucked over me at Catterick, saying the wrong thing about dezzies at Knettishall, getting hosed, stripped or queened, it was all the same thing. It was a long way from welcoming you into the wider military family, a long way from building a team, a long way from fostering trust. It was the absolute antithesis of the mutual respect that the military bangs on about nowadays.

It was just shit.

It was an absolute Freddie.

Very quickly, going out on the piss with my workmates lost any appeal it may have had, so after a while I just stopped doing it. And knowing what was in store for me if I did go, it wasn't like I had a *good* reason to want to go out boozing with the squadron. The other lads I'd been posted in with dealt with it better than me, and fair play to them. At the end of the day they had better social skills than me, they fitted in better than I did. They were right for the Regiment, and the Regiment was right for them.

It so wasn't the case with me. It simply isn't for everyone. I just didn't realise it yet.

*

Not long after the barbecue, Corporal Stewart told me a room had come up in the Rock Block. It wasn't multiple choice, it wasn't a question.

But even so…

'I'd rather stay in the Javelin Suite, Corporal,' I said.

Corporal Stewart's head flinched like he'd been bitch-slapped.

121

'What?' he growled in a low voice. The other NCOs in the flight office caught his tone and looked up. 'Don't you *want* to live with the rest of the squadron?'

'It's not that,' I said, lying utterly. 'I've just got here from Catterick, then I went out to Raynham, Corporal. I've been moved all over the place and I just want to stay put for a while.'

'That's all?'

'Sure it is, Corporal.' Even to me it sounded lame, but since being posted to 17 Squadron, I'd quickly learned how to become a grade A lying bastard. The first lesson was to keep it simple, which I'd just done. And it really didn't matter if they believed me or not, what was said was said.

Of course, what I *wanted* to say was that I didn't want to live in the same block as a bunch of crazy mad bastards who'd already stripped me and now wanted to sit their naked arses on my face for a laugh. And it's not like I was welcomed aboard with open arms either, so fuck off.

You wankers.

But whatever I'd said, we both knew that I was telling the whole squadron that I didn't want to live in the Rock Block, and I could see that Corporal Stewart didn't like it.

At least I didn't queen him.

LAC/SAC cadre

As an LAC on 17 Squadron, all I wanted to do was be an SAC and then hopefully I'd stop being treated like shit. Maybe Corporal Faith had been right, way back on Basics, but promotion to SAC would never come any quicker than the rules said, which was one calendar year after joining up.

And before that happened I also had to do a week-long cadre, which essentially meant getting beasted for five days alongside the rest of the squadron's LACs. But it was all LACs together, we knew each other and the only two people beasting us were Sergeant Ross, built like a brick shithouse, and Corporal Quinn, graduate of Corporal Stewart's weight loss programme. The cadre was one hundred per cent official, so no way were they going to strip us or queen us. Since my arrival on 17, a few more LACs had been posted in, including Vicar, the guy who'd called out the Basics instructors for actually feeling cold. Another new posting was Slade, who'd passed out with me on Meiktila. Slade, despite his flat-top haircut, broad shoulders and six-pack, had even more trouble than I did in making himself liked. His loud mouth and 'been there, done that' personality wasn't nearly servile enough for an LAC. And actually, in absolute fairness, when you're an LAC, you *haven't* been anywhere or done anything. Slade was to keeping quiet and not drawing attention to himself like I was to buying a pair of dezzies. While I'd been on my Rapier course, Vicar and Slade had been at St Athan to get their driving licences. They were both booked for the mid-August Rapier course.

The LAC/SAC cadre involved a re-run of our GSK from Swinderby, fire and first aid training, range work, marksmanship principles and lots of physical stuff. We did a CFT, went to the gym where the PTIs had us doing circuit training and we also went to the nearby American base at Mildenhall, where we were put over their assault course. While the British assault courses tended to be a traditional slog involving a lot of high walls to climb over and mud and water to fall into, the American versions were much more imaginative. Both types were bastard hard, but in different ways. At Mildenhall there was one obstacle called Dirty Names.

One bar was five feet off the ground, and the other was nine. All you had to do was climb onto the five-foot bar, then jump across to the nine-footer, which was four feet away, straddle it and then you were done.

All this after running a few miles and then doing all the other obstacles.

On its own it sounds easy, but believe me, it wasn't.

And if you fell off it at nine feet, you fell.

I was still an LAC at the end of it, but it was one less hurdle to becoming an SAC. And while I was no nearer to being accepted socially, the cadre had given me some excellent physical prep for something that just *might* do me some favours.

Peacekeeper

Peacekeeper was a mixed fitness and shooting competition run by the US Air Force, and it was open to units that specialised in airfield defence. The Americans, Australians and British all sent teams, and it was held every year in America.

America!

Not surprisingly, competition to get on the team was really high.

I applied for selection, which lasted a week at Catterick. Three of us went from 17, we were the only ones there from a Rapier squadron, and a good half of the rest were from 2 Squadron.

And I was absolutely the only LAC there.

It felt really strange going back to the Depot and glancing at the recruits being put through Basics. It had only been a few months since my passing out parade, but I still felt I'd progressed, despite being continually told by the sweats what a useless sprog I was. Strangely enough, though, none of them made the trip to Catterick to give Peacekeeper a try.

Selection activities were split right down the middle. Half shooting, half physical and the ten blokes with the highest overall scores got on the team. In the competition itself, the Americans tended to win at shooting, the RAF Regiment tended to win at fitness and the Australians were wild card random winners at either, but they always won in the bar.

The first shoot was with the Beretta pistol, which I recognised from the *Lethal Weapon* films. Then I had to re-acquaint myself with iron sights. At that time the Brits used optical sights, the Americans didn't, so no SUSATs were used in the interests of fair play. After lunch, it was circuits in the gym followed by a timed run in the CTA. Part of the run went past Meiktila's old trench positions from Omega. All that remained after four months was a fading line in the lumpy grassland, as the rolled-back turfs knitted into the ground. It was returning to nature, and Neil from *The Young Ones* would have been proud.

It was hot weather, hard exercise and high summer, and I probably hadn't hydrated as much as I should have. On the first toilet stop back at the Depot I started pissing blood. Pissing blood! Young, healthy and fit, it was the last thing I expected to see and I duly shat myself. To my non-medically trained mind, either my kidneys had packed up, I'd been poisoned, or my dick was about to fall off. The duty driver took me to the Garrison Hospital, and after a few checks, mostly revolving around a urine specimen, which was now normal, I was sent back to Knettishall.

A trip to the Knettishall Medical Centre didn't throw up any worries, a kidney scan was booked for the following month and I was sent straight back to squadron duties.

*

At around this time another room came up in the Rock Block and it would have been absolute suicide to refuse a second time. A couple of LACs had already moved over, and nothing bad had happened to them. I was still wary of the sweats, and they didn't seem to like me any better, but by then I was Rapier trained, I'd won for the squadron at the Rock Olympics, done the SAC cadre and at least shown willing on Peacekeeper selection. That had to count for something, right?

Not really. It was all counterbalanced by my weird dress sense and reluctance to socialise. For me, the NAAFI was a scary place where nothing enjoyable happened. The LACs that had been posted in since me all had to endure their ritual stripping on the Thursday bop nights. I wasn't going to watch that, and I sure as hell wasn't going to put it on anyone else. In a pushback reaction to what we could expect if we ever went to the NAAFI, a small LAC subculture developed, including myself and Vicar. We felt safer and had a much better time by driving to one of the massive American bases at either Lakenheath or Mildenhall. They were absolutely lux and like a small piece of America transplanted to the UK. They had a bowling alley, pizza shop and even used dollars on base. We changed our pounds into dollars, played the slot machines, ate pizza and then watched a band play in the bar, where nobody ever got stripped or queened.

What was not to like about going there instead of the NAAFI? Nothing.

Operation Granby, 10th August to 14th November 1990

On 2nd August 1990, Iraqi forces invaded Kuwait. Initially, there was the usual political frothing from presidents and prime ministers around the world about what a bad thing it was. Most people, though, including me, thought nothing would happen beyond words. After all, no one really did anything the stop the Soviets invading Afghanistan, and while the Falklands War was a singular, if politically expedient, example of standing up to aggressors, most of the time the world was simply a bad place where bad things happened and no one really stopped it.

Not this time.

The next day, US President George Bush announced he was sending ships to the region. A few days after that, Margaret Thatcher announced a British mobilisation.

Not that us Brits were actually needed. Let's face it, the Americans could have done the whole thing on their own without any help, and that's the opinion of British aircrew who flew right into the storm, not just me. We simply weren't in the same league as the US military and hadn't been for decades. Even Thatcher knew that, but in 1990 she was trailing Labour in the opinion polls, and she knew better than anyone the election-winning potential of sending in the troops.

But enough of geopolitics. On the ground, NCOs spread out around 17 Squadron's hangar and briefed everyone crew by crew. Warning order: go to Station HQ, collect your dog tags, get ready to deploy and don't tell *anyone* what this is about.

Like you'd need the brains of Alan Turing to connect the squadron drawing their dog tags with the biggest news story on the planet.

I was going to war and it was the weirdest feeling ever. I wasn't scared, just sort of numb. All that shit I'd convinced myself about, it'll never happen to me, most people go twenty years without seeing any action, didn't last long, did it? Reality smacked into me like a cricket bat in the face. It was like a sense of utter disbelief at being right in the middle of history as it happened. I probably actually should have been scared, but when you're young, you

127

think you're immortal. I believed in the team, in everyone around me, and no one ever thinks the bad stuff will happen to them. It'll happen to someone else, right?

The next few days were a haze of unbelievable activity. The main song on the radio at that time was 'Civil War' by Guns N' Roses. Every time I look back at that time, I always think of that song. Then the medics descended on the hangar and we were jabbed up to buggery. Both arms and both arse cheeks were used as pin cushions, and more than one rock-hard, pub-fighting bastard rolled his eyes and fainted. Photographers were allowed on to the base, and several of us had our pictures in the papers, posing in NBC suits. One newspaper called us the RAF Rapier Regiment, one paper claimed our missiles were nuclear tipped and another story said that the Rapier kit was so lux it could track a flock of birds.

All of those stories were about as accurate as my shooting, which was shite.

What did happen was seven blokes out of a squadron of a hundred and fifty suddenly got married, and one of the weddings was plastered all over the red top newspapers. Another wedding was one of the new LACs from El Al, Sean Willis, and he asked me to be his best man. I didn't even know what a best man did, but I was really flattered to be asked. It was a very quick job at Thetford Registry Office, then a posh dinner at a nearby hotel. Their honeymoon was a night at the hotel and then it was back to reality.

And all the while the whole squadron prepared to go to war. One Jaguar after another took off and flew out east, and from eight in the morning til nine at night, B Hangar's doors were permanently open. Truck after truck rolled in and dropped off kit. Each one of us was issued a Berghaus Bergen, a new respirator filter and jungle uniforms.

Jungle uniforms. For the desert.

That's because in 1990 the British military didn't have any desert uniforms. With an astonishing lack of foresight, they'd all been sold to Iraq four years earlier. The only hot weather camouflage the armed forces had were tropical uniforms, which was simply DPM on thinner fabric than we were normally issued. A lot of the sweats already had a set for posing around the base in, and they were great for the jungle, fine for Cyprus and not too bad for a British summer. But in a desert environment we'd all be sticking out like a bulldog's undercarriage, and everyone knew it. Individual body armour wasn't standard issue then either, but even more worrying than that were the NBC arrangements.

The standard issue respirator at that time was the S10, which was compatible with the Mark 4 NBC suit. The only trouble was that the whole squadron had been issued with Mark 3 NBC suits, compatible with the obsolete S6 respirator, which we didn't have.

That meant they didn't give an airtight seal at the hood/respirator junction.

So if we came under a chemical attack, they'd leak, which was a definite Freddie.

And if you're on a peacetime training exercise, that wouldn't matter a jot. But when you're about to deploy for real, against an enemy that was known to have stocks of nerve agent *and* had willingly used them against their own people, it was a much less than ideal detail. I mentioned it to one of the officers and he told me not to worry about it.

Who listens to LACs anyway?

The pace of preparation was frantic and no one really knew, or more accurately, no one was really telling us, where we were actually going. Some said Cyprus, some said UAE, some said Saudi. Every night, the whole squadron was paraded and the CO gave us the same tub-thumping pep-talk. This was going to be an air campaign all the way, he said, it would make the Falklands look like small change. And then, just to really focus our minds, he said he didn't think we'd all be coming back.

I had no idea what we'd be facing, but I was damn sure *I'd* be coming back. One part of my training had already kicked in: it never happens to you, it's always the other guy.

Then, in a crucial change from the 17 Squadron normal, the NAAFI became the focal point for everyone, even me. The old sweats actually shut the fuck up, left me alone and I started to bond. Crews were realigned to allow a mix of experience, and I was moved from A2 to A4. Like pretty much every unit in the armed forces, 17 Squadron was undermanned. That meant the numbers were bumped up to operational with blokes brought in from other squadrons, including an OCA who was rapidly dropped in from Wing HQ.

There was briefing after briefing after briefing. Leaving aside the kit compatibility issues, I filled my head with NBC lore. There was loads of first aid training. I was told about the importance of getting fluids into casualties, about treating shock. I was shown the emergency bottles of intravenous fluids, about how to connect them to IV lines. Sergeant Ross told A Flight how in an emergency you could shove an intravenous tube up a casualty's arse if there was no other way to give the fluids. Smiling, he added, 'Any man who tries that on a casualty who's still conscious will be charged.'

Not too many people on the squadron had any real experience of desert operations, or indeed, any operations. Plenty had been to Belize and Cyprus, and we were taught about acclimatisation, hot weather, snakes and scorpions and how they loved to take up residence in empty boots. Pretty soon I'd get used to the sound all around me of boots being thumped against any hard surface, then tipped upside down and vigorously shaken before being gingerly pulled on.

And in a great example of fear transference, I learned about camel spiders, which supposedly lived in the desert. Whatever actual stuff I got told about them, I magnified everything. In my mind, camel spiders had a leg span the same size as a four-tonner's spare tyre, they had a massive jumping capacity and if they looked at you, they'd jump on to your neck, bite paralysing poison into your jugular vein and then devour your face. Vicar and I actually believed that shit, and the first chance we got, we drove into Bury St Edmunds and found a hunting and fishing shop, where we each bought the biggest machete we could find. We dubbed them Anti Camel Spider Knives, even abbreviated them to ACSKs, and then laced them to our Bergens. We never went anywhere without them.

The days passed. We got ready, we were ready, we were all more than ready. Then the regular nightly briefing changed. The CO brought in an air officer from somewhere way at the top of the RAF food chain. He praised the whole squadron for our hard work and then dropped the bomb that we might not now be needed.

All this after a week of being told we were going to war.

The RAF high command really mess with your head.

All credit to the CO. Once they were discreetly out of sight, he apparently took the air officer to one side, had him up against the wall and told him exactly what he thought of him.

What followed was a few days of me phoning my family, telling them I was off to war, the next day saying no, I wasn't, and then back to saying I was. Magnify that by one hundred and fifty as everyone on the squadron had to make exactly the same phone call. The anguish for our families must have been a nightmare. Then, just before mid-August, we were told we were moving out to Cyprus. For definite this time. How much that had to do with the CO 'advocating' the need for us to go somewhere, anywhere to the visiting air officer, I've got no idea, but we now had to make our kit and vehicles Hercules friendly. The four tonners had to have their headroom lowered by two feet to fit into the Herc's cargo holds, and the whole squadron was split into chalks, the loadmasters' term for each planeload. It took thirty-six chalks to get the whole of 17 Squadron to Cyprus.

Well, the whole squadron minus one. Pete Jones, the archetypical sprog-bashing senior SAC old sweat. Always the first one to shout out 'Get the LACs', and the same arsehole who'd head-butted Steve Lake at the Easter party for no fucking reason whatsoever, didn't deploy with the squadron. I've got no idea why, but he stayed put at Knettishall and that was fine by me. It was one less dickhead to worry about when there were much more important things going on.

Once we'd been given our chalks, we knew our flight times. The runway was lit up right through the night, and at all hours a Hercules would land at Knettishall, load up and take off. In Basics the instructors always said anything could happen, a war could happen when you least expected it, and they were right. This was utterly unexpected, utterly unreal, and here I was, playing my small part in huge events that were unfolding all around me.

Cyprus

The chalk I was part of had a stupid, dark o'clock early morning flight, and it went all the way from Knettishall to Lyneham. Once there, we transferred from one Herc needing repairs to another one that was fixed. Then it was up in the air and a seven-hour flight to Akrotiri, Cyprus.

Flying in a Hercules was definitely not glamorous. It was loud as hell and I had to wear ear defenders for the whole flight. The high-mounted wings gave me an overhead view of the hydraulic rods, and the toilet was a curtained-off cubicle mounted halfway up the loading ramp at the back of the plane. In-flight meals were microwaved NAAFI meat pies.

Even though the UK summer of 1990 had been pretty hot, when the ramp came down at Akrotiri in August it was like an oven door had been opened. I stepped onto a sun-soaked pan surrounded by sandy soil and scrub bushes, universally referred to as bondu.

Akrotiri was and still is a huge airbase, occupying the entire southernmost peninsular of Cyprus and running up to the northern edge of a large salt lake. Its eastern end joined the Lady's Mile beach, which ran almost into Limassol, the nearest town and a big tourist location. Just north of the camp gates was Akrotiri village, a small collection of bars and restaurants that did a roaring trade from off-duty airmen and their families.

Over the years, the number of people based at Akrotiri changed. Sometimes it was a cushy backwater and an ideal posting, and other times, like Op Granby, it was a prime piece of real estate, massively crowded and busy as it took on the role of unsinkable aircraft carrier. It had plenty of buildings, hangars and accommodation to allow for rapid expansion, which was just about to happen.

The loadmasters got the kit unloaded, and we drove along Phantom Way to a storage yard and warehouse near the western end of the runway. This was 17 Squadron's new base, the replacement B Hangar. Once the Land Rovers and kits were safely stowed, we were taken to one of Akrotiri's transit barrack blocks, each given a camp bed and bedding and told to find a spot. Just like Knettishall, it was LACs, SACs and corporals together. Unlike Knettishall, it was ten men to each room and a wardrobe to stow your kit. It was basic and airy, it was Cyprus, I was on ops, the adventure of all adventures, doing exactly what I was trained for. I was just buzzing.

You can say what you want about the air force, and yes, they fucked the entire squadron about with their on-the-bus, off-the-bus, mess-with-your-head bullshit back at Knettishall, but once they did actually get their arses into gear, shit happened. We were shipped across a whole continent within a few days and as soon as the last chalk touched down, B Flight deployed their four kits straight away. Rumour was rife about where A Flight would go. 17 Squadron was always set up to operate on two separate sites. Would the same thing happen again out here? While B Flight were on the kits, A Flight were based at the compound making sure the other four kits were in good order and generally shaking down and settling in. We attended intelligence briefs, realigned our aircraft recognition skills and also worked on our tans. Even in a build-up to war, Cyprus followed tropical work routines. The seven-to-one working pattern and all weekends off never stopped while I was there.

One week after B Flight deployed, A Flight took over and spent a week on the kits. The Regiment's motto is *Per ardua*, which loosely translates as 'through hardship', but it absolutely did not apply to 17 Squadron's Op Granby tour. Deployed and living in a twelve-by-twelve tent in Cyprus with trips to the Airmen's Mess for food wasn't hard at all. And although there were live missiles on the launchers and the entire squadron was kept in a high state of readiness, there was practically zero danger of an Iraqi air attack. That's because they'd have had to get past Israel first if they wanted to hit Akrotiri, and there was *no* chance of that happening. I was moved again, from A4 to A3, which was deployed on the extreme southern end of the island. The site was pitched on a sandy clifftop in among the bondu, with an uninterrupted view of the Mediterranean sea. If you took the Rapier kits out of the picture, it was the kind of holiday scene you'd pay thousands for.

'Welcome aboard, Brindle,' Pete Andrews, one of the crew's corporals greeted me, along with a perpetual smile. His black hair and handlebar moustache gave him a piratical air. 'Stow your kit in

133

the tent and have a walk around the site. You're on the first run for nosebag.'

'Cheers, Corporal.'

'Pete,' he replied. 'It's Pete, all right?'

'All right,' I said, still not sure if I actually could call him Pete. He was the first corporal on 17 Squadron to tell me to ditch the rank. It felt strange and good at the same time, a slow, very slow, sense of being accepted.

One of the SACs on A3 was an enormous statue of a man called Tarzan. I never knew his real name, but his nickname fitted perfectly. With his shaggy black hair, marble-hard, six-pack abdomen and permanent grin, that's exactly what he looked like, even in DP, and especially when he was armed. The first time I saw him on A3's site, he was laid flat out on his camp bed, wearing nothing but male-model speedo briefs.

Tarzan was something of a legend. To begin with, he was probably the only sweat who was actually decent to the LACs. And although he was unbelievably hard as nails, he never threw his considerable weight around, maybe because of an underlying nice nature, or maybe because he didn't have to. He had absolutely nothing to prove.

But that's not to say he didn't have a dark side or demons to face, and like many the drink affected him. There was a story that one night at Knettishall, he was leaving the NAAFI drunk and was challenged by a scuffer with an SLR. Despite being alone and unarmed, Tarzan pulled the rifle away from the scuffer, hit him just once and put him in hospital with a long list of unpleasant injuries. I don't know how much of the story was true, or how much of it had been embellished, but what *was* true was that everyone, even Tarzan himself, said that he was on his last chance. If he fucked up just once more, no matter what it was, then he'd be booted out of the RAF.

And that happened in the second week of the tour, just after I'd been shifted across to A3. I woke up in the tent one morning and Tarzan simply wasn't there any more. Apparently his mail was being read – I don't know if it was everyone's or just his – and he'd been writing home about which officers he was going to shoot if it ever turned into a real war. He'd said it often enough on the site, and over time, over history, he wouldn't have been the first or the last to talk about it. Putting it in a letter was a step too far for the air force, though, and that was the last any of us saw of him. He was flown back to the UK, court martialled about a year later, sentenced to hard time and then discharged from the RAF.

Towards the end of August it became clear that air defences were needed further east. The bases in Saudi had good levels of protection, but Bahrain, from which coalition planes were also flying, had very limited SHORAD. The decision was made way above squadron level to pack four kits up and send them out there.

The crews selected were B1, A2, B3 and A4, along with half of HQ Flight, and half of Eng Flight. None of the LACs were sent to Bahrain.

Not that there was a huge pool of added experience to send east. 17 was very much a sprog squadron. A big chunk of the SACs had been posted in straight from Basics, including most of the sweats. A lot of the corporals and sergeants were also newly promoted to rank.

Not long after the squadron split into two, there was the only real episode of officially sanctioned, utterly pointless bullshit. It was for Battle of Britain Day, which usually fell on or around the 15th September. Understandably it was a big thing for the RAF as a whole, but just like bull nights and being shouted at for having your hands in your pockets, it kind of belonged to the non-operational side of life.

Not all the time, apparently.

As Akrotiri was in a kind of no-man's-land between war and peace, it still retained some of the traditions, and a church service had been organised for Battle of Britain Day. It meant that we had to do some kind of bollocksy march past, and before that happened, Chiefy B had got it into his head that he wanted to inspect the block beforehand.

Which meant a bull night, on a transit block, in Cyprus, on ops.

It was pretty much unheard of, but orders were orders, even idiotic, dumbass fucking stupid ones. Probably for the first time in its existence, the barrack block was scrubbed and cleaned from its roof to the flagstones. Shutters were hosed down, floors swept, toilets and showers scoured. 'Why the fuck are we doing this?' was whispered, cursed and muttered by everyone, and on the appointed day as everyone stood to attention by their beds, Chiefy B swept in and spent about thirty seconds silently glancing at what had been several hours of hard and completely pointless work.

At least it only happened the once.

With half the squadron now in Bahrain, the kits around Akrotiri were taken out of action and pulled back to the compound. The flight's office and telephone room were permanently manned, ready to call us out at short notice, and an air of semi-permanence took over. Logistics started happening, and the camp beds in the barrack block were replaced with regular ones.

And once the risk of imminent war receded, all the other shit came back.

One of the B Flight LACs, a guy called John Brown, was having even more trouble fitting in than I was, even though he'd served in the army before joining the air force. He had the shaved head and large build which certainly gave him the physical fit, unlike me, and while I never actually knew the reasons why, he'd been unpopular since day one.

One night at the block, Eddie Allan, his broken nose gained from boxing for the squadron, and one of the toughest blokes on B Flight, dragged Brown awake. Allan started telling him he'd been heard boasting in the NAAFI about his previous army life. I think the main gripe was that he'd been exaggerating, but I really had no idea. Brown kept saying he'd only spoken about stuff he did in the army, but Allan wasn't having any of it. I lay in my bed, my whole body trembling. In the darkness I heard the punches land one after another, after another. I was an LAC, just the same as Brown, and I wondered if I was going to be next. No one in the room spoke up, no one moved, no one did anything, including me. After a while, Allan stomped out.

And that's how it went. At the compound, there was the military discipline, but outside it was fend for yourself, and Christ help you if the sweats took a dislike to you. There was nowhere to run to, nowhere to hide. In the Rock Block back at Knettishall, at least you had your own room and a door to lock.

And it really wasn't every SAC who took a liking to labelling themselves senior, or who stalked the transit block looking for sprogs to bash, but it didn't need to be. Because it didn't matter if it was one bully, or ten, or a hundred, it never got stopped, and the chances were always that once it started, more would join in. All it took was one arsehole mixed with alcohol, and herd mentality would soon take over.

Not long after Brown had been visited the first time, they came for the poor bastard again. Same thing: night-time, no lights and alcohol. 'Brown!' But this time it was two of them: Geordie, the pseudo-northerner who'd told me and four others to strip at the Easter party, and John Haughton, another B Flight hard man. They dragged him out of bed and screamed at him to fight them. 'Get up,' they yelled. 'You're a soldier, and your job is to close with and destroy the enemy. So fight! Fight us now!'

Brown tried, but up against two he didn't have a chance. And this wasn't just punches hitting flesh; he was being rammed into furniture and thrown against walls and into wardrobes, as well as being whacked from two directions. Absolute coward that I was, I lay in my bed, shat myself and wondered how many more LACs were on the hit list that night. Should I have stood up and tried to stop it? Part of me wanted to, even though I knew it would achieve nothing, but I didn't have the balls. Everyone else in the room was awake, they had to be. In the bed-space next to mine was an Eng Flight corporal, seemingly asleep.

No one was asleep.

After a few minutes, but I really don't know how long, Pete Andrews appeared at the doorway. 'Get out, Pete,' said Geordie. 'This doesn't involve you.' They carried on beating up Brown. Pete stood there for a few seconds, walked out of the room and then came back a minute later and called Geordie and Haughton outside.

No one else in the room moved or made a sound. It was as though nothing had happened. Everyone, including me, carried on pretending to be asleep.

I thought that surely nothing else could happen that night, but some time later I heard Geordie's voice in the distance, and this time it was Slade who was being screamed at to fight. If anything, Slade was even more unpopular than I was. He didn't help things by acting as though everyone was his mate and equal and calling the corporals by their first names long before being invited. None of us were perfect, and Slade's mouth got him into trouble just like my dress sense did to me. Unpopular he might have been, and maybe he did need to think before he spoke, but did he deserve a kicking?

Did he fuck.

But apparently the sweats thought so. Slade's ordeal was happening at the other end of the block and it sounded as though the poor bastard was surrounded by a whole pack of them, led by Geordie.

Eventually Geordie was bawled at by one of the corporals who'd been brought in from 54 Squadron. 'Stop this shit, now!' I heard him shout, as I laid terrified in my bed.

'Stay out of this,' replied Geordie. 'It's not your business.'

'The hell it is,' snarled the corporal. 'I told you to stop. I'm *ordering* you to stop. Are you disobeying an order?'

'Fuck off.'

'I'm a *corporal*, you bastard.'

'Fuck you, you're not a 17 Squadron corporal.'

The stand-off continued until another corporal waded in and put a stop to it. Fucking hell, I'd rather have faced chemical weapons with an incompatible suit and respirator than have that night repeated on me. This was a hundred times worse than anything that happened at Knettishall. We were having chunks knocked off us by our own side, never mind the Iraqis, and it was LACs who were suffering. We were out there for real and *this* shit was happening! Even when the noise died down and everyone, including me, could make the bullshit claim that they'd been asleep through the whole thing, I lay in my bed, and the only thing I dared move were my eyes. If I kept still maybe no one would notice me. If there had been any food in my stomach I'd have thrown up. Was it my turn to be next? Was this my fault? Had I made this happen? Should I have stood up, said something? Was I gutless because I didn't? The next morning, Brown's face told the story of the night before, red marks and bruises everywhere. I walked over a patch of bondu to the Airmen's Mess and my thoughts were in freefall. Twelve hours earlier I'd felt like the luckiest person alive to be in the RAF Regiment, to be on 17 Squadron, but now, after the actions of others, and inaction by myself, everything had changed. This wasn't the Regiment I thought I'd joined, and I was ashamed of everything that had happened that night, including myself, for not doing anything. My first thoughts were that I wanted no part of this and I should just leave. But can you do that when you're on ops? I had no idea. I walked into the mess, shovelled an unseen breakfast onto my plate and sat down with no idea what I was eating. Pete Andrews came in and sat down next to me, grinning his pirate smile as though the night before hadn't happened. 'It's over, it's done,' he said. 'Brown deserved it.'

I looked at him with a neutral expression, already wise to not saying what I thought, which centred around *when will I deserve it?*

Christ, I thought, Pete Andrews was one of the good guys. A week earlier he'd welcomed me to A3 and told me to call him Pete. Would he still do the same when it was my turn to get stoved? Everything that I thought was good and right had been turned on its head. Having just found my place, having thought I could make this work, I had to ask myself all over again if I really was doing the right thing. Now, more than thirty years later, the memories still turn my stomach, still make me feel ashamed. But was I responsible for those fuck-bastards going medieval? No, I wasn't. And was it my job to rein them in? No, it wasn't.

And while I feel bad about something that was never my responsibility, I'd bet a million pounds the wankers who actually did it didn't feel a thing.

A few days later a story emerged that Brown had been stopped while riding a hired moped straight towards one of the cliffs on the southern edge of the base. It didn't take the brains of Socrates to work out what he'd been planning, and it wasn't much of a surprise. He'd taken more shit than any other LAC for sure, and everyone's got their limits.

Nothing was said about any of this officially. The only thing I ever heard was when I was duty driver and I gave an Eng Flight corporal a lift. 'Tell the rest of your LAC friends,' he said, 'tell them they've got nothing more to fear. We let you boys down and we're sorry. It won't happen again.' He sounded sincere, and I'm sure he meant it.

Shame that no one who actually did the bashing ever said sorry.

And nothing ever happened to them either. Nothing was said to them, none of them were disciplined.

And yes, there was also some context. Tarzan was on his final chance, but he'd only threatened to harm officers and he faced the entire might of the Queen's Regulations. But when a handful of LACs actually *did* get the shit kicked out of them, when it was witnessed by NCOs, the perpetrators got away scot-free. Go figure.

All of this was less than six months after the CO telling us that he was only too happy to deal with any bullies on his squadron.

Yeah, right.

On that point, he was never as good as his word, which I guess gave the green light to anyone who wanted to bash an LAC, because even if you got caught, and even if it was seen, there clearly wouldn't be any consequences.

A few weeks later, I woke up in the middle of the night and a B Flight LAC was sitting on one of the beds opposite mine. I could smell the beer, and he looked upset and angry. 'Are you all right?' I asked. It was dark and I couldn't see much more than his silhouette.

'No,' he replied.

'What's up?'

'What do you think?' he said, scowling at the doorway. I switched on the light and saw that his nose was bleeding. Another whacked LAC, only this time it had been done by a corporal.

Now, you might think this is all just part of being on a fighting unit and if you can't take a twatting how are you going to be when the bullets start flying? And you might be right. You might have a point. But you could *also* say that when you're getting nothing but shit and humiliation from your oppos, do you really think they'll ever risk their lives for you? Will they ever have your back? And more to the point, will you have theirs? If one of those wankers was lying out in no man's land and possibly wounded, would you really brave a hail of enemy fire to bring them in? And you'd *really* have to ask yourself, imagine what the humiliated, terrorised and still-bruised LAC might do if he's live armed and one of those tossers shows up in his SUSAT.

Shit like that didn't build bridges, it built walls.

And although the *actual* violence wasn't constant, it was the threat, the possibility of it that wore me down. So just like at Knettishall, most of the LACs socialised together, avoiding both the NAAFI and any beer calls at the block. There was nothing any of us could do about middle-of-the-night attacks, but any other time, if you weren't there, you weren't a target. The LAC survival clique that was born out of Knettishall's ritual stripping and queening was solidified by even more shit in Akrotiri. So okay, if they didn't want to know us, fine, we didn't want to know them. Which speaks volumes for the team building benefits to be gained from marginalising the new boys.

Sometimes we'd hook up with guys from Eng Flight and go into Limassol, but most times we went to the Akrotiri Arms, a bar in the village just outside the camp gates. A lot of the sweats didn't like it, or us, for going there. 'It's a 'Guin's bar,' they'd glare at us and mutter. And they were right, but you know what, no one ever got beaten up there either.

September wore on and 34 Squadron, the resident CVR(T) squadron at Akrotiri, moved east to Bahrain and were replaced by 2 Squadron. More and more kit and people were moved through Akrotiri and onwards. Air power built up at Dhahran and Tabuk in Saudi, and also in Bahrain, along with the Regiment. 1 and 26 Squadrons were sent to Tabuk, and 51 Squadron deployed to Dhahran. The rumours started again. Maybe the rest of the squadron would be moved out to Bahrain. Despite everything, I was still keen, still RAF Reg all the way. Sure, there were some wankers on the squadron, but I'd worked out how to avoid them most of the time, and besides, I was there, on ops and having the adventure of my life.

Then, in early October we were told to get everything Hercules-ready again. We were headed to Bahrain. Morale climbed. Akrotiri as a place had its plus points – no one was going to argue with the working hours, or the climate, or the really laid-back, holiday-camp atmosphere when we were actually getting ready for war – but Bahrain was the real deal, or so we thought. Going there put us a whole lot closer to any action, which was the reason all of us joined in the first place, the reason we were being paid.

Akrotiri also really reminded me of my time in Germany. It was a semi-isolated British outpost abroad, although the foreign country I was actually in was kept at arm's length. All the amenities were close to hand, cheaper and sometimes, like medical and dental, completely free. And all the real-world UK problems, which at that time included the poll-tax riots, were just stories to read about in the newspapers. Clearly not the real world, but a reality for me, and a familiar one, one that reminded me of a more comforting time, which in my mind offset to quite a large degree all of the more recent shite that had been going on. The only tangible problem I had was the money I'd wasted on tickets for the Monsters of Rock festival and Prince concert, neither of which I could now go to.

Akrotiri also had a cinema, another escape route from the barrack block sproghunts. I was there so often I occasionally got let in for free. One of the films I saw that had an explosive impact on me was *An Innocent Man*, a prison drama starring Tom Selleck. It was all about an individual being terrorised by his peers while the establishment did nothing to help. It didn't take much to draw the comparisons, and I was lifted by the central character's triumph against the odds, as well as one amazing line: 'You don't have to stand tall around here, but you've *got* to stand up.'

I don't know if I actually *did* stand up, but what I didn't do was break down.

With days to go before the rest of the squadron moved out to Bahrain, the cinema showed *Born on the Fourth of July*, which was probably *not* the best film to watch just before getting a whole lot closer to the sharp end. At the start of the film, I gloried in Ron Kovic's determination and will to become a soldier, but once the injuries started happening, the film gave me a real sobering reality check that I might very well come back from all of this in a wheelchair. The film utterly obliterated my 'it'll happen to someone else' belief, which was probably exactly what Ron Kovic thought. I walked out of the cinema in a daze, suddenly very grateful to be able to walk, and really, *really* wondering what the future held. Art had just imitated life in a massive, shocking, eye-opening way.

Bahrain

Bahrain's airport was surrounded by the city of Muharraq, right on the north tip of the island, and Bahrain itself was joined to Saudi Arabia by a fifteen-mile-long causeway. It was used a lot by Saudis who drove over to take advantage of the legally available alcohol. I'd regularly see lots of Mercedes parked up on the beach, with traditionally dressed Arab blokes pulling crates of beer out of the boot and then chilling on the sand with a cool one.

Surreal, but that was Bahrain all over.

If Akrotiri was a different world, Bahrain was a whole different universe.

The airport was a busy civilian hub which had been suddenly crammed to bursting with military hardware. The Herc pulled up and we unloaded the wagons onto a packed pan. Everywhere I looked I saw pink Tornados and Jaguars, while C-130s from a dozen different nations, with a dozen different military paint schemes, were dotted all over the place. Threading their way through all of this madness were civilian airliners.

A small-ish tin hangar had been set aside for 17 Squadron and we parked the kits up and were briefed by both the CO and warrant officer. 'You can forget about being welcomed here with open arms,' said the CO, still scruffy in his tropical DP, still the gravelly voice and still staring into my soul with his laser beam eyes. 'Half of this country might want us here, but the other half hate our guts, and they think Saddam's a hero for giving the West the finger over Kuwait. But like us or not, Bahrain's a police state, which we're probably being blamed for as well, even by the people who like us.'

'And don't stare too hard at the locals, either,' growled the warrant. 'On paper, homosexuality is illegal in Bahrain, but behind closed doors it's accepted and never talked about.' He paused. 'For the men at least. And if you see two Bahraini men holding hands, don't stare, don't comment and for fuck's sake don't laugh. It just means they're friends, nothing more.' He then did the warrant officer stare that froze my blood. 'But if I see any of you fuckers holding hands, you'll be walking back to the UK once the tour's over, via Baghdad.'

It didn't take long before jokes were being made about selling the LACs to rich Arabs for fast cars and lots of money. It was banter, it was good-natured and, crucially, it actually included the LACs.

Which was kind of a new thing.

'I don't want you working on your suntan, Chapel,' one of HQ Flight's SACs told Vicar. 'They like them pale over here.'

'What's my selling price right now?' he asked.

'Ten thousand US.'

'Is that all?' he replied. 'I'm worth double that *and* a Ford Mustang for this virgin ass.' He minced out of the briefing room and the wolf whistles followed him.

The last chalk had barely touched down before it was followed almost immediately by the order to deploy. B Flight were the first on the ground back in Cyprus, so this time it was A Flight's turn. Some would say it was about time we started earning our wages, and sometimes we did. Having to burrow the kit's cables into the rock-hard, semi-manufactured Muharraq beach was fucking hard work in the thirty-degree heat and near hundred-per-cent humidity. It made the trench digging on Omega seem like nothing.

The war plan was for six kits to defend the airfield, which was the reason the rest of the squadron was brought over from Cyprus. But until a war was absolutely, totally, utterly imminent, four kits were set up, two were kept back and two were to be used for spares. With eight Rapier crews, four on and four off made absolute sense from a manpower rotation perspective. So while A Flight spent a week on the kits, B Flight stayed on the airfield in a support role and slept in hotels.

Five-star, posh-as-hell hotels.

The Rapier sites weren't too shabby either. They'd been worked on for six weeks and as a place to fight a war from, they were absolutely lux. The launcher, radar and optical tracker points and missile dump were all banked up with sandbags and oil drums. Accommodation was an air-conditioned Portakabin with bunk beds, microwave and fridge. All meals were back at the airfield in the combined mess.

Per ardua? That's the last thing it was.

And it would really have to have gone tits up, with the Iranians *and* the Russians pitching in against us, for it to get hairy. So as long as it all went to plan I was pretty sure I'd be okay, but I also knew from the many briefings that Saddam was dead set on dragging the Israelis in, and if that happened, all bets would be off. The coalition could very well fall apart, and if it did we'd all be a long way from home in a country that wouldn't want us there. Another sobering sight sprang up just outside the airbase. On a large area of flat land stood dozens of olive-green canvas tents, all with a red cross painted on them. Right then they were empty, but they were there as a triage clearing station, set up in anticipation for the expected casualties. Hundreds, maybe thousands, of expected casualties. Some of my optimism faded and I remembered *Born on the Fourth of July* all over again.

But there really was nothing I could do about any of that, so I focussed on the hotel lifestyle and the job in hand. With four kits deployed it was time to make things permanent. As well as digging in the cables, we sank poles around the site and set up a double-height barbed wire perimeter. There were also rolls and rolls of desert netting to drape over the sand walls and oil drum protection. Despite the location, the beach that A3's kit was on was man-made, and the duty rumour was that the sand being used to build up our defences had been imported from Wales.

Along with the camel spiders, believing everything I was told carried on, way after Basics.

*

On 3rd October 1990, exactly one year after I joined up, East and West Germany reunited. The Cold War was ending, the Soviet threat was diminishing by the day and the world was changing fast. Then, a week later, Chiefy A came to the site one night to do flight commander's checks. Just before he went he said, 'Brindle, you're now an SAC.'

And that was it.

I'd been in the air force for a year and it wasn't so much that I was an SAC, but I was no longer an LAC. I sure as shit wasn't going to strip or queen anyone, but maybe things would be different now. Since I'd been in Bahrain there was no off-duty sprog-bashing shit going on, but then again there wasn't the opportunity. When we were on the kits, we lived as a crew under constant NCO supervision, and when B Flight were on the kits we lived in a five-star hotel, in plain sight. Even the most pissed-up, old sweat, brain-addled senior SAC couldn't get any ideas about bashing an LAC with impunity. And I suppose we were kind of almost nearly at war, which must have made even them recognise the need not to act like complete tossers.

After the first week, B Flight took over and I stayed at the Gulf Gate Hotel, which beat the shit out of any barrack block I'd ever stayed in. And because we were on ops, no one paid any food or accommodation charges. Every week, whether I was on the kits or in the hotels, I was given a hundred and fifty quid, in dinars, on top of my wages, supposedly to buy food because there weren't any established messing facilities.

I wasn't complaining, but really?

For our week on the kits, we were fed entirely by the combined mess. The following week, each morning started with a huge breakfast at the hotel and lunch at the combined mess. So I only had to buy evening meals every other week, and I quickly found Pizza Hut and Hardee's. That left loads of spare cash to spend and I don't think anyone on 17 Squadron actually touched their wages while they were in Bahrain. I sure as hell didn't, and I was in the lowest pay grade on the squadron.

As well as drinking beer in the hotel bars, evenings were spent at Muharraq's commercial district, which was a bustling warren of small shops that sold absolutely everything. A big chunk of us bought top-line cameras for a lot less than UK prices, and we were buying it with our food money. I got all of my Christmas shopping, and everywhere around us were whole streets crammed with gold shops. Popular purchases were his and hers cut-coin jewellery, and haggling was always the way to go. In Andy McNab's book, *Bravo Two Zero*, he described the Gulf airbases as a kleptomaniac's paradise, but if he'd gone to the local shops he'd have had to pay.

The CO was right about the place being a police state. MP5-toting uniformed paramilitaries loitered on every street corner, as well as outside the hotel. There was never any trouble in the town, although we drew hostile looks from the locals as often as we got smiles.

But you can't mention Bahrain without talking about the barbers' shops. They were amazing. I sat in one and watched Pete

Andrews get a haircut. To begin with it was your standard hair clipper and flat-top, which, unless you were a baldie, everyone on the squadron had. Then there was loads of talcum powder, then a head massage and then a face massage. I hadn't seen anything like it. A strong-fingered, middle-aged Arab kneaded Pete's face all over like it was a lump of dough. Pete didn't seem to mind, and afterwards it was my turn. I'd never had a face massage, and the barber's fingers working my facial muscles felt great. Pretty soon we renamed the experience. You weren't getting a haircut; you were getting a face-fuck.

For week three we were back on the kit, and the build-up and war preparations got more intense. There were simulated air attacks, and I spent a few hours wearing full NBC kit in thirty-degree heat, soaked in sweat and wondering if the presence of nerve agent would make it easier to keep suited up. We still had the Mark 3 suit and S10 respirator combo. Was I the only one who was worried about it? Maybe I was overreacting.

Slade, the LAC who'd been bashed by the sweats back at Akrotiri, was now part of A3. I'm not defending what they did to him, but it's probably fair to say that his mouth got him into trouble. That week, a plan was hatched to grab him one night and drag him into the missile storage bay, I guess to scare him. We jumped aboard an Eng Flight four tonner that was on the site and drove it towards Slade with the lights on full. We grabbed him, forced a sandbag over his head and then chucked him in a Land Rover. He struggled, but it was the usual thing: one against many, no chance. We then drove around the site before backing up to the missile storage bay. We lowered the tailgate and stopped at that point as it sounded as though he was crying.

We let him go.

We.

Suddenly I wasn't the victim any more.

I'd stood alongside the other SACs, of whom I was now one, and done just as much as them. I hadn't even realised I was going along with it. It was a very quiet, understated, not even mentioned change. No one said well done, or welcome to the dark side, it just happened.

But it's what I had to do to get accepted – do unto others what you've had done to you.

I should have known it was the only way; there had been enough signs over the past six months. Christ, was that all it had been since Basics?

The following week, back in the hotel, which this time was the really lux Regency, I'd been allocated a room with Sean Willis, whose wedding I'd done best man duties for just before we flew out. At the Regency, a band played in the bar every night, and the room service club sandwiches were bigger than a full meal at the combined mess. It was another affluent, excessive slice of unreality that was hard to equate with sort of, kind of, almost being at war. Sean was on A1, so we hadn't seen each other for the past week.

'We really put the frighteners on Slade last week,' I said, relaxing in the hotel room with a club sandwich.

'Oh, Christ,' said Sean. 'Did he get another kicking?'

'No,' I said. 'We just grabbed him, put a sandbag over his head and dragged him into the missile bay one night.'

'And then what?'

'Nothing.' I shrugged. 'We let him go. We only wanted to scare him.'

'*Only* wanted to scare him?' said Sean. 'Bloody hell, mate, you've really changed.'

I munched on my club sandwich and thought about what I'd been part of. Slade walking around the site on his own, doing generator checks, blinded by the four-tonner's lights and the truck driving towards him, the sound of our voices shouting out his name. Then jumping towards him, unseen in the headlight glare and dragging him into the back of a Land Rover. I shuddered as I remembered that in Cyprus, only a few weeks earlier, he'd been beaten up. I remembered my own fear rinsing through me, the disgust I'd felt at myself for being a bystander. And now, less than a month later, I was a perpetrator.

Sean was one hundred per cent right. I *had* changed, and I hadn't even realised it had happened. 'Let's get a beer,' I said.

We got in the hotel's lift, which was complete with a fitted deep pile carpet with the day embroidered into it. The service there was so absolutely spot on, I was sure it would be replaced with the next day's carpet before the clock even struck one minute past midnight.

The Regency's bar normally played host to businessmen, but in 1990 it was awash with flat-top haircuts and squaddies, all of them sunburned to various degrees. Office suits had been replaced by jeans and Fido Dido T-shirts, which became a 17 Squadron fashion item. Normally I'd take a spot in the bar with Steve Lake, drink a few pints and watch the Filipino band play cover versions. But first I had a job to do. I had to speak to Slade.

He wasn't hard to find. Unusually for a Muslim country, alcohol was legal in Bahrain, but pub crawls and bars on every street were a step too far for what was still a very conservative society. So the hotel bar was pretty much the only game in town for a drink, and most of the squadron gravitated there. Slade was ordering a pint.

'I'll get this one,' I said, paying the barman.

'Cheers, mate,' he brashed, always loud, always laughing.

'Listen,' I said, suddenly feeling uncomfortable, not sure what to say. 'All that shit that happened the other night.'

Slade grinned. 'That was nothing, that,' he said. 'I've had worse.'

'I know you have.' I paused, trying to find the words. 'It was out of order,' I stammered. 'I shouldn't have done it.' I gripped my beer glass and shoved my other hand into my pocket and clenched my teeth. I knew I'd done wrong but I still couldn't say the one word I wanted to say, the one word I should have said. Elton John was right, sorry really is the hardest word. And Slade might have been loud, gobby and at times his own worst enemy, but I guess he could still spot someone who was at least trying to apologise.

'Forget it, Brinders,' he said. 'I don't care about any of that. I just laugh it off and move on.'

Slade walked to his seat and I stood there alone with my thoughts. I'd learned a fine lesson about myself, and now I was back at the exact same crossroads. As much as I was still all for being in the Regiment, I had to be accepted as me, not what they wanted me to become. I realised that doing the job was the easy part, but everything that went with it wasn't. At least not for me. And I definitely didn't want to become a sprog-bashing, bully-boy, old sweat wanker that I'd very nearly mutated into. So it was time for me to decide what kind of person I wanted to be.

Once again, I was on a collision course with the squadron's culture.

By now it was mid-November. 17 Squadron's three-month tour was finishing and 66 Squadron were due to take over. Air defence-wise, Bahrain was to become a 6 Wing rotation. For however long it went on, 19 would take over from 66 and then it would be 20 Squadron. But right now, I was headed back home.

66 Squadron arrived and I met some mates from Basics and Rapier Training, along with Sergeant May, our sergeant from El Al who'd since been posted. The kits were staying put. We were flying back with our rifles and only one uniform. Everyone's second set of tropical DP had to be left behind. We posed for the obligatory flight photos with the parked Jaguars as a super-cool backdrop, then trooped on board a waiting TriStar for the flight to the UK.

On the plane, everyone was handed a tax declaration form to fill in. The Inland Revenue weren't idiots, and they knew exactly where we'd been and what goodies we'd been buying. Everyone had spent big, but on the flight back most only declared a fraction of it.

Until we landed and saw a whole phalanx of customs inspectors waiting for us. No one got through without being turned over, some were even dragged into side rooms for more detailed checks and a body search. By the time I got to the front of the queue my declaration form was watertight accurate. I was hit for an extra hundred quid, all still paid for out of my food money.

Coaches drove us back to Knettishall, where we put our personal weapons back in the armoury and were then signed off for a long weekend. The following week, with nothing but webbing and Bergens to rearrange and no Rapier kits to work on, there was very little to do except walk around the station and pose with our suntans.

So the whole squadron was given six weeks' leave.

Not bad for three months' work.

Guard duty

My annual leave was very quiet. My family were really relieved I was back home, and while I didn't want anyone to worry about me, all I wanted to do was go back to the Gulf. And why wouldn't you if it was hotels, air-conditioned sites and shedloads of extra wonga?

But the air force had other, less exciting ideas.

In January 1991, it was back to reality and I had to do a week of guard duty. For most of 17 Squadron that meant seven nights at Fersfield, a small camp five miles from Knettishall that had a small training area, barrack blocks and very little else. A corporal and two LAC/SACs patrolled the camp at night, challenged anyone walking around, checked that all doors were locked and reported any unusual or suspect packages. The amount of time spent out on the ground depended on the corporal you were with. Usually it was out for a few hours, back to the Guard Room for a few hours and so on. The night always ended at 7AM when we fronted up to the Airmen's Mess for a cooked breakfast, then slept in the daytime. Changeover was Friday lunchtime and then you had a long weekend off before being back at work the following Monday. It was an easy way to spend a week, made more memorable by Iron Maiden's single, 'Bring Your Daughter to the Slaughter', reaching number one in the UK charts. With two concerts missed because of the Gulf tour, I'd put my annual leave, and money, to good use by ordering several more tickets for the early part of 1991. I planned on seeing Cinderella, that's the band, not the pantomime, a few weeks after Fersfield, and I'd bought a second ticket for Ox, who was now on 19 Squadron, based at Brize Norton.

A few days back from my guard duty and the Gulf Crisis turned into the Gulf War. Rotations with other squadrons was out, 66 were there for the duration and 17 Squadron were designated as battle casualty replacements, so the only way I'd be going back out there would be, quite literally, to fill a dead man's shoes. And even when the footage of the downed Tornado pilots was shown on television and news of other aircrews dying in action filtered

151

through, I never ever thought beyond 'it'll happen to someone else'. Like many, I remained mad keen to go back.

In the meantime, 17 Squadron were ordered to guard the married quarters at Knettishall. It was a totally bullshit assignment, but really, what else was there for us to do? Our Rapier kits were in Bahrain, and while 66 Squadron's were an hour up the road at West Raynham, we were never ordered to take them over. The CO made a good fist of the new role, though, as he always did. 'Don't forget the IRA, lads,' he said. 'They'd love to have a pop at a squadron just back from the Gulf. We've also had some credible intel that the Iraqis might try and attack soft targets in the UK. You lads have been given special clearance to be the only live armed troops in mainland England outside of a military base.'

Right.

As if the Iraqis didn't have enough to do being bombed back into the Stone Age, they were really going to send a covert kill-squad to deepest Suffolk to run riot around an RAF housing estate?

Eng Flight were signed over to guarding the main base, HQ Flight did Fersfield, and A and B Flights now rotated through the quarters, one week on and one week off. I pulled nights on the first week, which pissed me off no end as it meant I missed the Cinderella concert. Ox always joked that he'd had a lucky escape.

At this point I'd been on the squadron nine months, I was now an SAC and I'd done my first tour of duty. I'd been put back with my original crew, A2, and after a fashion I'd settled into the squadron. With everything that had happened, I had a sense that things were working well. I was even comfortable going over to the NAAFI on Thursday nights. I kept a wary eye out for any bad stuff happening and I still left after a pint, but it seemed a good compromise. I showed my face and made damn sure I wasn't around for any of the other shit. I'm not so sure my presence was even noticed by most, though. The usual conversation the following morning was, 'Where were you last night?'

'I was there,' I replied and then validated by recounting a shirt that someone was wearing, or a joke that someone had told.

'Oh, all right then.'

At which point the subject was closed until the following week.

But personality-wise, I was completely unsuited to being in the Regiment. I wasn't aggressive, I wasn't outgoing and my post-Gulf confidence peak was only temporary. All of this was picked up on by B Flight's resident joker, Billy Saxe.

Saxe was an Australian ex-pat. He had the typical down-under accent and a permanently shaved head that showed off a horizontal Frankenstein scar running just above his eyebrows. He never took anything seriously and it was always his comments and jokes at other people's expense that made him popular, which at the same time put everyone around him on edge. In me, he found a perfect victim who wouldn't fight back.

It was February 1991, and I was one of two crews on daytime guard duty. The other section were out and I was sitting in B Hangar's crew room on down time. Saxe walked in and half turned, pouted and looked at me. Straight away it didn't feel right. Ever since arriving on 17 I'd learned to sense trouble, to instantly work out if things were going south. My heart rate sped up and the hairs on the back of my neck rose. My insides flipped and I felt sick. My fight or flight instincts were running in the red and telling me I was in danger. Trouble was, I'd always veer towards flight, every time.

'Brinders,' said Saxe, his voice soft and oily. 'You're looking mighty sexy in your DP. I've always thought you were my kind of man.'

Everyone else in the crew room started chuckling and I suddenly sat up in my chair and looked for an escape route. Saxe walked towards me, his movements surprisingly fluid despite his well-financed beer gut. He came closer and I didn't know what to do. I'm sure I looked either scared or uncertain, but what I definitely wasn't sending out were any signals of encouragement, unless showing no sexual interest at all in men was some sort of flip-flop message that I actually was. I should have got up and run, but all I could manage to do was stand up and look wildly left to right. He closed in and tripped me up. I crashed to the ground, he flopped on top of me and I felt my hands pinned to the floor. He kneaded my chest and panted in my ear. Everyone else started laughing and I tried pushing him away, struggling, but he was stronger than me, heavier than me. 'Fuck off!' I shouted. 'Fuck off! Just fuck off!'

'Oh, I like it when you put up a fight, Brinders,' he gasped in fake rapture. 'And you'll like it too, I know you will. Just give in to it, give in to meeee!'

'I'll give you a kick in the bollocks,' I hissed.

'No, you won't. I know you won't. *You* know you won't.'

And I didn't. God knows I should have, but I didn't. Saxe stood up, and still on the floor I backed away as fast as I could until I felt the wall behind me. 'You know where I am when you want some more.' He smirked, then sidled out of the crew room.

And so it went. That was my daily ordeal. Saxe would always seek me out. I could be busy on the kit, working with the rest of A2, collecting some gear from Supplies, or having a brew in the squadron canteen, and suddenly there would be a roar of 'Briiiiiiinders!' The thunder of running boots on the hangar floor, I'd look up and he'd crash into me, drag me to the ground, pin me to the wall, floor, cage door. He'd get into my personal space and tell me to stop fighting it, give in to it, I'd love it. It absolutely turned my stomach every time it happened. People thought he was joking, that it was all for an audience, all for a laugh and supposedly harmless. And if I'd been a standard, regular Rock, I'd have responded in either one of the two approved ways: play up to it, react in the same way and eventually he'd (hopefully) back down, or plan B, twat him. I did neither. I passively resisted, tried to push him away and it failed dismally. It was great viewing for everyone watching, but for me it was a perpetual nightmare.

And as if one of the bastards wasn't enough, it quickly doubled.

Herd mentality and need for approval being what it is, one of A2's crew, Tommy Harpen, the moustachioed, cleft-lip Argentine/Irishman, also saw this as a great way to raise a laugh with everyone apart from me, and he started doing the same.

It started in February 1991.

It stopped in November 1992 when I left the squadron.

As far as I was concerned, then and now, thirty years and more later, it was unwanted sexual attention, it was sexual harassment. Unwanted sexual attention is mentioned in the Queen's Regulations in 2019, but was it illegal in 1991? I'd like to think so, although given the impunity with which LACs were bashed in Cyprus the year before, legal or not wouldn't have made much difference.

154

And it didn't.

My hope at the time was that pretty soon Saxe and Harpen would get fed up with the joke, and either give up or move on to someone else. But really, why the hell was this even happening at all? This was 1991, for fuck's sake, not the Dark Ages.

So why did it happen? Why was it tolerated? Even with the benefit of years to reflect, I'm not entirely sure. My best guess is this: everyone else found it funny, and herd approval gave it implicit permission to continue.

If you don't fit in, if you don't comply with the culture and lifestyle, then you're a legitimate target, so that's why it happened to me.

And I just took it, so it didn't stop.

In a world where heterosexuality was all that was allowed, sexual humiliation, weaponising sexuality and using it as an insult, or worse, was absolutely permitted. Saxe and Harpen were never viewed as being gay, despite what they did. But at best I was viewed as being less than a real man, which in the narrative of the time made me the one who was gay because I didn't fight back. I was seen as either compliant or encouraging them. Thirty years ago, being gay and somehow less of a man meant the same thing.

Combine that with two bastards who sought group approval through a prism of humiliating someone else, on a squadron that did nothing to protect its own, and it was always going to happen. If not to me, then someone else.

I'm not saying it was right, because it fucking well wasn't. But that's how it was.

I didn't realise it at the time, but that was the fracture point. As unsuited as I was for the RAF Regiment, I think I still could have made a go of it. I was slowly settling, very slowly gaining confidence and very gradually assimilating.

Until Saxe and Harpen started their shit.

After that it all went downhill and I retreated into myself. Any admittedly small chance there was of me making a success of being in the Regiment was now gone.

*

With the end of the Gulf War, the squadron was no longer needed to guard the married quarters, which meant on 1st March I got to go to Wembley Arena for the David Lee Roth concert. After having to miss Cinderella's show, and with Saxe and Harpen's shit just starting, I really needed the lift, and Diamond Dave was the absolute right person to do that. The flamboyant American showman had been booted out of Van Halen five years earlier, and he'd shown everyone that he was doing just fine without them, thank you very much. But he also proved that it was so much more than him, his music, his stage show. Once the Gulf War kicked off, quite a few American performers cancelled their European tours through fear of some kind of Iraqi-sponsored terrorist threat. David Lee Roth made a big thing about this at the start of his show, saying there was no way anyone was telling *him* to cancel out on his fans. Everyone in the packed arena loved hearing it, and for me, having just come back from the Gulf, admittedly as a hotel warrior, and admittedly two months before the shooting started, it was still a very personal thing to hear. And that was just the start of the show. For two loud and glorious hours, Roth scissor-kicked, cheesy-smiled and sashayed non-stop around the stage. It was a whole night of acrobatic, long-haired, pre-grunge, early '90s metal done to absolute perfection.

Ten days later, I went from the twelve-thousand-seater Wembley Arena to the nine-hundred-standing-room-only Norwich Waterfront, to see Uriah Heep, stalwart British grebo rockers who'd been around for ever. They were no less good than David Lee Roth, but in a completely different way. It was solid, sweat-stained Brit metal that hit me like a 7.62 chest shot. I managed to worm my way right to the front and even shook hands with guitarist Mick Box at the end of the show. Brilliant.

I might have been getting a shit time on the squadron, but that didn't mean the music was going to stop. And it didn't.

And thank Christ for that because it was the exact one thing that got me through.

Missile Practice Camp, Hebrides

To prove both the kits and crews, every squadron went to Missile Practice Camp in the Hebrides once a year and fired live missiles at towed targets. Usually each squadron went en masse with all kits and personnel, but 17 Squadron's gear was still in Bahrain, so in March 1991 those of us that hadn't fired a missile the year before were tagged on to 19 Squadron's trip to Scotland. It meant more missed concerts for me, as my tickets for Deep Purple and Judas Priest were now worthless, dammit.

But the good news was that Saxe and Harpen weren't going.

17 Squadron's contingent drove up in three Sherpas, the military's ubiquitous minibus. From Knettishall, it took two nights and three days' driving. We overnighted in a truck stop in north England for the first night, and the second night at the Faslane naval base.

Faslane.

If you're not used to a naval base, and I wasn't, Faslane was a surreal place. We were assigned our transit accommodation and then I spent the next hour looking for the toilets. Nobody thought to mention that in the navy they were called heads. And in their equivalent of the Airmen's Mess, halfway through our meal an all-base tannoy announcement reminded us that it would be sunset in half an hour. Sean Willis and I looked at each other with absolutely no idea what the hell that meant. Some of the navy guys told us it was all about facing the flagpole at sunset, which was weird stuff to a bunch of visiting Rocks.

But that wasn't the half of it. The nearest town to Faslane is a place called Helensburgh, and there was a bus that ran there from Faslane. It pulled up outside the gates and we got on and started chatting with the navy lads.

'Yeah,' they said. 'Helensburgh's a good run ashore.'

'Have you come off of a ship?' I asked.

'What do you mean?' they replied. 'Faslane's the ship, and Helensburgh is the shore.'

'But Faslane's on dry land.'

'It's still a ship, lad. Every naval base is a ship, even if it's on land.'

Right.

Suddenly, guarding the married quarters against an intercontinental Iraqi murder squad seemed positively normal.

We piled into a Helensburgh pub and this time I didn't leave early. I couldn't because the bus didn't come back for us til closing time, and by then I was well pissed. Which would have been fine if I wasn't duty driver the next day. I was still hanging the following morning, and there was no way I was legal to drive. Secretly, it felt very good having to hand the Sherpa keys over to one of the sweats, while I collapsed on the back seat and farted stale alcohol for the rest of the journey.

How to make yourself popular, Regiment-style.

19 Squadron were already established at the army-run Benbecula camp when 17's Sherpas pulled up. I was now getting used to mixing with other squadrons, having rubbed shoulders with 2 and 34 in Cyprus. Ox was the first person I sought out, easily visible by being a head taller than most people around him. His height and history had made him ideal for the QCS, but perfectionists that they were, his glasses had saved him from a lifetime of bulled boots and drill. We grabbed a table in the Airmen's Mess, or whatever it was the army called it.

'How's it going on 19, man?' I asked.

'The usual fuck-around.' He grinned. 'We all had to bring webbing and Bergens with us.'

'What for?' I asked.

'Prep for our Gulf deployment once 66's tour is up.'

'Shit, man.' I sipped some tea. 'Isn't that, like, all over now?'

'Try telling our CO that.' He laughed.

'Same old, same old,' I said. 'So how did they welcome you from Basics?'

'No problem,' said Ox. 'We went to the NAAFI, drank beer, got pissed.'

'And that's it?'

'Sure,' said Ox. 'All that bollocks we got fed on Basics was just to scare us, the wankers.'

'So they didn't make you strip on the first night out?'

'What?' Ox put down his tea and looked at me.

'And they don't have queening on 19?'

'What the fucking hell is queening, Brinders? Is this more of your heavy metal, dope-smoking, hippy shit?'

'No way, man,' I said. 'It's real.'

'What's real?'

'Queening,' I said. 'What they do is this…'

I watched Ox's jaw drop as I explained it. Although I'd seen it happen and had no choice but to live through it, it was only when I described it to someone else and saw their universally disgusted reaction, the 'Stop right there, I'm gonna puke' moment, that I really, finally realised just how utterly fucking sick the whole thing was.

'Jesus H Christ, Brinders,' said Ox. 'That does *not* happen on 19.'

I didn't mention Saxe and Harpen. Some things you don't tell anyone, not even your mates.

*

While I was in the Hebs, Vicar and Slade had been on their Rapier course, re-scheduled from the year before because of Op Granby. As soon as their course was over they were flown up to Benbecula to fire their missile. In the plane with them was a corporal, Ricky Devon, who'd been posted to 17 Squadron from 58. Vicar and Slade hadn't long before been at Catterick on Basics, and so they all spoke about their time there.

'Yeah,' said Ricky. 'There was one recruit who was there last year, what a cunt. He used to wear a long flasher mac and cowboy boots all the time. We didn't speak to him, we didn't even know the fucker's name, but just looking at that tosser really pissed us off. Dressed like an absolute knob-jockey and he wanted to be a Rock? I hope he got binned, the bastard, or failing that, I hope he never comes anywhere near me.'

Vicar and Slade kept quiet and let him find out the good news himself.

Most of the time at the Hebs was very quiet and actually quite boring. You'd spend all day on the firing point, playing cards in the troop shelter waiting your turn to fire and then it was literally all done in a heartbeat.

'Brindle!'

I scampered out of the shelter, took my seat at the optical tracker and pulled on the headset. Seconds later I heard the alarm tone and I jammed my eyes against the binocular sights.

Beepbeepbeepbeepbeepbeep! 'Alarm, narrow, in cover,' I called out. I couldn't see a thing but the kit could. Beepbeep…beepbeep…beepbeep! 'Target lock, radar tracking.'

'Free to fire.'

I pushed the button. With my eyes still glued to the binoculars and the headphones stuck to my ears, I had no idea if the missile had left the rails, if it was flying true or if it had gone rogue. It was cloudy and low visibility. I couldn't see a thing and seconds later it was all over. The missiles never actually hit the towed targets, the cancel switch was hit back in the control tower long before then, and the missile blew up in mid-air.

My one missile had been fired, rumoured to have cost anything between twenty and sixty thousand pounds. As soon as enough of us to fill a Sherpa had fired, we were sent back to Knettishall the way we'd come.

I found the toilets at Faslane a lot quicker the second time round.

Running

The squadron's kits were shipped back to the UK in April, and with their return, the post-Gulf excitement quickly died down and routine took over. That meant checking the vehicles, running repairs on equipment, sweeping the hangar floor, emptying bins and occasional T's and A's. A tour of duty so soon into my career gave me a stilted view of what life in the Regiment was like most of the time, because heading out on ops within a year of joining up just wasn't what it was like back then.

After coming back from the Hebs, I applied for a Command Post Signaller course. It would have meant two weeks at Catterick being trained up, followed by a six-month tour in Belize. After that you automatically got your choice of posting, which for me would have been 3 Squadron, Northern Ireland. That was the plan anyway, and all I had to do was wait for my name to get to the top of the list.

While I was waiting, Saxe and Harpen didn't let up with their pseudo-sexual advances. Saxe would be all slimy with his fake, mincing walk, softened voice and hands all over me whenever I was cornered and caught. Harpen was blunter, affecting a boss-eyed smile, a lumbering, lurching approach and then demanding a blow job. Both used their physical strength to force their way into my personal space and stay there. Everyone else loved watching it, thought it was a great laugh, but for me it was an absolute fucking Freddie. Grabbed, groped, held down, whispered demands in my ear, asking if I wanted to be fucked. It was pretty apparent that I didn't like it, but beyond struggling, I also wouldn't fight back, so it carried on, and carried on. One time the 2iC watched me being held against a wall by Saxe. He just laughed and said, 'Brindle, are you the passive partner in this relationship?'

The 2iC didn't make it stop.

And if the 2iC, a flight lieutenant, wasn't going to put a stop to it, no fucker was.

In (some) fairness, I was advised that the best thing I could do was to punch them and maybe they'd leave me alone. That's Regiment thinking for you. In order to put a stop to sexual harassment, which was illegal, I had to resort to physical assault, which was also illegal.

But I never did. I was never aggressive, never really cut out to be a Rock, so I just took it. The last time I went to the NAAFI for my pint-and-then-leave mission, Saxe grabbed me from behind. My arms were suddenly pinned to my sides, my pint went flying and everyone turned and laughed at me as I struggled and fought and tried to get away. At that point I pretty much gave up trying to socialise.

As well as listening to my music and going to concerts, another crutch I leaned on was running. I was always a decent runner, which got me a spot on the station team and then took me to different bases for any organised races. In April 1991 I did three runs in a week: The Halton Hill Race, Knettishall CO's Cup Cross-Country and The Brüggen 10.

Throw more than one Rock into the mix though, and even that retreat went sour.

The Brüggen 10

Brüggen was one of four RAF stations in Germany, and each year it hosted a ten-mile road race, which was two laps of the peri-track. Seven of us from 17 Squadron went across, including myself. We loaded up two Sherpas and drove to Dover. We were Flight Sergeant Adams, Corporal Field and five SACs. One of the SACs was Dave Wilkins, who'd passed out on El Al, was posted to 17 at the same time as me and then queened at the block barbecue the year before. Despite that, Dave had really settled in, embraced everything air force and was destined for a lifetime in the Regiment. Fair play to him.

The IRA threat meant we weren't supposed to be off base in uniform or do anything to advertise us as military. But believe me, there was zero imagination or effort ever made. If they wanted, the Provos could have spotted and whacked ninety per cent of us in civvies, and the trip to Brüggen was no exception. Apart from me in my jeans, metal tour T-shirt, biker jacket and cowboy boots, everyone else had the regulation RAF Regiment rugby shirt, green fleece jacket, Ronhills and dezzies. Our haircuts were military all the way, flat-top and number one at the sides, or number one all over, and both Sherpas were green.

Piss-easy to spot for any terrorist that could have been bothered.

Back in the BFG days, any jolly to Germany always involved a Deutschmark max-out on German beer. That meant our first stop on the continent was the huge NAAFI at Rheindahlen. Forming a human chain from the shop doors to the car park, we filled the Sherpas up with crates of Warsteiner, the RAF Regiment's adopted and universally favourite beer. After that, it was a short drive to Brüggen.

37 Squadron were Brüggen's resident Regiment unit. We parked the Sherpas in their MT shed, which was where we'd be sleeping the night. Well, apart from Flight Sergeant Adams who copped a spot at the Sergeants' Mess. We stowed our gear and walked over to the NAAFI.

With the race the next day and no wish to get pissed, I left the NAAFI early and headed back to the MT shed. The others came back later, with beer and herd mentality firmly in control. The overhead lights exploded into brightness, I felt my feet lifted skywards and I was poured out of my sleeping bag, a crumpled and suddenly cold tangle on the concrete floor.

Only just awake, I looked up and saw Dave Wilkins standing above me, wearing a dust mask that covered his mouth and nose. 'Target acquired,' he droned, his Manc accent muffled by the mask. 'You know what to do.'

'Knowing what to do' meant three sets of hands dragged me down into the vehicle inspection pit and pulled my clothes off. Somewhere between Dave's face above me and forced naked I became fully awake, but by then it was way too late to get free. My hands were held behind my back, and a pair of quickly secured cable ties kept them there.

'Come on, lads,' I said. 'Let me go, hey?'

'We've only just started,' said Dave, taking pictures of me with my own camera. 'It's way too early for sleep, right, lads?'

'Right,' said one of the others. 'Over here, Brinders.'

I looked left, then closed my eyes as a cold, jelly-like substance slapped into my face. I smelt the oil-based product, opened my eyes and saw green splodges of Swarfega being slapped all over my now shivering body. Three drunken Rocks slimed me, MT shed-style. Utterly helpless to stop them, I had no choice but to try and laugh it off as they carried on taking photos.

If Saxe or Harpen had been there, I'd have shat myself, really shat myself.

And it wasn't like I was the new boy, or even an LAC any more, but somehow I could never get away from being everyone's target. Even Dave Williams, who I'd been on El Al with, who'd joined the squadron on the same day as me, he'd progressed, but I hadn't. He'd morphed into a sweat while I remained left behind, stuck forever in the victim squad.

Cable-tied and naked, the bastards could have done what they wanted, although believe me, I think they'd already done enough. I was utterly friendless in that shed, when all I'd done was turn in early to do a good run the next day. And call me old-fashioned, but wasn't that the point of being there?

As for Corporal Field, he saw the whole thing, laughed just as loudly as everyone else and did fuck all to help. Not that I expected anything else by that point.

So at least I wasn't disappointed by his utter inaction.

Once the film in my camera was all used up, and there was no more Swarfega to chuck over me, they eventually cut me loose. Naked, cold and covered in green gunk, I squelched over to a small sink in one corner of the shed and sluiced myself clean.

'Oi, Brinders,' called Dave. 'Turn the lights out, mate, we're trying to sleep.'

I towelled myself dry, gathered my clothes and returned to my sleeping bag, which had mercifully escaped the Swarfega. All around me were blokes I'd been to the Gulf with, one of whom I'd gone through most of Basics with. You'd think there would have been something, but as I switched off the lights and climbed into my sleeping bag, I never felt so alone.

Reality was now starting to set in. I wasn't hard, I wasn't a threat, and that made me an easy victim. As long as I took it and didn't hit back, this shit would never stop. Would I ever be accepted, or even just left the fuck alone? I could so easily have changed, like Dave Wilkins had, and picked out my own victims. Fucking hell, I even did for one microsecond in Bahrain. There were now quite a few on the squadron who were junior to me, and I could have turned myself into a little wannabe sweat without any problem, but that was never what I was.

What was I supposed to do? Keep taking it forever? Change into something, or someone I wasn't? I didn't know the answer, but I was trying to work it out.

*

As runs go, the Brüggen 10 is, or at least was, really good. A smooth road surface, all on the level, it was fast and really well attended, so lots of good competition. Everyone who took part got a medal and certificate, and if you finished in less than an hour you got a free T-shirt. I came in at just over an hour, missing out on the T-shirt by ninety seconds, but I was really happy with my time.

And happier still that I came in before anyone else from 17 Squadron.

Once the run was over, we piled into the Sherpas and headed back to Knettishall. At a pit stop in Belgium, the Swarfega squad taunted me with the roll of film. 'You want this, Brinders?' crowed Dave. 'No fucking chance, mate. We'll develop the pics, put them up in the canteen, maybe send a few to the WRAF block, *then* you can have them back.'

I hung my head and my arms flopped to my sides, faking defeat. Dave chuckled and looked over at the drinks machine. The second he took his eyes off me I lunged forward and grabbed the roll. I shoved it into my mouth and bit down hard in an attempt to break the casing and ruin the film. I was instantly pounced on and dragged, struggling like hell, into the toilets. I bit and bit and bit into the film casing. 'Let it go,' panted Dave, kneeling on my chest and holding my wrists. 'Give it up, mate,' he said. 'We won't let you go until you do.'

Satisfied that I'd mangled it as much as I could, I spat out the film, with its now dented casing. It was soaked in my saliva and hopefully ruined.

All of this was in a Belgian motorway service station. Christ knows what they thought was going on, but back then there were thousands of British servicemen on the continent. The dezzie boots, Ronhills and green Helly Hansen fleece jackets made us instantly recognisable. Well, apart from me in my cowboy boots. And while a grown man being dragged, struggling, into the men's toilets might normally have raised *some* eyebrows, I guess the Belgians had seen plenty of stupid squaddie behaviour before and decided to leave us to it.

*

It was now clear to me and probably already clear to many others that I wasn't fitting in with the squadron's way of thinking. Unofficially at least. Officially, I polished my boots, ironed my uniform, did what I was told. Unofficially, Saxe and Harpen made my life a misery, while everyone else thought it was an absolute hoot, watching me get chased around the hangar, groped and told what they'd do to me if the lights were ever switched off. And because I didn't fight back, other than struggle when they caught me, push them away and tell them to fuck off, I suppose in everyone else's eyes that made it at best consent, at worst my fault.

And the lurking threat of a beating was always there more than the actual thing, which in a way wore you down even more. After the NAAFI closed on Thursday nights there would be the usual rampage through the block, with every room door tried. If you'd gone to sleep without locking up, you'd be anything from dragged out of bed and woken up to…anything. It all depended on who came in, if they liked you and how many there were.

Taking care of myself if things got even worse seemed like something I needed to do better. I enrolled in a local karate school in Bury St Edmunds with the thought that if I was ever cornered, if it looked like I was about to get a real kicking, then at least I'd have a chance of doing something before I was stoved. After Cyprus, I knew that if they did come for me, it wouldn't be in ones, and even if they saw it, the NCOs wouldn't intervene straight away, if at all. I went to karate classes every Monday night, didn't tell a soul where I was going and got to orange belt by November '92. But who the hell was I kidding? Steve Lake told me one day that if I ever was provoked – like I hadn't been already – I'd have a really savage return punch. But I never fought back, I never lashed out. It just wasn't in me.

PVR

Not long after the Brüggen 10, there was a hangar party for everyone at Knettishall who'd been involved in the Gulf. And there were a lot of veterans by the time it was all over. It was a long way from being just 17 Squadron, and unlike 17 Squadron, most of the others had actually been there for the whole thing. All of the Jaguars had been out there, big time, and lots of the support trades had been as well.

A bar was set up in a maintenance hangar, with a Jaguar undergoing a refurb serving as a backdrop. A band was playing and it was well attended, a bit like a NAAFI bop but in a bigger venue. I remember standing there with my pint and looking at various groups from 17 Squadron. I meekly walked from one knot of Rocks to another, but I just stood on the periphery. I was engaging less and less, and now I was even having trouble starting conversations.

'What are you doing here, Brindle?' asked one of the SACs from A3. We'd done generator checks and T's and A's together in Bahrain the year before, but now that was forgotten. 'You just don't fit in at all,' he sneered.

I stood in the crowded hangar, and for me it might as well have been empty. The words finally hit home and they were right. I didn't fit in and I realised I never would. The way I dressed, my personality, my interactions, none of it even said RAF, much less RAF Regiment.

I was third-generation military and it was a hard thing to confront, but I realised I had to. What the hell was I doing there? Really? And what the hell did I want to do with my life? I wasn't finding the answers straight away. I accepted I'd never be an officer, and my one-time thought that I'd reach the nine-year point as a sergeant was so unrealistic it was laughable. Even getting to corporal by that point? Sure, it was possible, but not for me.

So what then?

Take all this shit, get chased round the hangar for the next seven years by the likes of Saxe and Harpen? Constantly live under the threat of a careers brief, a drying room party, kangaroo court, or any of the other euphemisms for being beaten up?

And for what?

Why the hell, I thought to myself, did *anyone* have to be humiliated and worse, just to keep the bastard sweats happy and laughing? And who the fucking hell was stopping it? No one. Not one single fucker from the CO down who saw us stripped and Steve Lake head-butted on the first night out had lifted a finger. But then again, that was initiation and that was accepted, although what it did was give everyone else implicit permission to do whatever they wanted.

Which they did. Like in Cyprus when Brown and Slade were both slatted. The corporals only stepped in eventually, and even then they said it was actually deserved.

And like a lot of coercion, control and physical abuse, it didn't need to happen every day, you just needed to know that it could. It was a bit like living under Genghis Khan's Mongols. They weren't everywhere all the time, but you never knew when they'd ride into sight and make your life a misery.

And if your first experience of your new mates is a very public and officially sanctioned humiliation, then you just know that culture will carry on. The ones doing it won't stop, and the ones being inducted will do the exact same to those coming in afterwards.

And if you didn't, you'd suffer.

Love it or leave it because you sure as hell won't change it.

Six months earlier I was on top of the world. I had everything I wanted. Now I faced a kingdom of misery with no way out. How could it have changed so completely and so quickly? How could it have been so good, and so right, at Swinderby, Catterick, even Raynham? And how could it turn so utterly, utterly wrong on 17 Squadron?

I didn't have the answer. Or more to the point, I wasn't accepting the answer.

Yet.

Maybe it would have helped if I'd had a plan. Well, a realistic plan, instead of what I thought I wanted. That weird, childhood, utopian ideal of simply living the cocooned forces lifestyle? It only ever existed if you lived in places like Germany and Akrotiri, and even then, only if you weren't actually *in* the forces.

Sure, I had the cheap food and accommodation, free uniform, massively subsidised travel, leisure facilities. I was cosseted and provided for like civilians never were, but the price for all that was one hundred per cent acceptance of the lifestyle and values, many of which were utterly alien to me. It didn't even matter if I was good at my job or not, just so long as I stripped a sprog at the NAAFI. I was starting to realise that the world I was in was completely wrong for me. I didn't fit in and I never would.

Worse, every time my parents and grandparents spoke about their positive memories of the military, I felt like an absolute failure, a traitor even, because my opinions and experiences were suddenly way different to theirs.

I was outwardly still keen, still RAF Reg all the way, despite still being chased, groped, propositioned by Saxe and Harpen, as well as residually expecting a kicking most days. But inside I was in turmoil. I accepted I wasn't right for the Regiment, that the RAF Regiment wasn't right for me, but what to do instead, I had no idea.

I needed some perspective, some place away from Knettishall. I needed a concert.

On 25th May, Vicar and I drove to Hammersmith Odeon to see the Little Angels, and the timing couldn't have been better. Vicar had never been to a concert before but I talked him into going, telling him how great they were. The Little Angels were really at their peak then, breaking into the UK big time, and while it sadly didn't last, in 1991 they ruled. The fanaticism of the fans was apparent straight away. At most metal gigs, you'd see a real cross-section of band shirts and badges, but that night, all the T-shirts, all the jacket patches, all the merchandise, it was Little Angels everywhere you looked. And the band were so sure of themselves and their music that they even had a horns section onstage, which for heavy metal was utterly unique. But they made it work. Toby Jepson led the band in a sonic assault on my ears, including 'Boneyard', a song they'd written about the Gulf War. It was just what I needed, the life-renewing injection my soul craved, a feel-good escape from the misery surrounding me and my other world. I got the amazing lift I always did when I went to a live show. I don't know if the concert made up my mind, but around that time the decision was made.

That music, that feeling, those people around me and the personal freedom. It all meant more to me and connected with me a lot more than life in the military ever did. What was unthinkable even a few weeks earlier had now become reality.

I was going to leave the RAF.

And I'd just have to work out for myself what I was going to do afterwards.

Because I wasn't an officer I couldn't just quit. I had to buy myself out, a process called PVR, which stands for Premature Voluntary Release. It might be different now, but back then you signed on for either six or nine years as a regular, plus six years as a reserve. If you wanted to leave the air force before your time, you put in a PVR request, which then brought forward your transfer to the reserve. The length of time it took to get out varied, depending on how short of manpower your particular trade was. The Regiment was always short of troops, so the notice period was always the maximum, eighteen months.

To PVR from the Regiment would take eighteen months and cost six hundred pounds. About a month's net pay.

I went home and told my parents that weekend. I agonised over the conversation I'd have to have with them. My grandfather had served twenty-two years in the Artillery, including war service, my stepfather was lifelong Royal Signals, joining as a boy and working up to major, and my father had done the same and made captain. Two whole generations before me had lived the military life all their lives, and I was bailing after eighteen months.

'I thought you were enjoying it,' my mum said.

'It's not for me,' I replied, evasively. 'I just want to do more.'

'Well,' said my stepfather. 'If it isn't for you, you'd better think of something that is.'

And that was it.

Christ, I thought to myself, *that was easy*. Easy or not though, there was no way I was getting into the whys and wherefores with them. Parents or not, supportive or not, there are some things you really don't want to tell them. Shit, there are some things you don't want to tell *anyone*.

On Monday 3rd June 1991, I was back in the hangar. I told Kris, one of A2's corporals, that I wanted to PVR.

'Bollocks.' Kris sat in A2's Cage and looked up from his computing magazine. 'You don't want to PVR.'

'I do,' I replied. 'I want to PVR.'

'Right,' snorted Kris. He went back to his magazine. 'Look, we all have shit weekends, Brinders, so get over yourself and check the generators. And stop calling everyone on this crew "man", including me, you mad bastard.'

'Sure, I'll check the gennies,' I replied. 'But I still want to PVR.'

'You're joking, right?' He put down his magazine and looked at me. 'Has Vicar put you up to this?'

'No one's put me up to it. I want to PVR.'

'Bullshit, Brindle.' Kris still wasn't having it. 'You've watched a Steven Segal film about an ex-forces hero, and you want some of that, or maybe you met a woman at the weekend? Fried your brains, did she?'

'Nope, I want to PVR.' Even I was getting bored of saying it.

'You're serious?'

'Hundred per cent.'

'You're even more fucking nuts than usual,' said Kris. 'You really want this?' I nodded and he shook his head slowly. 'Fine,' he said. 'Stay there, I'll get the forms.'

I loitered around the hangar floor and two minutes later Kris came back, without the forms. 'The flight sergeant wants a word.'

I knew what was coming. The endless conversations about nobody wanted to stop me from leaving if I didn't want to be there, but actually, that was exactly what they were doing. Anything to make a drawn-out process even longer and more complicated, and sometimes it worked, sometimes people did change their minds and soldiered on.

'If you really want to leave,' said Chiefy A, 'we're not stopping you.' Known for liking a drink, his nose glowed like a Christmas reindeer. I could have predicted what he was going to say next. 'Just tell me why.'

The truth: I was wrong to join the Regiment, I'd never be accepted as a Rock, I didn't fit in and I never would. I wasn't going to change, no matter what happened to me, and I'd be wasting my time staying where I was. Oh, and I'm also fed up to fuck with being sexually harassed every day by a pair of complete tossers.

What I actually said: 'It's not what I thought it would be, Flight. I'm fed up with sweeping the hangar floor.'

I wasn't lying to Chiefy A, because I really *was* fed up with sweeping the hangar floor. I just didn't tell the whole story, and what would be the point anyway? Christ, he was the one who asked me if I'd had a good night after watching me get stripped the year before. Good night, was it? Oh yeah, it was fucking fantastic!

So after a few hours of cajoling and a lot of NCO attempts to talk me out of it, the documents finally appeared. The first official step was to complete a General Application, or GenApp, which always started with 'I have the honour to request that I be allowed to be considered for...' Then you added whatever you wanted, whether it was a pre-para, special duties, or PVR. Then it went to OCA, and after *he'd* try to talk me out of it, and if he was happy with what I'd written, the application went to the CO. He'd do exactly the same, and only then would he say yes or no. And then, *if* he said yes, the documents would go off to squadron and the process could actually start for real.

In reality, while they were always going to delay it and try to get you to change your mind, if you were adamant, they were never going to turn down your PVR, because why have unwilling troops? But, weirdly, they also didn't want your GenApp to actually sound negative. They wanted you to write something like 'I want to leave the RAF because I actually really like the RAF.'

My stubborn nature redlined when my GenApp was sent back. OCA didn't like what I'd written, so I re-wrote it, saying in more detail why my job was boring and unfulfilling. It was sent back to me again so I re-wrote it a third time with even more specifics about why I wanted to leave, this time mentioning how I was regularly used as an unskilled labourer.

I wasn't going to say anything good in my GenApp and I think they finally realised that, so after a couple of weeks of back and forth, it went upstairs. First stop was the WO. 'What would it take to get you to stay, Brindle?' This was the warrant officer, the most powerful man on the squadron and everyone, even the CO, knew that. He was practically begging me to change my mind. Me! The most unlikely and unsuited Rock ever to say *Per ardua*. Tells you all you needed to know about how short of blokes they were. 'What if I could get you anything you wanted?' he asked. And the WO had the power to make those things happen as well, which was one of the reasons a lot of people PVR'd: to get the posting they wanted, or the course they wanted. It was a gamble if your career path really was the Regiment. A lot of times it gave you some leverage and as often as not it worked, but not with me. I wanted to leave and that was that, so I was finally sent in to see the CO.

The CO absolutely didn't like my unskilled labourer comment and he knew what it meant. 'If you don't like sweeping hangars,' he growled, 'do some fucking courses.'

'And when the course ends, Sir, I'll still be sweeping the hangar floor.'

'I know that.' He looked down at my file on his desk. 'I know your qualifications as well. Why don't you try putting your fucking head down and going for a commission?'

'I've thought about that, Sir,' I said. 'I've tried it in the past. I'm not officer material, and I think we both know that.'

'So you just want to fucking leave?' he asked. He looked at me and shook his head. 'Are you married?'

'No, Sir.'

'Kids?'

'No, Sir.'

'And you know there are three million unemployed out there right now?'

'Yes, Sir. I'll take my chances.'

'Then you're fucking mad,' he snapped. 'Application approved.'

The paperwork was processed and I was given a leaving date and a price, neither of them a surprise. 17th December 1992, six hundred pounds.

Eighteen months to find a job. Eighteen months to decide what to do. And eighteen months to come up with the money.

I was regularly told that I could withdraw my PVR at any time, but as long as it was in place I wouldn't go on any jollies, trips, detachments. It was standard procedure.

A few days later, coincidence or not, my Command Post Signaller course came through. Two weeks at Catterick, then six months in Belize, followed by 3 Squadron if I still wanted it. My ship had come in.

I thought about it, really thought about it. I asked myself if my experience on 17 Squadron was unique, or would it be the same wherever I went? Whenever I spoke to my mates from other squadrons, they'd not gone through the same level of sprog-bashing, or at least they hadn't said anything. But then I always glossed over what was happening on 17, so maybe they had as well. I remembered the Christmas party from Basics. Christ, I was having beers chucked over me just for being there, before I'd even said anything. I'd also heard that Jimmy Hendricks, another stubborn individual, was having a hard time on 48 Squadron. True or not, I wasn't sure. But the fundamental questions had to be asked, was the RAF Regiment right for me? Would I ever really fit in?

It was a no to both. I turned down the course and my PVR stayed in place.

Just like most workplaces, once someone decides to leave it goes round the shop floor in seconds. The comments I got ranged from 'non-hacker' to 'well done'. I stopped trying to fit in, I gave up even thinking of going to the NAAFI on Thursday nights. Saxe and Harpen didn't let up though. It was good entertainment for the troops, and it gave both of them a lot of positive attention. As for me, fuck it, I didn't fight back so it was my own fault for encouraging them, and besides, I was a PVR boy now, I didn't matter.

The Rugby Club

Knettishall's Rugby Club was just another RAF bar that got its name because it was next to the rugby pitch. It played host to various functions: birthdays, weddings, pre- and post-detachment piss-ups, leaving nights and of course, anything to do with rugby. In the summer of 1991, two SACs from 17 Squadron had just passed their pre-para, and their leaving night was at the Rugby Club. Vicar and I were both adamant we wouldn't go.

If you're not there, you've got nothing to fear.

But as the night wore on we sat in the largely empty barrack block and had a change of heart.

'We could just stand at the back,' I said.

'No one'll be looking at us anyway,' said Vicar.

'Better than being asked why we didn't show up.'

'Yeah,' said Vicar. 'We'll stay near the door and if any shit comes our way we'll just fuck off.'

Despite being on 17 Squadron for over a year, despite having a tour of duty under our belts, despite being SACs and despite LACs having been posted in, we were both still outsiders and still targets. Quite how being singled out and then isolated from your oppos made you a better soldier is still beyond me, but it wasn't me or Vicar who made the rules.

We walked out of the gates, along the road and turned left onto the playing fields. We could see the Rugby Club.

'Are we sure about this?' I asked.

'One drink,' said Vicar. 'Stand at the back and then it's prep to move.'

We got closer and we could hear one of the departing lads making his leaving speech. He sounded pretty pissed and so did the roaring crowd that cheered him on, sometimes even louder than he was.

'Are we sure about this?'

We got closer and closer, and the cheering got louder and louder. We got to the club door and reached for the handle. We looked into each other's eyes, still nervous, still not sure if we were doing the right thing, and from out of the opened windows we heard the dreaded cry, 'Queen him! Queen him!'

Vicar and I both knew if we stepped into a Rugby Club that was full of pissed-up Rocks shouting 'Queen him', it didn't matter that we weren't the intended target, we soon would be. We'd have been queened before we had time to shit ourselves and try to run away. So we didn't go in, but we *did* shit ourselves and then we turned around and ran away.

Just to be really safe, we buggered off to Mildenhall for the rest of the night.

And if you're thinking we were overreacting, or that somehow a bunch of drunken men rubbing their naked butts into other drunken men's faces isn't too bad, if you think that we should have just got with the programme and took an arse in the face for the team, *you* try doing it.

And predicting the outcome of events when 17 Squadron were out on the piss was an impossible task. It was never something that was entirely self-policing. Sometimes the consequences happened a while afterwards. Sometimes people would get so legless that they'd piss the bed when they got back to the block, which was known as swamping. Even worse, if you got really wankered and ended up pissing, shitting and even puking the bed, it was called grand slamming. You wouldn't be thought any worse of if it happened to you, but you could expect to pay the bill for a new mattress if any of the stains were still there when you left the block for a new posting.

And sometimes the madness attracted a higher force. The NAAFI was there for everyone, not just 17 Squadron, but if things got out of hand and impacted on another unit's night out, it meant trouble. I never actually saw what happened because I'd largely stopped going to the NAAFI by then, but one time the CO paraded the entire squadron in the hangar and bollocked *everyone*, even the sergeants, even the officers, even the married guys. He said that unless things settled down at the NAAFI, every Thursday morning he'd CEMO tab the whole squadron to Fersfield, where he'd have us bivvied up in the training area overnight while the rest of the station enjoyed the bop night and then we'd have to tab back the next morning.

That bollocking worked.

The more I found myself isolated and out on a limb at Knettishall, the more I craved live music, and no more so than festivals. On 17th August I went to Donington for the Monsters of Rock. I'd missed it the year before because of the Gulf tour. It was the third festival I'd been to and the second since joining up. It's always better going in a crowd, but us loners never mind going anywhere on our onesie. The first band to play, Black Crowes, were my favourite that day, with their super-cool blues rock. Queensrÿche were a little bit boring and took themselves way too seriously, and Mötley Crüe and Metallica were so-so. I only actually wanted to see AC/DC, as I'd missed seeing them earlier in the year, but I struck out again. After Metallica, I went back to my car to pack away my cool box and get my coat, and security wouldn't let me back in, bastards. It was a bit of a rookie mistake, but you live and learn.

Not the shot in the arm I could have really done with, but still better than nothing. I finally got to see AC/DC in '96, and they were amazing.

Bergen run

Having to give up the radio on Omega still weighed on me, and now that I'd PVR'd I was desperate to prove that I wasn't leaving because I was a non-hacker, even if only to myself. So when the squadron asked for volunteers to do a sponsored Bergen run to raise money for charity, I was well up for it. The objective was to do 23 miles inside a target time of five hours, with 20-kilos weight in a Bergen, which in my case was a third of my body weight.

Stuff like this was what I imagined happening all the time in the RAF Regiment, and it was the kind of thing I thought I'd be judged on. To a point I was, but being part of the terminally masculine, alpha-male, beer-fuelled social life was also a part of it, a big part, and that's where I fell down every time.

But a Bergen run was still a Bergen run, and they were never easy. Eight blokes out of a whole squadron stepped forward, which tells you everything. It felt good to be part of it, even if one of the eight was Spanner, the man responsible for bringing queening to 17 Squadron. Being able to complete a Bergen run was all down to training and preparation, and I made sure I did loads. PVR boy or not, I'd always done plenty of fitness. After knock-off time at the hangar, it was straight to the Airmen's Mess for the evening meal, and my standard routine most nights was weight training in my room for an hour, then a run. I was used to doing between five to seven miles most nights, so I built up the distance and added a few ten-milers with my Bergen. This time round, my Karrimor Condor was set up properly.

When you're young and fit, when you're dead set determined to do it, you can do stuff like that. You can do anything. As fit as I was before, I felt myself getting stronger, more resilient. Practising and training for the run did more for my confidence than the sprog-bashing, stripping, queening NAAFI culture ever did, which I found demeaning, demoralising and isolating. I couldn't have cared less about doing this run for the squadron, the Regiment or the air force. This was for me, this was proving to myself that I could do it.

179

The run was set for 6th September 1991. It was an early start and we formed up in the middle of Thetford Forest at seven-thirty. We were paired up and set off at five-minute intervals. I was teamed up with a guy from HQ Flight called Ice. Ice had a completely shaved head, and unlike me, he was built to carry a Bergen all day long. I never knew his real name but I did know he'd been on 26 Squadron during the Gulf and he was a decent guy. We'd agreed to switch between walking and running, and we also had to work out our route and make sure we didn't get lost. We had a map, we were told where the next five-mile waypoint was and it was up to us to get there.

When you're carrying a loaded Bergen, it doesn't take long before you feel your spine being compressed, your legs ache and your shoulders burn. Then your lungs start to strain as the weight presses down on your thoracic cavity. And when that happens, all the fitness in the world only gets you halfway there. I'd say that after one mile, the pain starts and then it's all down to willpower.

And fighting through that barrier was the biggest rush of all. Ice and I kept each other going and we stuck together. Our timing was pretty good. At the water points, it was one drink down your neck, the other over your head and carry on to the next checkpoint. Run, walk, run, walk and keep on going. After a while the pain turned into numbness, then determination kicked in and took over.

At some point, I don't know if we caught up with them or if they caught up with us, but we linked up with another pair and did most of the run as a four. The 2iC who'd organised the event was way out in front, then it was us, then it was three others behind us.

After the last waypoint it was individual best effort. I didn't need anyone's support by then, and there was no way I was quitting this close to the end. None of us did. I crossed the line in fifth place out of eight, ahead of Spanner, which was a little victory, and a time of five hours fifteen. I grabbed a Stim, dropped my Bergen and, knackered as I was, completely knackered as I was, I felt great. I'd done the fucker.

I don't suppose the chosen charity was too happy with me though. I raised less than a tenner in sponsorship.

And sure, it wasn't a pre-para, it wasn't the Cambrian, but it was still something. And for years afterwards, in fact even now to a point, if you told me to take load A from point B to point C, I could do it, and I'd know I could do it.

I could barely move for the whole weekend after, but there wasn't a feeling like it, and definitely in a good way. I guess I needed to get out more.

Which for me, meant another concert.

On 28th September I went to the NEC in Birmingham to see Magnum. I had unbelievable seats, right at the front. And because it was seated, it was a guaranteed front row in the mosh pit. Normally, if you want the front row you have to cop your spot and stay there all night and then after an hour decide if you want to lose your place to use the toilets or piss yourself. The support band were Kiss of the Gypsy. At most concerts, you were lucky if the support band were any good, but Kiss of the Gypsy were amazing. British blues rock par excellence, it was class music and they had future headliners written all over them. I was sure they'd make it big, they definitely deserved to, and I bought their debut album that weekend.

But Magnum were the band I'd paid to see, and they were better still. 'Old England's Eyes' kicked off the set and they ruled the school with their pomp-rock Brit metal. It was the biggest venue I'd done the front row at, and I soaked up the experience. Coming as it did at a low point, having trouble saving my PVR money, still getting massive unwanted attention from Saxe and Harpen and with absolutely no idea what I was going to do in civvy street, a top-drawer metal gig was just what I needed.

Battlecamp

Shortly after the Magnum concert, I had an early start to go on a run with the station team, so I missed morning parade. I got back to the hangar that afternoon and A3's Detachment Commander, Sergeant Morris, called me over. He looked concerned.

A sergeant looking worried? That was unusual.

'Brindle,' he said. 'Is there a reason why Vicar would run away?'

'What?'

'He wasn't on parade this morning and his room's empty.'

'Shit, Sarge.' Shit. Really, shit. Vicar wouldn't do a runner, he wouldn't go AWOL. Would he?

'Where is he?' asked Sergeant Morris.

'I don't know.' And I didn't. And Vicar wouldn't, he just wouldn't.

'You're sure?'

'Sure I'm sure,' I said. 'It's news to me.'

An hour later the mystery was solved. Vicar had been admitted to the RAF hospital at Ely the night before with acute appendicitis. They phoned the squadron to say he was out of surgery and stable. I was given the barrack block pass key and told to pack a bag for him and take it to the hospital. It was the usual Regiment shopping list of things a patient would really need: wash kit, crisps, Stims, spare underwear, change of clothes and a huge stash of porn mags. The ward staff at Ely, all RAF, were utterly unsurprised at his provisions.

Vicar made a good recovery, but best of all he was discharged on light duties, which got him out of Battlecamp.

*

Every RAF Regiment squadron did a Battlecamp once a year, which was a two-week refresher of the infantry skills that all gunners were trained in. 17 Squadron's 1991 Battlecamp was an October trip to Sennybridge, in Wales, which was ideal for training, because it rained there, a lot. For all I knew it had been since I was last there in July on a tracking exercise. That's aircraft tracking, not SAS-style man tracking.

But before we went, there was the usual fuck-around bull night at the block. I walked into the flight office to collect my mail and saw the order written on the noticeboard. 'What the fuck,' I moaned. '*Another* fucking bull night.'

'That's right, Brindle,' said OCA. OCA was almost as unlikely a Rock as me. Overweight, a former technician, and like many officers in the '90s, possessed of that vague disconnect with anything or anyone below the rank of sergeant. 'We can't leave a minging block behind when we go away.'

'How can it *ever* be minging?' I said. Seeing the smile disappear from his face, I belatedly added a 'Sir'. 'We've got a cleaner who goes in every day, for fuck's sake.' And despite debating with an officer to the point of insubordination, I had a point. The block *did* have a cleaner who went in every day, which made me constantly complain about the frequency of bull nights, even more so since I'd PVR'd.

'That may be,' replied OCA. 'But we don't want anyone leaving stale cabbages, or anything else under their beds for a fortnight, now, do we?'

'Sure,' I grumbled. 'And I suppose, Sir, the Officers' Mess has got a bull night and room inspection as well?'

I might have been a PVR boy and imminent civilian, but I was still pushing it. Standing behind OCA, Sergeant Morris was pissing himself laughing.

Two days later the squadron moved out to Sennybridge from Knettishall. It took hours by road and would have been a trip too far by four tonner, even for Rocks, so we went by bus. The accommodation at Sennybridge was basic. Each flight was allocated a wooden hut and bunk beds, but it was warm and dry.

Our daily trips to the ranges were made by four tonner. There and back, we were serenaded by a boombox radio playing the musical duel at the time, between Bryan Adams' ballad, 'Everything I Do', which felt like it had been number one for the whole year, and 'Winds of Change' by German metal band, Scorpions. 'Winds of Change' stayed at number two. I kept hoping it would take the top spot, but Bryan Adams won out in the end, dammit.

Battlecamp was a lot of range work, starting off by blatting live rounds at static targets. Then there were Close Quarter Battle drills

183

in singles and pairs. Section attack and defence were eight-man, shoot 'em up, second childhood fantasy times. Ambush and anti-ambush were done with blanks so we didn't actually kill anyone, and there was also a good amount of phys. There was one run in particular where groups of eight were set up roughly according to ability. I was in the same group as Harpen and I didn't care where I finished, as long as it was in front of him.

I finished in front of Harpen.

Little victories and pride.

*

Despite our lux Gore-Tex waterproofs, there were loads of tactical situations when you couldn't wear them, like pretty much every shoot we did. The trouble was, they rustled when you moved in them. Not as much as traditional waterproofs, and certainly not as loud as actual gunfire, but the end result was that they stayed rolled up and bungeed to your webbing, leaving you, most days, piss-wet through.

And just like on Basics, the training area was spider-webbed with streams. It felt like I'd crouched, kneeled or advanced to contact in or along every single one of them. After each shoot my feet were squelchy soaking wet. I was glad I still had a spare pair of socks that I'd stuffed into my webbing in Basics and hadn't used since. They didn't really help, though, because in the afternoon I did the same thing all over again and got soaking wet all over again.

One of the things that was drummed into us way, way back in Swinderby, was that you never ever left your weapon out of reach, and better to be queened by the whole squadron than lose it.

But that's what OCA did. He just left his rifle on the ground and walked off. And when an officer loses their weapon, the attention is magnified a hundredfold, although the penalty was usually diminished by a similar amount. As soon as we realised it was his rifle, we chucked it in the back of a four tonner and threw Bergens and kit over the top of it. Everyone was in on it, from Sergeant Morris downwards. When OCA walked back a few minutes later, only just able to get his webbing belt secured and asking if anyone had seen his rifle, nobody knew a thing.

I don't know what happened to him, but for an officer it's only ever embarrassing. If it had been an NCO, probably some extra duties. If it had been an airman, charged, jankers and/or a fine.

Rank has its privileges.

The final exercise of Battlecamp was a squadron-strength dawn attack on a FIBUA village. We headed out at an absolutely stupid time, something like one in the morning. OCA was grinning wide enough to swallow a whole Wagon Wheel as he said it, the bastard. I couldn't think of an earthly reason to head off at that time, other than to piss us off, which might well have been the objective. It certainly worked on me.

And it wasn't like we had to leave at that time, either. The whole squadron spent bloody hours holed up in a leaky, deserted group of farmhouses waiting for first light. No breakfast, no ration packs, cold, wet, pissed off and starving. It wasn't just the PVR boys who were grumbling that night.

But there's nothing like a squadron-strength urban assault to focus the mind. We really went for it at dawn, and let's face it, when you're fully cammed up, festooned with blank ammunition and there's no enemy, who wouldn't enjoy it?

The ladders went up, we climbed up to the top floors and piled in, blatting off rounds all over the place. Corporals and sergeants shouted orders louder than the gunfire as we cleared each room, with bangs and flashes everywhere. Then we snaked downstairs to the ground floor. Fashion items that year were Petzl helmet-mounted head torches, and inside the dark, dusty FIBUA houses they sent random beams of light into sandbagged nooks and crannies. In the cellar we threw a blank grenade into one room, then three of us piled in and back-to-back we circled the room and opened fire. Complete cowboy stuff, and if it had been for real the ricochets alone would have killed all three of us.

We weren't working up for Northern Ireland, we weren't about to go on ops, so we really couldn't take it *too* seriously. After two weeks of ranges, bunk beds, pissing rain, shit rations, no sleep the night before and wet socks, it was just a great fun way to end the camp.

Freddie Mercury

In one way, 1991 was no different to two years before: the whole of the military was utterly homophobic and in a totally hypocritical way. Before 23rd November, about eighty per cent of the forces were Queen fans. Twenty-four hours later, all you heard was one anti-gay comment after another about Freddie Mercury. And all the while, HM Forces' collective record/CD collections were rammed with Queen music.

Go figure.

Anyway, I was a real big music fan and I loved my metal, which is a *very* broad church. I loved a lot of Queen's stuff, and no way was I denying them like some kind of faithless apostle. I was shocked to my core when it came out he'd tested positive, and I was absolutely gutted when he died the next day, aged just 45. I couldn't believe it. I can still remember sitting in the Airmen's Mess at breakfast when the news came through on the TV. I watched the story in stunned silence, my breakfast forgotten.

It was without a doubt the worst news I'd heard all year, ever, in my entire life. I was numb with disbelief. Freddie Mercury was dead. Holy shit. Never mind my PVR, never mind those wankers trying to shag me against my will, never mind the Soviet Union had disintegrated and nuclear weapons were disappearing into the ether, or that the Balkans were fracturing into civil war. All of that was bollocks. Freddie Mercury had died, and *that* was the news, the *real* news.

It took a long time to sink in, maybe even more so as no one around me seemed even nearly as bothered. Something as completely unrelated to the military as a musician's death really reinforced to me that, no offence to either side, but I was in the wrong place, and it was best for everyone that I moved on.

Freddie Mercury, an absolute legend. Rest in peace.

Satellite TV

For all of its downfalls, and there were many, life the barrack block also had some plus points. Mostly around how cheap it was. A nominal charge for food and accommodation was taken out of your pay before you saw it, and in theory you didn't need much more beyond that to live. You could eat as much as you wanted in the Airmen's Mess. Apparently it was a chargeable offence to leave the mess hungry. Accommodation-wise, your rent covered maintenance and upkeep, water, electricity, heating. Basically, every other bill apart from the community charge. You even got free bedding *and* got your free bedding laundered for free. How I ended up skint and overdrawn every month is still beyond me.

In theory, you also had to buy a TV licence, but I never bought one during my RAF service, and I don't know anyone else in the block who did either. What we did have to pay was two quid a month block fees, and that covered the use of and repairs for a washing machine and tumble dryer, and also satellite TV.

Satellite TV.

There was one box for the whole block and it was usually set on a film channel. The block sergeant was called Seth Franco, Mauritius-born, a veteran of the Dhofar War, and one of the very few Regiment NCOs who'd actually led a section under fire. Seth's favourite saying whenever the block needed to be cleaned was 'It's not a clean-up, lads, it's a bull night,' followed by his characteristic staccato laugh, 'Ah! Ah! Ah!' I asked him one day if he could tune the satellite box to the adult channel. 'Fucking hell, Brindle,' he roared. 'Ah! Ah! Ah! If I did that, you boys'd be wanking every night.'

Did he actually think we already weren't?

But having a film channel on your TV at night was brilliant. I watched *Bill and Ted's Excellent Adventure* and I loved it. I liked the characters, their happy outlook on life, their stand against the odds, the establishment, the man. I liked the way they talked and I loved the music. Grunge might have been just around the corner and ready to spoil the party, but no one had even heard of it back then.

And having the film channel on tap was a great escape if you had to lock yourself in for a while. One time I walked out of my room and coming into the corridor were Spanner and another sweat called Jim Murray, who was stark naked apart from a peaked leather cap and a fucking enormous fireman's axe. Murray laughed when he saw me, and Spanner sort of leered, which was what he tended to do. I turned around and shot back into my room and locked the door. Seconds later they were beating on it from the outside. 'Let me in,' wailed Spanner. 'Let me iiiiiiiiiiin!'

Yeah, right. More chance of me pulling my PVR.

Time to watch Sky Movies and ignore what's happening outside.

That episode was a joke and even I realised that. A joke in as much as they probably weren't going to beat me up, just scare the shit out of me. And while I didn't think they were going to axe me, I'd still have been queened and my room would definitely have been trashed if they'd got in. But there was always the chance it could have escalated and there was always the chance that others could have piled in. That's when herd mentality takes over and anything could have happened.

It was a joke, Regiment-style, which I sometimes had trouble seeing.

Like I said, I didn't really fit in, and it's not for everyone.

A bit like the joss sticks, really. I'd taken to burning them in my room. I wasn't overly fond of them, but they were another part of my hippy, non-conformist image, and I was damned if I was going to stop using them just because I was told to, which I had been. Even two years in, I was having trouble getting my head completely around the small fundamental of obeying orders.

Anyway, on 15th December 1991, I went to the Waterfront in Norwich to see Wolfsbane, an up-and-coming British metal band. It was pretty much peak time for them. They didn't break it big, and in 1994 their singer, Blaze Bayley, joined Iron Maiden. Before I headed out to the show, I lit up a joss stick and left it burning in a plant pot on top of my television.

Musically, Wolfsbane weren't for me, but the show itself was good. In between each song the crowd shouted out, 'You fat bastard!' at Blaze, who regularly hung upside down from power cables that were nailed to the ceiling. Not sure how safe it was, but it looked impressive. This was an era of stage-diving and crowd-surfing, and every couple of songs someone would get past the bouncers, run onto the stage and then launch themselves into the audience. I always bought a tour T-shirt at concerts, and the back print on the Wolfsbane one said 'Shitheads on Safari', which was a very tongue-in-cheek reference to Wolfsbane fans. Years later, wearing it in Sainsbury's earned me a polite request to leave.

After the concert, I drove back to Knettishall through a horror-film fog and a maximum speed of thirty miles an hour. It took bloody ages, and walking up to the block I saw that my light was on. My first thought was that someone had opened my room door, got in and wrecked the place. I walked into the block and I smelled burning. Inside my room, the smell of melted plastic was overpowering. I looked over at my television and saw the reason why.

The joss stick I'd left burning hadn't gone out.

But they *always* burned themselves out.

That night though, it hadn't. It had carried on glowing, right through the plant pot, which was full of dried earth, and then it set light to a sheet of paper which I'd put down to catch the ash. Then it started cooking the top casing on my television.

As the casing melted, it gave off fumes and filled the corridor outside with clouds of nasty-smelling smoke. No one was sure if I was in or not as the door was locked, so some of the lads in the block forced open the window, saw I was out and chucked the smouldering joss stick into the sink. By the time I got back, the station's fire engines had been called out to declare the block safe. It must have been a real piss-take for them. They were exquisitely trained to stop fires on burning aircraft and get the crew out alive, and they'd ended up having to deal with a joss stick that wouldn't go out.

Just like all good news, it went right round the squadron before I even got to the hangar. Straight after morning parade I went looking for the Seth, but he found me first.

'Brindle!' His voice shot across the hanger. 'Get over here, now!'

'Morning, Sergeant.' I doubled over.

'Something to tell me, Brindle?'

'Yes, Sergeant.' I slammed to attention in the best drill move of my career. 'I nearly set fire to the barrack block last night.'

'Fucking right you did,' fumed Seth. 'And you're fucking lucky that no one got hurt. If it was up to me you'd be locked up. Now fuck off out of my sight, you bastard.'

'Yes, Sergeant.'

I fucked off out of his sight.

The television still worked and I could still get satellite TV, but I didn't ask Seth for the adult channel again.

Squadron Christmas party

A few days after my television melted, the squadron's Christmas party was held at the NAAFI. Wives and girlfriends were invited and there were no new LACs to strip, so hopefully it wasn't going to be too bonkers.

Although Vicar and I both had a beer from time to time, we never went to the NAAFI, so we were seen as teetotal. As a result, we were asked to drive people home in the Sherpas after the party. It seemed a pretty safe duty and we agreed. Smart dress was expected and half of the squadron, myself included, wore Regiment blazer and tie, although my added earring raised a few eyebrows. The 2iC smiled but didn't make an issue of it.

Smartly dressed or not, though, it was the NAAFI, it was the Christmas do, people got pissed. I remember seeing Harpen clinging to two sets of shoulders as his legs gave way underneath him, slurring at the top of his voice, 'RAF Reg, you know it makesh shensh!'

There was also a huge buffet laid out, and with plenty of it uneaten and left over, Vicar and I siphoned loads back to the block. At the end of the night, the numbers thinned as people left to go home and the Sherpa taxi service filled up. Vicar and I climbed aboard and we headed off to the outlying estates around Watton and Fersfield. In my Sherpa was Eddie Allan, one of the bashers from Cyprus who really had it in for Brown. He generally left me alone, but he had a fearsome reputation and was unbelievably hard as nails. If there was one person I didn't want to piss off, ever, it was him.

'Where to first?' I asked, as we cleared the gates.

'Back to the block and start some trouble,' growled Allan. He was sitting next to me and he started fumbling with the gearstick and indicators. In the seat behind him, Saxe, who normally chased and groped me in the hangar, tried to calm him down. Suddenly, my easy duty turned into an absolute Freddie. I was stuck in a Sherpa with a boxing team sprog-basher and a sex offender. They were both pissed, and I had to drive them back home while one of them tried grabbing the controls from the passenger seat.

I focussed on the road and my driving. Suddenly I felt fingers stroking my neck. It was the kind of shit Saxe would regularly pull back at the hangar when I was cornered and when he had an audience to egg him on. But this time it was Allan doing it and all I could do was sit there and drive.

'You're a good lad, Brinders,' he whispered, still stroking my neck. 'But you take a lot of shit.'

You don't say, I thought. *Like right now, you mean?*

'You know what you need to do?' he said. Then he suddenly shouted, 'You smack them!'

Allan switched between gentle advice and shouting, and at one point he squeezed my throat. After a few seconds I told him I couldn't breathe, and I really *couldn't* breathe. My vision starred and I took my foot off the accelerator pedal. A few seconds later Saxe made him let go. Fucking hell, talk about unpredictable. I don't remember how long the drive was to his house, but I made damn sure Allan was the first stop. I dropped him off and he walked around the Sherpa, gripped the wing mirror, ripped it clean off the vehicle and chucked it into the passenger seat. Then he walked around the other side and did the same. I wondered how the fuck I was going to hand back the Sherpa the next day without having to grass him up. But that was a problem for later.

The rest of the drop-offs, even Saxe, were simple, thank Christ. I parked the Sherpa outside the hangar and walked back to the block.

The MT corporal went ballistic the next morning.

'What the fucking hell happened to the wing mirrors?' he asked me, which was a perfectly reasonable question.

I looked at the Sherpa and shrugged. 'I don't know,' I said. 'They were there when I parked up.'

I was lying, and he knew I was lying. He looked at me, sighed and told me to piss off.

In fairness to Allan, he didn't 'fess up to the mirrors, but he did apologise to me for being a pissed-up dickhead the night before.

Shame Saxe never said sorry for anything he ever did.

Open University

My plan to leave the air force with a degree wasn't going to happen any more, but I had no intention of giving up on my studies. So in February 1992 I started my first of six Open University modules, titled Society and Social Science. It was the first time I'd done anything academic for six years, and even though my study skills were really rusty, I was totally up for it. At that time, all the OU offered was a degree. It wasn't in any particular subject and you picked the study modules according to your needs. I'd done well-ish at A level geography, getting a D at my second attempt, so that's the road I went down. There weren't too many physical geography modules at the time, so human geography it was, starting with the foundation course.

The Open University is geared towards people who work, which meant you studied in your spare time. It's all do-able, but there's no teacher standing over you and you have to put the work in yourself. For the next eight months it also gave me an easy excuse to avoid the NAAFI, pleading either study time or evening classes, which I attended religiously to get my head back into learning mode.

The course comprised eight essays to be submitted at roughly monthly intervals, a week-long summer school and an exam. In absolute fairness to the air force, they paid eighty per cent of the tuition and the entire summer school. I was pretty surprised, but I wasn't saying no. I even told them that I was leaving the RAF that year, and they still paid.

I absolutely soaked up the knowledge on that course. It taught me stuff I'd never even thought about and made me question everything I believed, everything I thought I knew. It was a foundation course, so while it didn't go into exhaustive detail, it introduced me to aspects of sociology, social policy, environmental geography, politics, economics and psychology.

At the start of the course I knew a bit about geography and the environment. I'd been a real tree-hugger since the mid-'80s, but who was listening to that song back then? The course also opened my eyes about other topics I thought I knew about, but really didn't. I learned about free trade, free will, the power and the responsibility of the state. I learned about it at a much deeper level than I ever did by watching the television or reading the newspapers. And once I began to work out what it meant, I had to decide what side of the fence I stood on. The conclusions I came to about my emerging beliefs didn't put me where I thought I'd be and definitely not where I'd been for most of my life. The course ran until October and it gave me some focus, prepared me for what was coming. It taught me a lot more about life and the world, the real world that I was soon going to enter.

*

In March '92, the squadron was due to head up to Spadeadam for Exercise Elder Forest. There had to be enough manpower to crew the kits, so a leave ban had been put in place months earlier. Cumbria in March sounded like lots of wind, rain and mud, so Vicar and I pre-empted and lied. We made up a fictional wedding that we had to go to, and despite the ban the lie worked and we got annual leave for the week. Even better, one of the nights involved a trip to Hammersmith Odeon to see Swedish soft-metal gods, Europe. Always known for 'The Final Countdown', there was a lot more to them than just that, and they were a lot heavier than their image suggested. In 1986, the metal magazine *Kerrang!* claimed that Europe were louder than Motörhead. I've seen both bands live and I totally agree. Back in 1992, unplugged was the fashion, even in metal, so for part of the show the band sat onstage with acoustic guitars and played a few songs. It wasn't my kind of thing, and I'm glad they don't do it any more. The first highlight of the night for me was when the singer, Joey Tempest, called out one of the audience to tell him that his wife was about to give birth and that he'd better quit the gig and get to the hospital. Later on in the show, the guitarist broke a string, but rather than just getting a spare instrument brought on by a roadie, he changed the string onstage while Joey ad-libbed at the front and got the crowd singing along. Utterly unnecessary, but fabulous entertainment. Vicar had a great time, and after rocking out to Little Angels the year before, he was fast becoming a concert convert.

Exercise Olympus Rock, Cyprus, 24th March to 21st April 1992

The Europe concert marked the end of mine and Vicar's ill-gotten annual leave, but not the live music. The following week, on 19th March, I went to the Norwich Waterfront, this time to see Baby Animals. They were an upcoming Australian band fronted by the excellent Suzi DeMarchi, who not only sang like a pureblood wildcat from Hell, but also played a mean Telecaster guitar. I'd seen them on the late-night TV programme *Raw Power*, and their video single 'Early Warning' was pure class. The concert was massively entertaining, they had loads of raw energy and just ripped through their set, although disappointingly, they never broke through to the big time. But they never gave up, and as of 2021 they were still going strong and still rocking out.

Five days later the good news ended and the squadron flew out to Cyprus for a month-long training exercise called Olympus Rock. I was absolutely dreading it and I'd been trying to get out of it for weeks. 'We're not there yet,' Vicar and I kept saying after each attempt to avoid the exercise failed.

In most jobs, a works trip to Cyprus sounded ideal, but not to me. Saxe and Harpen's persecution hadn't let up. It was getting worse. And on a detachment with no room door to lock, no Mildenhall or Lakenheath to bug out to if it got nasty, there was nowhere to run. Every day at Knettishall, at every briefing, or aircraft recognition lesson, or in the squadron canteen, anywhere we were in the same location, I'd be targeted. 'It's Brinders,' Saxe would say. 'Give him to me, I want to fuck him.' If him or Harpen ever got close they'd grab me and grope me, tell me I'd love to do it with a man, they'd say whatever they wanted. I never responded with violence. Maybe I should have. Saxe especially left me in no illusions that he couldn't wait for Cyprus and what he was going to do to me if he ever got the chance. And sure, homosexuality was illegal in the armed forces at the time, but that didn't stop it from being used as ritual harassment or humiliation. It wasn't a contradiction, or a paradox, or complicated. It was hypocrisy, which everyone saw, everyone knew about, but no one stopped.

Including me, but what was I supposed to do? Report it to my superiors who had already seen it and knew it was happening? They were impotent to stop the beatings on Op Granby, and how long would I have lasted in the block if I'd grassed Saxe and Harpen up to the scuffers, or got the station involved? I'd have had all of their mates out to get me, and it would have been in numbers. I wouldn't have stood a chance. Every time I unlocked my room door I'd be targeted. And even if I was moved to another squadron, the news would soon follow me, and so would the trouble.

Reporting it was out. It would have made things even worse.

How many other victims of abuse have said the same thing?

And if you didn't like it, then you were the one being thin-skinned or over-sensitive. It was only banter, so the argument went, so just suck it up.

Should I have responded by taking a swing at them? Because fighting was also illegal in the forces. Chinning the fuckers would have entertained the people watching, but the chances are that I'd have been charged. Saxe was probably better at fighting than me, and Harpen definitely was, so I'd have got beaten up as well as everything else.

Better to just avoid it as much as I could and wait to get the hell out.

Same shit, different day.

So all in all, I really wasn't looking forward to Olympus Rock. Planning ahead, I'd applied for a job as a civilian air traffic controller. Ultimately I didn't get it, but my best hope was that the entrance tests would be at the same time as Cyprus. Unfortunately they were held about a month after I came back, dammit.

One bloke on the squadron did manage to escape though. On the day we flew out, a Sherpa went to Watton to collect the married men who lived there. The duty driver knocked on Dave Luther's front door only to see a note. 'Dear 17 Squadron. Gone fishing, enjoy Cyprus.'

Blokes doing a runner really didn't happen very often, but Dave Luther's escapade was AWOL with a capital A, and it was done in spectacular style. He turned himself in a few days later and spent some time inside, but what the hell, he'd got out of Olympus Rock, which was what plenty of others, not just me, wanted to do. What a hero.

The trick to going AWOL was either don't get caught, or come back before you were dragged back. Ox told me a story about a bloke on 19 Squadron who'd gone AWOL for over a year. He left a handful of German coins in the waste bin in his room, then fucked off to Germany. When he reappeared one day in the flight office, he just asked if there was any mail for him. He was locked up for a while and then welcomed back to the squadron with a stellar reputation.

However, on the other side, a guy from 17 Squadron went AWOL and didn't come back on his own. He'd gone to ground in his parents' house, which was where ninety per cent of the sliders went, and it was always the first place the scuffers looked. He was brought back, locked up and then kicked out of the air force.

All of which made it so much more sensible to just do your time, even if you've PVR'd, even if you're facing daily persecution. No matter what kind of hell I was going through, I knew that trying to make a break for it outside of the law would have made it a thousand times worse.

And a criminal record, even a military one, would have done nothing for my job prospects in civvy street.

*

Unlike Op Granby, for Olympus Rock the squadron flew out to Cyprus by TriStar. Once there, a bus took us from Akrotiri to our home for the next month, a place just west of Episkopi called Radio Sonde. It was sat in the middle of the Cypriot bondu on top of a hill, a sun-blasted and rusting collection of six metal huts, one office block, showers and pretty much nothing else.

It was hugely ironic. On Granby when the shit was for real, it was laid-back and cushy. On Olympus Rock, not even close to being on ops, it was endless fuck-arounds, pointlessly long hours, shite accommodation and basic food.

Each flight was allocated a metal hut. Bunk beds, sleeping bags for a month and one wardrobe between two definitely wasn't a glamour detail and it definitely wasn't a holiday. We were up for PT in the mornings, but not hard PT, just pointlessly early in the morning PT that wouldn't even have made a spacey break into a sweat.

Then it was refreshing on stuff from the training book. Signals, weapons training, marksmanship principles, navigation, fieldcraft, first aid. And in a master class of utterly meaningless fuck-around, we also had to work on Saturday mornings. You might think I'm moaning about nothing, and you might be right in the big scheme of things, but really? In Cyprus? We must have been the only unit in the island's entire history to work on Saturdays. At least half of the squadron had done Granby and could see the differences.

And a different CO might well have had something to do with it. Squadron Leader Dillon, who'd been the CO when I joined 17 and who commanded the squadron for the Granby tour, had just been posted out. And apart from doing jack shit to stop the bullying, sexual harassment, initiations and sprog-bashing, he actually wasn't that bad. He was a real warlord, he swore in front of his troops, he was a bit like a Moshe Dayan without the eyepatch, and he stuck up for his men. Well, apart from the ones being bashed.

The new CO was…well…different.

But it was what it was, and the RAF Regiment remained constantly under-strength, possibly because of a combination of dumbass official decisions like Olympus Rock and sickass unofficial activities like Saxe and Harpen.

Even in the wilderness of Radio Sonde there was still a NAAFI hut. In keeping with the character of the place, it had a lopsided bar, a rickety pinball machine and a half-dozen mismatched tables. Vicar and I went there the first night. As soon as we walked in, Geordie, the sprog-bashing sweat who'd squared up to/mutinied in front of the corporals the last time we were in Cyprus, looked up from his beer and smiled. 'Hello, boys,' he crowed. 'Fucking wankers' and 'pair of sprog poofs' was muttered from most others, so we shipped over to the pinball table, thought small and avoided attention.

A new posting to A Flight was Dan Reid, a fresh-faced SAC from 58 Squadron, and although he definitely wasn't straight from Basics, it didn't stop Geordie from giving him a hard time and calling him a sprog. Dan quite rightly spoke up, saying he wasn't an LAC and he wasn't on his first posting. Geordie spluttered indignation and stood up. Eye-to-eye personal space contact came next, and it took a corporal to intervene, again, and keep it friendly. A year later, Dan had also put in his PVR.

Wonder why.

Most week nights on Olympus Rock, Vicar and I would walk down to Happy Valley, a leisure complex on the garrison with a sports ground and the odd bar and café. There we found a sports bar that was open to all units, more diverse and less threatening.

After lunch on Saturdays, it was free time until Monday morning. Radio Sonde was close to Limassol, and most of the squadron headed there for the bars and a chance to get with the women who were out from the UK on holiday. Some blokes hired rooms for the night, while Vicar and I instead went to Akrotiri and booked transit accommodation. It was free and it was safe. Kevin Costner was having a good year at Akrotiri's cinema in '92. We saw *JFK* and *Robin Hood, Prince of Thieves* and also *Star Trek VI*. Afterwards we'd relax at Lady Lampson's Club, a small coffee shop café next to the cinema.

For one night a week, there were no sweats, no sexual harassment, no threats of violence, no social exclusion, no bullshit.

But it wasn't like we didn't make an effort to socialise. We did. One night, the four tonner took an A Flight truckload to the Akrotiri NAAFI. Vicar and I went along as well, did the usual thing, stayed sober, stayed on the periphery and kept the fuck away from any trouble-radar signs of danger.

An Eng Flight corporal was the four-tonner driver, and there was room in the cab for three.

'Can Vicar and I sit in the cab on the way back?' I asked him. Cyprus it may have been, but a night-time trip back to Radio Sonde in the back of a four tonner was bloody cold in March.

'First come, first served, lads.' He smiled. 'And you're it.'

Result. After time was called, Vicar and I sat in the four-tonner cab and looked forward to a warm, comfortable trip back to Radio Sonde.

Until Harpen came out of the NAAFI and clambered up to the cab door like an oversized spider. 'Get out, you fuckers,' he growled. 'That's my spot.'

We kept the door locked. I wondered where the hell the Eng Flight corporal had gone, and we stayed put.

'Get out, now!' blazed Harpen, starting to get angry. 'I'm riding back in the cab and you two bent sprog fuckers are sitting in the back. Open the fucking door, now!'

I was starting to shit myself, but what the fuck, it wasn't Harpen's decision, and really, what was he going to do, smash the window?

'I won't say it again, you cunts,' he shouted, holding onto the cab structure like he was in a tree. 'Open this door or I'll smash the window and slash you fuckers.'

He wouldn't do it, he wouldn't. He was pissed and he was just beating his chest. He wouldn't do it.

Harpen switched on his bayonet face and pulled back his fist. His lips peeled over uneven teeth in a rictus snarl, and a mad gleam blazed in his eyes. Christ, the mad fucker really was going to punch through the window. Vicar and I looked at each other, nodded and unlocked the door. Harpen yanked it open, grabbed us one at a time and threw us out onto the road. Like a predator claiming his territory, he perched in the cab and folded his arms while Vicar and I fled into the bondu. Our bluff had been called and we were definitely the losers. The four tonner filled up and from our vantage point we saw that Harpen wasn't any happier for having the cab. As the four tonner filled up and we stayed put, I could see the corporal's indecision: wait for us to show up or head back?

'Chapel! Brindle!' roared Harpen. 'Get your fucking queer arses back here now!'

Yeah, right.

We waited for the four tonner to pull away, then got a taxi back to Radio Sonde.

We stuck to Happy Valley after that.

*

Back in the UK, there was a general election on 9th April. Before the squadron flew out we were told what to do to if we wanted to vote, although I'm not sure how many did. I didn't, but with my OU studies really starting to kick in, I was becoming more aware both of politics itself and what the parties stood for. I was starting to learn what things like minimal state, egalitarianism, sovereignty and power really meant. I was learning about liberal and conservative traditions and ideals, Marxism and social reformism. It was an avalanche of ideas that two months earlier I knew nothing about. We've all got our own views, and at that time mine started to change, grow and evolve.

It was springtime in Cyprus, not as hot as I remembered from Granby, but still a damn sight warmer than the UK, and there were the usual briefings from day one about sun protection. Sunburn was considered an avoidable, self-inflicted injury and therefore a chargeable offence. Very early on, OCA's back and shoulders turned lobster-pink and he was diagnosed with sunstroke, which in the military's eyes was subtly different from sunburn. Officers' privilege? Maybe.

OCA still hadn't picked up the habit of keeping his rifle in sight. One time on the range he again left it lying around. Harpen picked it up and totally obliterated the zeroing. OCA was normally a really good shot, but all he managed that day was to dig rounds into the dirt twenty metres from his firing point.

A great retreat for many of us, myself included, were Walkmans, and we all had our favourite music that got us through. For me, it was Ozzy Osbourne's album, *No More Tears*. Its title track was absolutely amazing stuff, well known as a single with its killer bass riff, but the rest of the album was also real quality. For that long, long month, listening to it was a salvation.

But there were two events from Olympus Rock that really stick in my mind. One involved Harpen, one involved Saxe.

Harpen was on A Flight, and Brown, the poor bastard who was beaten up on Granby to the point of near suicide, and who was still getting a hard time, was on B Flight. It turned out that while at Radio Sonde, Harpen had joined in with the abuse and whacked Brown. Brian Docherty, an A Flight SAC, decided that this reflected badly on A Flight and it was time to take action.

The specific action was to put Harpen before a kangaroo court, which is a completely unofficial trial with no legal basis and where the outcome is pre-determined. This meant that Harpen was already guilty. The whole thing was endorsed by Corporal White, and nobody outside A Flight's metal hut knew anything about it.

With fantastic irony, I was made prosecuting council.

I thought at the time that it was a pretty unusual response. I mean, yes, someone should have done something to help Brown, like maybe the officers or NCOs, but why help him now? The poor bastard had been taking shit for two years. No one had ever stepped in before, and no one on B Flight had ever given Saxe any shit for what he'd done to me. Brown and I were probably both on

201

a similar level of unpopularity, so I don't know what spurred this action. It may have been something as simple as a way to relieve the boredom.

Much like the violence and abuse, the retaliation was equally sporadic.

It was dark outside and Harpen came into the hut. At that point, half of the flight were on adventure training so there were about fifteen of us there. Harpen was asked by Docherty if he'd given Brown any grief.

'Yeah.' Harpen shrugged, drawling the words in his soft Irish accent. 'I gave him a backhander. So what?'

'You've made the whole of A Flight look bad,' said Docherty. 'You're out of order and you need to pay for what you've done.'

'Fair enough.' Harpen sat on a chair in the middle of the hut. There was no sense of malice anywhere, no sense of the hairs sticking up at the back of my neck, no sick feeling I always felt when Saxe came anywhere near me, a feeling that I was cornered, trapped. Whatever it was that was going to happen to Harpen, it wouldn't be violent. I'd seen the look in people when it was about to get nasty. The lip-curl, the sneer, the clenched fists, and it just wasn't there.

Docherty was the judge and he laid out the court's proceedings. Defence was followed by prosecution, then verdict and sentence, as though any of it would make a difference. Everything was already decided. The court was just a way to waste some time.

Defence council was Corporal White, who spoke up for Harpen. After he finished, it was my turn as prosecution. I started with a rip-off quote from *Tango and Cash*. 'Corporal White has spoken very eloquently,' I said. 'And I wish I could be as forgiving. But I can't, because this here is a kangaroo court and nothing Corporal White can ever say will change that. In fact, I direct the court to ignore his words. Harpen's guilty as fuck, so let's just get on with this.'

'Quite right,' said Docherty. 'Harpen, you're guilty of acting like a twat, and in doing so you've made the whole flight look like a bunch of cunts. Therefore, it is the decision of this court that the whole flight exacts punishment. SAC Harpen, you are hereby sentenced to lie on the floor of this very building and accept a queening from every man in A Flight. You will make no resistance and you will exact no retribution.'

I stared wide-eyed at Harpen. He sat in his chair, utterly calm, even laughing at the proceedings, and I wondered if he'd actually do as Docherty said. On the one hand, it seemed as though the whole flight was against him and he had no choice, but on the other hand, if he decided to challenge everyone to fight him, what then? I'd never actually seen him in action but I guessed he was pretty tasty. Would we physically force it on him? I didn't know.

As it turned out, we didn't have to.

Harpen stood up, then laid down on the concrete-slabbed floor, arms wide and looking as unconcerned as if he was lying on the beach. 'Let's get this over with,' he said.

It was one hundred per cent surreal, and Harpen was really lucky that half the flight weren't there, but that still meant fifteen arses were about to be rubbed in his face. Normally a queening involved alcohol, group chanting, violence, struggle and eventually, inevitable humiliation. This time it was orderly and actually humorous. For me there was a sense of justice. Harpen was being punished, not just for Brown, but for everything he'd done to me. It was payback time. We queued up and waited our turn. Then one by one, everyone in the hut from LAC to corporal stood over Harpen, dropped his shorts and queened him. Each time it happened there was a cheer and even Harpen laughed. Looking back, I'm amazed he took it so well, but many things in the Regiment simply defied explanation, and that night was one of them.

I'd like to hope that reading this, you haven't queened anyone yourself and you don't know what it's like. I can tell you that as well as feeling the facial contours of nose, lips and forehead from a very unusual perspective, if you're queening a man, then the best way to describe it is like wiping your arse with sandpaper, especially if, like Harpen, there was stubble and a moustache involved.

When it was done, Harpen went off to the shower block to wash. He came back minus his moustache. I'll leave it to your imagination to work out what he must have found lurking there after having fifteen rusty bullet holes rubbed in his face. I don't know if Brown ever found out what had happened that night in his name, and looking back as I write, it feels utterly weird to say this, but I hope he did and I hope he appreciated the gesture, if that's the right word to use.

It was rough justice, very rough justice. But in all my admittedly very short time in the Regiment, it was the first and only time I'd ever seen anything like that done in a good way. You might think that's weird. *I* think it's weird and I was there. But like I said, some things defy explanation.

The other thing that happened was worse.

My two main problems on 17 Squadron were Saxe and Harpen. They'd both been chasing me, stalking me, grabbing, groping and propositioning. All I'd heard from them for over a year by that point was that they wanted to have sex with me. However much I was told it was just a joke, it felt fucking real to me, and I was shit-scared that if they ever did corner me with nowhere to run, well, Christ knows what they'd have done.

Just for a laugh. Just for a joke.

And despite the moves I was learning at my Monday night karate classes, who was I kidding? If what was already happening wasn't going to trigger a response, nothing would. I wasn't aggressive and I never would be. At nine and a half stone, even when I was ringing wet, unless I was actually Bruce Lee, I was no threat to anyone.

And quite frankly, I wasn't Bruce Lee.

One night Saxe appeared at the A Flight hut door. And this time he wasn't just standing there, he was standing there naked, and he didn't look pretty. He stared at me with hooded eyes and his mouth hanging open. 'Brinders.' His half-whispered down-under accent was unmistakable. 'I'm here for you.'

I was like a rabbit caught in headlights. I always was when he pulled this shit, but at least he'd kept his clothes on before. This was sick and scary all rolled into one. Christ, I thought, could it get any worse than this? The bunk I shared with Vicar was in a corner, so my flight options were already short. He sashayed towards me, an utterly unattractive sight as his beer gut flopped and wobbled, and while Vicar was struck dumb, everyone else tuned in for the entertainment. Would I just take it like I always did, or would I lose it and fight back just this once? Everybody watching shouted encouragement, some for Saxe, telling him to fuck me, and some were telling me to be a man and stand up.

He reached the end of the bunk bed and stretched his arms out towards me. I tried to push him away. I stepped back but he followed. He grabbed my head, pulled my face towards his and tried to kiss me. I clenched my teeth so tight I thought my jaw would break. I felt his lips on mine, fucking gross. He tried shoving his tongue in my mouth, I kept my teeth clamped shut and struggled wildly. I closed my eyes and all I could hear were cheers as Saxe tried and tried to French-kiss me, like I was showing *any* sign of encouraging him, like I was showing *any* sign of wanting it. I don't know how long the bastard was there, but eventually he gave up and walked back out of the hut. I stood at my bunk, shaking. This had gone way beyond sexual harassment, this was sexual assault, no fucking doubt. As if the harassment wasn't bad enough, this was a whole world and universe worse. I felt dirty, used, violated. All the words that victims have used for years and were never heard, but always blamed for, I felt them all.

And all of it was done just to give the lads a laugh.

All for a joke.

Some fucking joke.

After Saxe left, a weird silence descended. I think even for a bunch of Rocks, there was a sense that it had gone too far, way too far. Of course, if you were to ask me, it had been going too far for over a fucking year. Docherty, who'd presided over Harpen's kangaroo court, called me over to his bunk.

'Are you all right?' he asked, displaying a massive talent for rhetorical questions. I didn't answer. I didn't talk, I *couldn't* talk. 'That was fucking awful,' he said, now mastering understatement. 'I gotta tell you, Brinders, I hated watching that shit.' *Really?* I thought. *Try fucking well feeling it!* 'I can't stand him, either,' said Docherty. 'But you need to deal with this yourself, and you need to do it properly. You need to fight that fucker and you need to twat him.'

Again and again those words from *An Innocent Man* crashed through my mind, 'You don't have to stand tall around here, but you've *got* to stand up.'

But that was the trouble. I never did.

Then another line washed through my head. 'Get yourself a piece and make a move.'

'He's right,' said Corporal White. 'Just fight him.' He shrugged. 'It doesn't matter if he beats you up. He'll leave you alone.'

It would have been nice if Corporal White had actually done a bit more than offer me verbal support *after* he'd watched me being sexually assaulted, but that's how it was. Looking back, and again, just like *An Innocent Man,* it all seemed very similar to prison. In that film, if a prisoner had a problem, it was up to him to deal with it, and he could expect no help or protection from the guards. And so it was in the RAF Regiment. The NCOs and officers, even if they knew it was going on, just like the last time we'd been to Cyprus, just like all the other times, and just like right then when a corporal had even fucking *seen* it, to expect them to actually do anything, that just wasn't the culture.

How do you feel after something like that? What do you do? Where do you go?

A few years later, and it wasn't even lyrics that perfectly expressed how I felt at that time. It was the WASP song, 'I Can't'. Blackie Lawless' wordless, barren scream completely summed up my sense of utterly hopeless helplessness. No words, just raw, heartbreaking emotion. It was everything I felt back then. And every time I hear that song, it takes me right back to that awful, horrible, bastard moment that no one should ever have to go through.

*

The next day at the range, Saxe was sitting with a group of B Flight SACs in the troop shelter. Thankfully he had clothes on this time. 'You hate me, don't you, Brinders?' He chuckled.

Get yourself a piece and make a move. The line from *An Innocent Man* shot through my mind.

I looked at him. I looked at my rifle. I looked at the neatly stacked ammunition on tables close by. I looked at all of the potential witnesses and then I looked back at Saxe. I thought about it all and I weighed up the angles and possibilities.

I thought about it.

And I wasn't for one second the first person to ever think about it. Plenty enough guys in the past had actually done it. During the

Vietnam War it happened so many times the US military even had a name for it: fragging. And less than a month after that shit happened to me, a British soldier in Northern Ireland shot and killed his sergeant major. There had been allegations of bullying at the time, and the soldier ended up walking free from court with a suspended sentence.

But I over-thought things way too much, and as usual I did nothing.

Which was probably a good thing.

And to give you some idea of just how screwed-up the military perception was, everything that happened to me was seen, tolerated, allowed, but not stopped. It was never stopped. But if two blokes were sitting on a bed and their feet weren't on the floor, that was considered to be an overtly homosexual act and expressly forbidden. So on a typical Olympus Rock evening I might be sitting on my top bunk, reading up on how politicians gave speeches, Vicar might be sitting on the same bed listening to his Walkman, and you can guarantee it would send the very next corporal who passed by into apoplexy. 'Get your feet on the floor, you fucking poofs!'

Bemused looks of disbelief would only wind them up more.

'Now, you pair of cunts, what the fuck are you doing, having a daylight gay orgy?'

But a naked Saxe trying to kiss me against my will, so utterly against my will, that's okay.

Six hundred quid to leave? An absolute fucking bargain. I'd have paid six thousand.

Not long after, Vicar and I were walking back from Happy Valley one night. Radio Sonde was locked up with a guard detail at the gates. On guard duty that night was Mike Ellis, a sweat from HQ Flight with a burn scar up his left arm that earned him the nickname Inferno. He gave us the usual shit about being sprogs and not mixing with the lads. This being the same lads who'd stood by and watched a full-frontal Saxe try and force his tongue into my mouth. 'You do know you're pissing a lot of people off,' he said.

Really? I thought. *Really, you wanker? I'm pissing people off, am I? And I suppose all those bastards who're the same rank as me, including you, you cunt, who've spent the last two years telling me how shit I am, you aren't beginning to piss* me *off?*

I thought it, but I didn't say it, as usual.

Just past the gates stood OCA, and an officer out at night was the last thing you saw. He called me and Vicar over. 'You two are a bit isolated on the flight,' he said, once we were out of earshot. 'But I can't help you, there's nothing I can do. If you don't change, you're on your own out there.' It was nothing we didn't know already, but even the illusion of our flight commander showing an interest in our welfare was now out of the window. Back in '92, duty of care simply didn't extend to 17 Squadron. 'What are you going to do?' asked OCA.

'They won't break me,' said Vicar. And he was right. They wouldn't, and they didn't.

'And I'm out in December,' I said. I was scared, I was sick of everything, I was so close to breaking, but fuck the lot of them. Fuck the bastard who did it, fuck those who watched and cheered him on and fuck every single one of my so-called leaders who did fuck all to help.

Vicar and I both knew the score, so I suppose it just made things official. The chain of command was washing its hands of us, but it wasn't exactly news. OCA was just the latest in a long line of officers and NCOs on 17 Squadron who'd done absolutely squat to look after their own.

For the rest of Olympus Rock, Happy Valley at nights and transit accommodation at weekends remained safe boltholes, and so was guard duty. Guard duty at Radio Sonde was a twenty-four-hour stint. Two airmen and a corporal, much like Fersfield, only the weather was better while everything else was shittier. The guard detail kipped in a tent behind the armoury, and let's face it, we weren't going to get attacked by anyone, so for me, it was ideal. I even did other people's guard duty for cash. They were only too happy to give me a tenner so they could drink in the NAAFI, and I was only too happy to take their money and get the fuck out of the way.

I pulled even more guard duty a few days later just for doing as I was told. We'd all been given a few days' down time in Happy Valley, whether it was water skiing, sailing, volleyball or other sports-type stuff. OCA said there was no pressure, we could just sit by the beach and do nothing if we wanted, so I chose to do exactly that. But it didn't last. OCA walked up to me as I was reading my book and relaxing. 'Brindle,' he said. 'If all you want to do is sit there and do nothing, you can do guard and let someone else spend some time down here.'

Result! Another night on guard duty was another night with no danger of any more shit from Saxe or Harpen.

*

Olympus Rock's final act was a two-day exercise. It started off with the whole squadron being trucked to a small military port where we boarded a landing craft.

A landing craft.

The last time the RAF Regiment had done a beach landing was probably Overlord, and we definitely weren't marines. Most of us hadn't even seen a landing craft, and we sure as hell hadn't had any prep, training or anything else. And despite the Health and Safety at Work Act having been around for eighteen years, by that point we weren't given anything in the way of floatation aids, life jackets, nothing. What we did have were weapons, blank ammunition, and enough kit and rations for a couple of days in the field. Anything that lent itself to sinking like a camouflaged stone, we were either wearing or carrying.

We trooped on board and were off. A cruise-and-return was out so I guessed a beach landing was coming up. It was a shame that no one had the first idea how to do one. Still, how hard could it be, right?

After a while the ramp came down and I did a massive double-take. The landing craft was still what looked like a mile away from the shore. What the hell did they think we were, the SBS? The crewman walked to the front of the craft, raised an arm over his head and with a judo-chop hand-strike, he pointed at the shore.

It looked a lot like an order to storm the beach, and we ran forward as one. The first five blokes jumped clear of the ramp and instantly disappeared into the sea. The crewman screamed, 'NO!', and the second row lurched back from the brink and scuttled away from the ramp. 'I was signalling the skipper,' shouted the crewman. 'Not you.'

The landing craft shifted into reverse and out in front I saw five soaking wet heads just above the water. At least they hadn't drowned, but they'd all gone right under when they jumped off the ramp. They were loaded up with kit and they'd had a luckier escape than a bat getting through an Ozzy Osbourne gig in one piece. I felt massive relief at seeing them still alive, and also that it hadn't happened to me. Along with the rest of the landing party I fell down laughing.

There were some simulated enemy ashore and they started firing at us. With a man on either side of the ramp returning fire, the landing craft approached the beach. I heard the sand crunching underneath the steel, and the crewman came back. 'Now you can go,' he called out.

We ran ashore and went to ground, a hundred per cent dry. I looked right and saw one of the five-man scuba squad, soaking wet and coughing his guts up. We shook out into sections and moved inland with no real idea of what was coming next, what we were doing or where we were going. We tabbed through the light-scrub bondu, and as the morning wore on a hill rose up in front of us. We got closer and it needed less and less of an archbishop's brain power to work out we'd be headed for the top. It was a hot, sweaty climb through long grass and dried-up bushes. Once there, an old Wessex helicopter was waiting, and we harboured around it as each section in turn was flown out.

The Wessex was a Brit-built version of the Sikorsky H-34, and even in '92 it was old. The loadie crammed eight of us in and we sat along a small bench either side of the hold, backs to the fuselage, toes in and looking at each other. A thin waist strap kept me in my seat. I put my kit on the floor and my feet on my kit. And that's how you flew Wessex-style. The loadie crouched by the open side hatch, and we were off.

The flight only lasted a few minutes but it was absolutely insane. The pilot flew so low he could have used his kite as a quad bike, hugging the hillsides, flying *underneath* electricity pylons and throwing us from side to side as though he had a dozen Stingers on his tail. One second I saw sky through the side hatch, then hillside. The loadie was laughing his head off while everyone else screamed in pure terror. Even Len Daley, our section corporal, turned greener than his camouflage.

The Wessex touched down and we gaggled out and collapsed into all-round defence. Slowly, my queasy guts subsided, I scrambled to my feet and we moved into the squadron's harbour for the night. Vicar and I still had our ACSKs from Granby, and they were put to good use as we cleared the scrub and set up our bivvies. We brewed up and waited until it was our turn to go on patrol.

It was dark when Len kicked us awake. We rolled up our kit and formed up. The temperature had dropped and it was raining. 'Even the weather hates us, man,' I said, imitating Neil from *The Young Ones*. Len looked at his map and we moved out.

By this point I had zero interest. As one of our corporals was fond of saying, I didn't give a flying monkey's fistfuck. It had been an absolutely shit month. We'd been pissed about more than usual and things had happened to me that I didn't even want to think about again. Now, I was wandering around the training area in the middle of the night on a pointless exercise, and on top of all that it was bloody raining. In Cyprus! It never rained in Cyprus, but it did when 17 Squadron came out to play.

We were walking in a roughly diamond formation. I fiddled aimlessly with the trigger on my rifle, and suddenly there was a loud bang and a muzzle flash lit up my BFA. The rest of the section instantly disappeared into the darkness and I was left standing up on my own, looking around and wondering where everyone had gone.

'It's okay, guys,' I whispered, sounding like a soggy hippy as the rain gently pattered down. 'It was me.'

'You wanker,' growled Len from behind a bush with a rain-soaked cockney accent. 'Form up, lads. Let's go.'

As dawn approached we went to ground near a ruined village that was slowly disintegrating into the bondu. The rest of the squadron was dotted around in the undergrowth. We crept along a wall, keeping low. On the other side were more sections, getting closer to the objective. While we were being as tactical as we could, maintaining cover and keeping quiet, a few yards away an officer from HQ Flight was standing on a large rock like a DP-clad meerkat, chewing gum and holding his rifle one-handed, pointed up at the sky. It was early morning and there was still some mist and condensation around, so I guess the rock he was standing on was damp and slippery. He suddenly lost his footing and fell flat on his arse, accompanied by a flight-strength ripple of tactically quiet laughter from one side of the farm wall.

Then the attack went in, and with a thunderflash as the go signal, we climbed into the nearest building, over a crumbling window ledge and took the house. It was empty anyway, so no real drama. There was some sporadic firing up and down the village and then it was endex. It was over almost before it began, and a definitely lower-key episode than the FIBUA attack we'd done at Sennybridge the year before. On the plus side, the weather was a bit better once the rain stopped, and we also had some rations to munch on as we waited to be trucked out and taken back to Radio Sonde.

So, finally, eventually, after an utterly shite month, there was only one thing left: an end of detachment piss-up. A Flight went to the Akrotiri Beach Club on Lady's Mile, and after everything else that had happened at Radio Sonde, actually, thankfully, there wasn't too much to say about it. The flight commandeered one long trestle table, and there was more or less a descending rank order of seating. Chiefy A grabbed his own stash of Coccinelle, and along with the sergeants copped one end. The corporals, SACs and LACs milled around at the other end. It was public, it was open air, so the risk of any bad shit happening was way low. But even so, when the four tonner came to take everyone back, Vicar and I still jumped out at the gates and headed for transit accommodation again. Just because nothing had happened up to that point, we weren't so forgiving, or gullible, to think that was it. Back at Radio Sonde, two of the guys grand slammed in their bunks in a typically 17 Squadron farewell to Cyprus.

And that was it. Olympus Rock was finally over. For years afterwards it remained the worst month of my life, and if I was isolated and introverted before that month happened, I was even more so afterwards.

Summer 1992

I didn't know it at the time, but Olympus Rock was the eye of the storm, and things never got that bad again. Cyprus is a fantastic place and Akrotiri had the potential to be an excellent posting, but for some reason it turned certain people on 17 Squadron into complete wankers.

By this point I was seriously damaged goods, and probably was long before then. Withdrawn, reluctant to communicate, nervous of my peers, just what you want from a soldier. Damaged, yes, but not completely broken, and still a hundred per cent stubborn.

Not long after the squadron returned, the station had its annual formal inspection. It had been deferred the year before due to the Gulf War taking a slight priority over bullshit, but it returned with a vengeance in '92. Cue loads more hangar polishing and kerbstone painting. And of course, it wouldn't have been the same without a bull night and block inspection. 'It's not a clean-up, lads,' said Seth, chuckling. 'It's a bull night. Ah! Ah! Ah!'

Just before the block was due to be inspected by the visiting top brass, it was looked over by the adjutant and Seth, and I was dicked to be a block warden. Like many things in the military, it was largely symbolic. When the block was inspected, the adjutant and Seth used pass keys to get into the rooms, and I was there to stand to attention whenever they walked past and also to make sure they didn't steal anything from anyone's room.

Like they were really going to do that.

And even if a sergeant and a flying officer actually did rob anyone, what the hell was I, an SAC, ever going to be able to do about it?

But what really pissed me off was the adjutant's reaction to one of the rooms he'd inspected, which belonged to Jeff Grant. Jeff was a real keen RAF Reg all the way bloke, whose room was like a shrine to the air force, with military prints on every bit of wall-space. 'There was dust along the top of his picture frame, Sergeant,' said the adjutant, indignantly. 'It's really not good enough when we've got an air officer inspecting the station. I want him to have an extra bull night and room inspection.'

I did my usual thing and kept it inside. Wisely this time. But what the hell, I thought. Who the fuck was the adjutant to come into our home and tell us we'd missed a bit of dust? Christ, we paid rent, admittedly not much, but we did. We paid the poll tax, and we had a bloody cleaner, which I suppose was paid for out of our rent. Just how minging could the place get? And even if it did, we fucking well lived there, not him.

Once I'd calmed down I realised that the military way and my way weren't going down the same path, and as I was leaving anyway, best to just count the days.

The inspection went well enough. Apparently the air officer was pleased, and the CO paraded the whole squadron to tell us it had been 'bloody marvellous'. It became his signature comment, and from then on if anyone on the squadron said 'bloody marvellous', you knew they were talking about the CO.

As 1992 progressed, politics actually impacted on the armed forces, which, compared to the rest of the country, was very rare. Options for Change kicked in and the forces were cut back, meaning a lot of army regiments were either amalgamated or disbanded. The navy and air force were also scaled down, two airfields in Germany were closed and the RAF Regiment started to see squadrons disbanded.

Every branch of the military was now scrambling to justify itself as the cuts began to bite. As a sweetener for two of the Germany squadrons being disbanded, the Regiment took over security at the RAF's three nuclear bomb sites, Honington, Marham and Brüggen. Termed 814 Duties, it was a rolling pattern of four days on, four off, then four nights on, four off. It wasn't a million miles away from the times the RAF Regiment used to guard the American cruise missiles at Greenham Common and Molesworth. It appealed to a lot of people, and Vicar was one from 17 Squadron who applied. I was glad he'd made the move and got the chance for a fresh start. He wouldn't be going there as an LAC, so maybe there'd be less shit for him to go through. He left 17 Squadron, and Knettishall, on his own terms, as his own man, which says everything about him and nothing about the wankers who tried to break him and change him. I wished him the best, but I had to accept I was losing my wing man, although it was now only months to go before I left.

214

For me, 1992's film of the year was *Wayne's World*. Following on from the success of *Bill and Ted* the year before, it showed just how accessible heavy metal had become in the late '80s and early '90s. Of course, metal was never a hundred per cent mainstream, but that was as close as it got. Sayings like 'schwing', 'party on', 'not' and the ever-present 'excellent!' were commonly used, at least by me and Vicar. And heavy metal itself was a living paradox. It glorified the individual, and in doing so, it united those individuals. It also had a double impact on me. It emphasised my individuality, which made my life in the military infinitely more difficult, but listening to it and seeing it live absolutely definitely got me through.

One such lifeline was on 19th June. I went to Birmingham's NEC to see Gary Moore. He was an amazing guitarist, he had a great voice, and along with his duets with Phil Lynott, I'd grown up with his classic album, *Corridors of Power*. 'Out in the Fields' is a colossal song even now, but by 1992 Moore wasn't doing metal any more, having evolved to playing blues. The first song of the concert was 'Cold Day in Hell', and the show just soared from then on. Blues was never my first musical love, it was always metal, but I still had a great night. Gary Moore, a huge talent, taken way too soon in 2008, aged just 58.

Away for a month

From mid-July, I managed to get away from the squadron, the hangar and Saxe and Harpen for a whole month. If there was a way to avoid it, I was all for it.

The first week was a trip to Catterick for my second shot at Peacekeeper selection, which since 1990 had changed a lot. Back then, 17 Squadron was the only Rapier squadron who had a presence. In '92, about half the guys there were Rapier. Another difference was the Head of Training Wing: it was Squadron Leader Dillon, our old CO from the Gulf, now promoted to wing commander. He gave his usual no-nonsense address at the start of the week: 'I'm a bit disappointed only one officer turned up, fucking wimps.'

The selection events were the same as before, half shooting, half physical. It was a really good week, although there was no way I was good enough to be selected. On the physical tasks I was in the middle of the pack, but my shooting was way down the list. Not that it really mattered. Even if I had made the list, they'd never give a PVR boy a jolly to the States.

One of the range tests was a Gimpy shoot. It started at 600 metres in full webbing, carrying a Gimpy and forty-five rounds in three strips of fifteen. The orders were to run to 500 metres, lie down and fire fifteen rounds at the target, run to 400 and do the same, and again at 300. Out of the forty-five rounds I fired, I didn't hit the target once.

I knew I'd never make the team but it was still a fantastic week. I didn't piss blood this time, and I really enjoyed the physical push. There were road runs, cross-country, runs with webbing and also running up and down the tank ramp on the CTA. In every one of the physicals I really went for it, raced for my best time, and given the competition – these were the best blokes in the Regiment, apart from me – it felt really good to be in the same ball park as them, in fitness if nothing else.

And strangely enough, no one gave a shit that in the evenings I was wearing cowboy boots and jeans.

*

The next week couldn't have been more different. I went to the University of East Anglia in Norwich for a week-long OU summer school.

The UEA is like a massive glass and concrete jungle, all paved walkways and open courtyards with high-rise modern structures. The whole thing was built in the same '60s style. I was allocated a room, I had a roof over my head and all meals were provided on site. In that sense it was a bit like being on base, although of course there was no one roaming the corridors wanting to strip me, grope me, or queen me.

And the people there were totally different. They came from all kinds of backgrounds, were all different ages and had all different views. It was a real eye-opener to hear so many people complaining about the government and really moaning about the recent election result. 'Why would *anyone* vote for them?' was a regularly asked question, which was something that would *never* be asked in military circles. It was a whole new insight for me, and I soaked up the experience. In the classes it was the same, with everyone expressing their opinions, saying what they thought, no arguments. If I'd had any opinions of my own to express, I would have, but at that time I was still working them out. And for a whole week there was no swearing. *That* took some getting used to.

The third week of my magic month away was at Fersfield. By this point I'd learned that Fersfield guard duty was another ideal and legitimate way to get away from the squadron. There was also lots of spare time and relative peace and quiet to catch up on my OU studies and assignments. In the two and a half years I was at Knettishall, I was on guard duty at Fersfield seven times. I don't know if that was a record, but it was a lot. It worked for me and I don't suppose I was missed back at the hangar. It was the usual quiet week. All the excitement would happen the next time I was there. Fersfield was followed by a week of annual leave and shipping some of my stuff back to my parents' house in preparation for December.

Alconbury Air Show

Before 9/11, there were air shows everywhere, every summer. Even Knettishall, a relatively small station, played host to one, but the American shows were enormous. With massive civilian footfall at any one of them, they were an ideal recruitment opportunity. Not in an overt way, simply a place for any unit that wanted to, to set out their stall and show the public what they did. Knettishall and Alconbury were relatively close to each other and 17 Squadron was the nearest Rapier unit, so when Alconbury did their air show on 22nd August 1992, A2 were chosen to deploy their Rapier kit by the runway.

We got there by mid-morning, so at lunchtime it was nosebag, USAF-style.

The Americans love to do everything bigger than everyone else, and their version of the Airmen's Mess was no exception. Even their plates were monster size. I put what was a normal meal on my plate and it only took up quarter of the available space. The word of the weekend was 'succotash'. I'd heard Sylvester the cat saying 'suffering succotash' in the Bugs Bunny cartoons, but I didn't know it was actually food. It was some sort of bean-mix, it was freely available at Alconbury and was instantly adopted as A2's go-to staple at mealtimes. It went with anything, and I had it with everything. Succotash? I liked it.

As well as the static displays, there was loads and loads of flying going on. Once that started, it was straight back to the kit, then taking it in turns to either track the kites as they flew by, or simply to watch the plane-porn flypast. An F-111 zoomed through the air, a Dutch F-16 crawled along the sky, practically sitting on its tail with its nose pointing upwards, amazing skill. There was a really scary rescue scene involving a downed pilot, which for the purposes of the display was a dummy. Attached to the dummy was a long line of rope that went into the air via a small balloon. Then a Hercules with a huge metal nose fork flew along and snared the rope. The dummy was yanked into the air as the rope caught, got dragged behind the Herc and then was winched into the cargo hatch.

218

If it was me, I might have preferred to walk home.

There were also two air display teams that day, the Red Arrows and the Patrouille de France, and we had ringside seats. Both teams did an amazing show, but in different ways. And I know a lot of people wrap themselves in whatever flag they want and say one team was naturally or traditionally better than the other, but personally I thought both were equally good.

The show ran for two days and we camped there overnight. We had our standard twelve-by-twelve tent set up, but right next us was an American medical unit with an absolutely lux tent. The groundsheet was some sort of foam padded thing, like a duvet, and they let us sleep in it overnight. We didn't need telling twice.

That night, Radio 1 was being played in the twelve-by-twelve. As I sat there and caught up on my OU studies, I was listening to that year's Monsters of Rock festival. It had been on for most of the day and I managed to hear WASP and Skid Row. WASP had recently released their brilliant concept album, *The Crimson Idol*, and for weeks I'd been driving everyone in the hangar mad by singing the chorus to 'Doctor Rockter'. They played it that night at Donington, and Skid Row also sounded awesome. I loved their singer's banter with the crowd. 'I'm gonna stay out here til they drag me offstage by my fucking ball-sack,' growled Seb Bach. Classic stuff. Their latest album was called *Slave to the Grind*. I loved it then and I still love it now, and a big chunk of it got played that night. But despite Seb Bach's comments, eventually they gave the stage over to Iron Maiden, that year's headliners.

Applying to become a nurse

Time was getting short and I still didn't know what I wanted to do with my life. My application for Air Traffic Control had crashed and burned, and unemployment loomed as a real possibility. Then, in late summer I chanced on an advert in the newspaper for student nurses. Anyone who had five O levels or GCSEs could apply. It wasn't something I'd even considered before, but I thought about it, thought about it some more, then thought to myself, why not?

Maybe I had a choice, maybe I didn't. But time, and options, were getting short. Either way, it seemed like something I could do, so I sent off the application. They gave a timescale for the recruiting process and I reckoned on an interview while I was still at Knettishall, so I applied to the nursing schools at Colchester and Orsett. I didn't know anything about either location, but one seemed as good as the other, and if it was a closer drive for the interview, fair enough. Of course, I then drew the usual comments about wearing stockings, all male nurses were gay, so I must be as well. I could have predicted every single one of the lines, but I really didn't give a shit. I had a couple of months to go and I was totally NFI by that point.

*

On 5th September, soon after applying for nurse training, I went to Birmingham's NEC to see Black Sabbath.

Black Sabbath, dude.

I'd last seen them when Tony Martin was their singer, back in 1989, and less than a month before I joined up. So there was a kind of diabolical symmetry in seeing them again just as I was about to leave. In 1992, they'd reunited the classic Mark 3 *Mob Rules/Live Evil* line-up, which included Ronnie James Dio on vocals. He was my absolute favourite singer and I also loved Sabbath whatever the line-up. As far as I was concerned, in the world of heavy metal you either got with the programme of line-up changes, or you missed out on some great music. And while the purists might have thought otherwise, Sabbath did some amazing stuff post-'79. The party definitely didn't end when Ozzy Osbourne left, and there was no way I was going to miss this gig. The latest Sabbath album,

220

Dehumanizer, wasn't their best, but live, it was incredible
Ronnie James Dio several times before, and Tony Iommi t
years earlier, but seeing them both on the same stage togeth.
chemistry was unbelievable, the truckloads of sheer talent between
them was beyond amazing. It was like I was watching *Live Evil*.
Brilliant.

Ronnie James Dio, a heavy metal messiah who passed away in
2010 aged 67. Rest in peace.

Final guard duty at Fersfield

My seventh and final stint at Fersfield for guard duty was in September 1992. I'd specifically asked for it to avoid having to refuse an order.

One of the sergeants had organised some sort of survival training session, involving killing and eating a rabbit in the field. To make it all work he'd bought a large supply of baby rabbits from all of the nearby pet shops.

I wasn't there, but I'm pretty damn sure he didn't tell the pet shop owners why he was buying them.

And quite frankly, I didn't want to kill a baby rabbit.

A few words are needed here about the RAF Regiment. The first part of the Corps' title is the giveaway. Sure, we worked outside the wire – sorry to disappoint the haters – but we were rarely so far from an airbase that ration packs would run out, or that resupply was so impossible or erratic that we'd have to lay snares and do a Lofty Wiseman on the local wildlife. So in the first place, there was absolutely no tactical reason for us to go out and kill lunch. Add to that my peace-loving world view and generally Regiment-incompatible outlook on life, as well as the fact that it was only weeks to go until I became a civilian. It meant there was no way I was going to kill an animal just to learn a skill that I would never, ever need. And even if it was World War Three the very next day, they were *not* going to chuck 17 Squadron behind the lines and turn us into Chindits, it just wasn't going to happen.

All of which meant that if I'd been there, it would have been a show of defiance. I'd have refused the order to kill the rabbit, there would have been all sorts of military ramifications and I'd have ended my illustrious RAF career in the Guard Room.

Which wasn't what I wanted to do, and really, what was the point of making an example out of someone who'd be long gone by the end of the year? So after a quiet word with the sergeant organising the whole thing, I was put on guard duty at Fersfield and everyone was happy.

Besides, I'd already done my share of animal homicide on the drive back from the pub in King's Lynn two years before.

The week on Fersfield guard duty followed its usual course. I was there alongside Trevor Vane, who I'd been on El Al with back at Basics, and a B Flight corporal called Spike. We wandered around the camp at night, checked that the doors were locked, prowled around barrack blocks that weren't and raided their insecure fridges for food. And then in the mornings, after the traditional breakfast in the Airmen's Mess, we either slept or watched videos. I brushed up on aspects of free trade and social reformism in preparation for my OU exam, which was scheduled for the following month, and nothing much else happened.

Until.

It was mid-afternoon and we were strictly on down time. The 'Guins and RAF Police had security during daylight, and we were relaxing in our crew room when the guard commander, a corporal, poked his head in the doorway. 'We need you lads outside right now.'

We picked up our rifles and rushed into the Guard Room, where a scuffer told us to follow him. We ran across the road and behind a high fence. I was wearing jogging bottoms, moccasin slippers and a T-shirt. Trevor and Spike wore Ronhills and dezzies. I peered through a hole in the fence, and at the gates was a lone male, standing in front of his car with a holdall at his feet.

'He's RAF,' said the scuffer. 'He's come from another station and he's saying he's got a bomb in the holdall.'

My heart flipped over and I felt it switch to rapid fire inside my chest. Bombs in bags were a very real threat with the IRA campaign still active. If there one thing we'd all had hammered into us since day one at Swinderby, at every guards and sentries brief, it was terrorists and bombs. We *all* knew the rules of engagement. This guy, air force or not, joking or not, had just turned himself into a legitimate target. If we thought his actions were about to endanger life, actions like reaching for his holdall with a supposed bomb inside it, then he could be shot.

One of the gate guards was trying to talk him down when he picked up the holdall and ran behind the guard block. 'Back inside, now,' snapped Spike.

We ran to the crew room, chucked on our uniforms and laced up our boots in Olympic time, then sprinted back to the Guard

Room. 'He's barricaded himself in the NAAFI,' said one of the guards.

'Let's go,' said Spike.

We rushed out of the Guard Room, across mowed grass borders and past empty buildings, then ran round the back of the NAAFI where Spike called us to a halt.

'Load.'

Three magazines clicked into three rifles.

'Make ready.'

Fucking hell.

The shit just got real, really real. The only other places I'd made ready was on exercise with blanks and on the range with live. We were metres away from a suspected bomber and we'd just made ready.

We moved round the building and knelt just outside the front door. The scuffers were already there, but then again they had a Land Rover. Spike spoke with the scuffer. 'The padre's inside with him,' he said. 'They're talking.'

Talking about what?

Trevor and I knelt in front of the door. My rifle was locked into my shoulder, I gripped the handguard, my finger hovered over the safety catch and my eyes were just over the SUSAT, fixed on the door to see who came out. What was going to happen next, I wondered. Shit. Christ on a fucking bike, I was weeks away from being a civvy and I was just about to shoot someone. The seconds stretched out in agonising silence while we waited, waited.

An RAF policeman came out first. He clocked three kneeling Rocks with rifles trained and held up his hands. 'Stand down,' he said. 'The bag's clean, he's coming out.'

'You sure?' asked Spike.

'We've got this, Spike. Stand your fellas down and get clear.'

Get clear. They didn't want us shooting him by mistake now that it was safe, and seeing three armed gunners as he was being led away might not have kept things calm. We took off and kept out of sight, while Spike watched from round the corner just to make sure. The Land Rover drove off with a disarmed bomber inside.

'Make safe,' said Spike.

A complete unload followed by a load. Magazine off, working parts to the rear, check empty chamber, check empty bolt, check no magazine fitted, bolt release, safety off, pull trigger on an empty rifle, safety on, fit magazine. My hands were shaking as I did it and I walked back to the Guard Room on jelly legs that barely carried me upright. What would I have done if Spike had ordered us to fire? I know what I'd have done. My training would have taken over, just like everyone said it would. I'd have been a good soldier and done it. I'd have shot that guy stone dead, and afterwards I'd have been messed up for the rest of my life.

And he would have died, too. There's no such thing as shoot to kill in the military. It's shoot to hit. Aim for the target, hit the target. It doesn't matter if your enemy's dead or wounded, they're out of the game. But at a range of less than ten metres, even a lousy shot like me wouldn't have missed. None of us would have missed, and no one survives three rounds to the chest from that close.

I wouldn't kill a rabbit, but I'd have shot a person.

I was so unbelievably glad it hadn't come down to it.

A few weeks later I sat my first OU exam, passing the module overall and absolutely nailing the free trade question. Rick Brindle, Open University undergraduate. I was on my way.

Gulf medal parade

In October 1992, it had been nearly two years since 17 Squadron had come back from the Gulf, but no one had been given their medals yet. And yes, we did return to the UK two months before it kicked off and we definitely did not come under fire, but if you did twenty-eight days either in theatre or were part of the show back home, then you qualified for a gong. If you *were* there after 16th January, you got a medal with a bar on the ribbon.

17 Squadron were due the medal, very much without the bar, and there was no shame in it. You went where you were sent, it's as simple as that. And home was where 17 were sent in November 1990. But we'd also put up with NBC suits that wouldn't have sealed with our respirators, jungle uniforms in a desert environment and more blue-on-blue sprog-bashing than *A Few Good Men*.

So we sure as hell deserved *something*. Shame it took two years to arrive.

On most other units, the gongs would have arrived in the internal mail, been stashed with the flight sergeant and then dished out at work. No fuss, no hassle. But not the RAF Regiment.

By this time about half of those who'd been on Granby had moved to other squadrons or were in civvy street. But for those who were still there, there had to be a parade, a presentation and even a special guest to dish out the metalwork.

Which meant lots of drill.

Bollocks.

If there was one thing I hated, it was drill. Mostly because I wasn't any good at it.

Even worse, all the practice was done in the hangar, which had these weird acoustics and echoes, combined with a SWO from the Highlands of Scotland with an accent you'd need an interpreter to understand. All of this meant that whatever order he gave, by the time it had echoed into my ears, the last thing it was was English, and the best I could do was guess what he said.

'Squadron!' he roared. 'Into line, @*&%£$^ turn!'

Everyone else understood and turned right. I tried my best, I really did, but I swore he said left. So while the whole of the rest of the parade turned right, I turned left, quickly realised I'd bollocksed it up and my ninety-degree turn swiftly changed into a two-seventy, while all around me laughter rippled up and down the parade line.

Oops.

Lesson learned, and on the day the parade went as rehearsed. A guest USAF lieutenant colonel who'd flown F-15s in the Gulf pinned our medals onto our chests. At each one of us he said the same thing. 'Well done, thank you.' There was a speech from the CO, although for once he didn't say 'bloody marvellous', and an air force photographer pictured each of us getting gonged. Everything that was happening now was happening for the last time, and that was the last time I wore my number ones.

Not long after the medal parade, I returned to UEA, not to study but to see the Quireboys – my last concert as a Rock. I'd seen them at the Reading Festival back in '88, and I liked them a lot. I also really liked their debut album, *A Bit of What You Fancy*. It was sleazy, bluesy, Stones/Faces stuff, and even better than that, they all wore cowboy boots! It was a world away from the huge arena-like NEC and Black Sabbath, but just as good in a whole different way. With two months to go before my discharge date and six weeks before my terminal leave, the next time I'd see a band my hair would be longer.

JMC, Scotland

JMC stood for Joint Maritime Course. It was a large tri-service, and often multinational naval/air exercise, held around the north coast of Scotland at the end of November every year. That was about as much as I was told, other than 17 Squadron were also taking part.

November + North Scotland = shite weather.

This was absolutely my last hurrah in the RAF Regiment, and what a cold, wet way to go. It was a three-day trip there and back, and 17 Squadron's part in the exercise was five days. We drove up from Knettishall, stopping at Edinburgh on the first night and Lossiemouth the second, before arriving at the high ground around Loch Ewe.

A2's kit was set up overlooking the loch. We parked the Land Rovers in a semi-sheltered, boggy depression on either side of the twelve-by-twelve tent, where we put the radio, chairs, and ate our meals. A striker tent was hooked up to the side of a Land Rover which served as the barrack block. Once everything was up and running, it was the usual endless generator checks to make sure the kit had constant power, and trying to keep out of the weather as much as we could. Although why we needed power for the kit was debatable because it hardly worked all week.

Rapier kits had differing levels of functionality called fireability. Fireability Alpha means everything's working well. Bravo, and the radar tracker is down, so you can only engage in daylight and only if you can see the target. Charlie, and the surveillance radar's out and you're down to the pointing stick or synchro-clutch to track the target. Fireability Delta means nothing is working, Eng Flight are needed right now, SHORAD is down to a Gimpy on a louch pole and you'd better hope there are no incoming Maverick missiles.

Of course, on exercise there were no incoming missiles, but there was plenty of fireability Delta. And it wasn't surprising. Rapier never travelled well. Sure, it *can* be hooked up to a Land Rover and towed all over the place, but once it gets there, don't expect it to work anywhere near properly for at least a week. It really is that temperamental. Or that fragile. Or even that crap. Once it settles down and gets a bit of love from Eng Flight, then it works a lot better, which lent itself much more to the RAF Regiment's world of point defence.

The highlight of the day was T's and A's. The rest of our time was spent on site admin, making sure the high winds didn't blow anything away and having to constantly pull the cam-nets back into place. The weather was absolutely, utterly shite, constant wind and rain that made Wales seem like nothing.

'Soon you'll be telling your civvy mates about all this crap weather you lived through, eh, Brinders,' said Harpen. Those of us who weren't on the kit were hunkered down in the twelve-by-twelve and sharing a hot meal. The tent was dry and the paraffin heater kept out most of the cold.

'I doubt they'll be too interested,' I replied. The memory of OU summer school was still fresh with me, as well as the diverse outside world, which really didn't spend too much time thinking about a bunch of rained-on Rocks. I'd had to explain to most people what the RAF Regiment actually was and did. And quite honestly, I'd be the last person to boast about it. Another crashing difference between me and Harpen.

'What do you mean?' Harpen's chest puffed out and his eyebrows met above his ginger-tache nose. 'You can wear your Gulf gong with pride and tell all them civvies that you're a veteran.'

'And how many civvies do you see wearing a bloody gong?' I asked. 'Christ, it's not like we even earned it.'

'Hey, Brinders.' Harpen's Irish accent took on a sharper edge. 'Stop talking that shit right now, all right. We worked fucking hard out there.'

'But we didn't actually come under fire, did we?'

'What the fuck are you talking about? We were fucking there.'

'Yeah, there,' I said. 'And we came back two months before it kicked off. So like I said, if we'd come under fire, then maybe we had a gong coming, but we didn't. All I'm saying is we didn't earn it.'

'You shut the fuck up right now, Brindle, before I kick the shit out of you.'

'Settle down,' snapped Murray, A2's new sergeant, who'd been posted in from one of the disbanded Germany squadrons. 'And change the subject. Brindle, generator checks. Harpen, secure the tent-lines.'

It was my last run-in with Harpen, low-key and almost anti-climactic, not that I was actually looking for any drama. For the rest of the exercise we stayed out of each other's way.

*

On exercise, the rules and regulations were never followed to the letter in terms of dress. As long as you were in DP, that was fine, which allowed for lots of after-market smocks to be worn. The same applied to your webbing. As long as it carried your kit and was either green, or DP if you were a real cabbage, no one had a problem with it. I pushed the envelope a bit on JMC with my headgear. I tied my sweat rag around my head and used Arnie's diagonal face-stripe cam-cream technique from the film *Commando*. On one occasion the 2iC visited the site. I was doing some admin in the distance.

'Who's Hiawatha?' he asked.

'That'll be Brindle,' Murray replied, with a sigh.

The 2iC walked away, shaking his head and muttering to himself.

Before being posted to 17 Squadron, Murray had done a few detachments to the Falklands, and down there, they know a thing or two about lousy weather. And with that experience, he brought with him two tank crew oversuits which were like fur-lined super-warm onesies that went over your uniform. Thanks to Murray, if you were on A2 and manning the kit you wore one, and they were amazing. Because let's face it, when you're on a Rapier squadron, it's not like any of this cool field stuff where you're running around and playing war and things. All you're doing is sitting at the optical tracker with your helmet on and waiting for the kit to alarm. Once, I tracked a pair of Buccaneers flying in at what looked like sea level, which was pretty awesome, but that was it. Ninety-nine per cent of the time it's utterly boring, and if I didn't have Murray's lux kit to wear I'd have frozen my nads off as well as being bored.

Not that it was ever actually completely warm, or dry. Anyone who's stagged on for more than an hour in crap weather knows that

230

whatever you're wearing, sooner or later the cold and the rain finds a way in. My lasting memory of JMC is standing at the kit in the pouring rain with nothing to do except wait to be relieved, when a Land Rover parked up in the low ground. The adjutant jumped out in his spotless windproof smock and strode around the site in his still-polished boots. He came up to the kit and posed for a picture next to the Gimpy, then looked down at my piss-wet-through, bedraggled appearance. 'Bloody hell, Brindle,' he said. 'You mean to tell me you're giving all this up to be a nurse?'

You're fucking A right I am, I thought, although all I said was, 'Yes, Sir.'

'You must be mad,' he said, before bounding back to his nice warm wagon.

A little over ten years later, he was commanding a squadron in Iraq. Fair play to him.

The exercise squelched to an eventual end, which then signalled the hardest part of a Rapier deployment: taking the kit out of action. It was bad enough putting a pristine, clean kit into action, but when it's covered in crap and the wet canvas is as flexible as MDF, and everything's wet and slippery as well as bloody heavy, you just can't get it put away quickly enough. We then had a short drive to the compound, which was a collection of wooden huts, but they had hot showers and bunk beds, which was a definite improvement on striker tents and damp DP. We were up early the next day and drove back to Knettishall via Lossiemouth and Edinburgh.

On our overnight at Lossiemouth we parked in and around 48 Squadron's hangar. Every spare bit of their tarmac had a filthy, rain-soaked 17 Squadron Land Rover and trailer parked on it, dripping mud everywhere and giving 48's WO palpitations. The squadron canteen was our bunk down room for the night. I copped a squat and then walked out onto the main hangar floor.

'Oi, slaphead!'

I turned around and saw Jimmy Hendricks walking towards me. I broke out the biggest smile I'd cracked since Basics. Fucking hell, Jimmy Hendricks. I knew he was on 48 Squadron, but I didn't think I'd see anyone I knew while I was there.

'All right, mate?' I said. We shook hands. If it had been twenty years later I'm sure we'd have man-hugged. I stepped back and

231

looked more closely. He was also in DP and actually pretty minging. 'Did you stow away with 17 last week?' I asked.

He laughed. 'Bloody call-out this morning,' he said. 'Just as it started raining. The fuckers kept us out half the bloody day. Jesus, mate. I bet you don't get that with 8 Wing and the Jags, right?'

'Right.' I laughed back, and it felt good to laugh. 'They never send us to Loch bloody Ewe in the middle of winter.'

'So how was Donington '90?' asked Jimmy. 'I was so looking forward to it when we bought the tickets on Basics.'

'Don't ask me,' I said. I didn't feel tired, didn't feel cold, didn't feel the ingrained dirt from a week's exposure to Scotland's winter. That's what happens when you see an old mate after two and a half years and all sorts of shit in between. 'I was at the Op Granby beach party. What about you?'

'Belize.'

'What was it like?'

'Fine til the Walkman ate my Yes tape. So what's happening, mate? What's next for you on 17?'

'Civvy Street in ten days.'

'Bollocks!' Jimmy took a step backwards. 'No way, man. Not you. I don't believe it.'

'Believe it, mate. I'm a PVR all paid up. I clear station as soon as I get back.'

'What are you going to do?'

'I've got interviews next week to be a student nurse.'

'Fucking hell, mate.' Jimmy smiled and shook his head. 'You sure know how to drop the news on a guy. Think of me out in Belize again next year.'

'Buy a new Walkman, you'll love it.'

'Hendricks!' a deep-boom voice that could only have belonged to a sergeant echoed around the hangar. 'You want me to wipe your arse for you as well?'

'Gotta go, mate,' said Jimmy. 'You know how it is.'

'I heard that. Take it easy, man.'

'You too.' Jimmy smiled. 'Stay in touch, you hear?'

'Roger that.'

I'd been on Meiktila Flight for just three weeks, but it was enough for Jimmy and me to bond and become lifelong mates, when all we had in common was a love of the same music and floor-length raincoats. As he disappeared into the hangar to do his sergeant's bidding, I felt a warm rush of friendship flowing through me. I wasn't expecting to meet Jimmy, and I definitely wasn't expecting the strength of feeling when really, we'd only been on the same flight for a short while more than two years earlier.

In that sudden blast of positivity, of time-defying friendship, one small moment told me that not everything in the RAF Regiment was crap. It was a surprising but still thoroughly good feeling. There was no going back, though, and I knew I was doing the right thing. Why the fucking hell couldn't they have been that accepting on 17 Squadron?

Endex

From Lossiemouth the roads took us ever south, and as one filthy Land Rover after another rolled through the gates at Knettishall, past the Javelin gate-guard and then on into B Hangar, there was only one question in my already civilian mind: when can I start my clearance card? A clearance card was a blue, A5-sized card, and once it collected the required signatures, it meant I'd be free to leave the station, I wouldn't be chased and brought back by the RAF Police, and more importantly, I'd receive my final month's salary.

Murray made a very reasonable deal. As soon as the kit was turned around, which meant cleaned, all parts repaired or replaced and ready for an immediate deployment, then I could clear.

Which was fine by me, and that's what happened.

I didn't know if I was supposed to, but the first clearance signature I got was after I returned my uniforms. That meant I had to wear civilian clothes for my last few days. It lent a surreal touch to the morning parades as I stood alongside the rest of the flight, them in OGs and jumpers, me in my hippy/heavy metal civvies. Nothing ever looked as stupid as me screaming out 'Corporal!' as my name was called out, then slamming my cowboy boot into the concrete hangar floor as I stood to attention, wearing faded jeans and a Baby Animals T-shirt.

I foreswore the usual leaving tradition of beer call and figurine, even if I had paid for it. Everyone put two quid a month into the flight fund, which bought a stock of beers, as well as a pewter figurine of a gunner, one of which was given to you when you left the squadron. No one ever got hammered at a hangar beercall, it was just a few tins in the squadron canteen, while the real carnage happened later on at the NAAFI. I didn't want a final leaving present from Saxe or Harpen, so thought it best just to leave quietly.

No beercall, no figurine, no leaving do. I just left.

I think I did it on good terms with most. There were lots of handshakes and good lucks on my last day, although that might well have been combined with glad to see the back of me. It was the end of November 1992, and my accumulated annual leave ran until 17th December, my last official day.

So what had I achieved?

I'd got through Basics and earned the right to wear RAF Regiment on my uniform. I got through Rapier Training, I ran for my squadron and my station, I did Peacekeeper selection, I did a tour of duty, I did a 23-mile Bergen run. I went wherever I was sent and I did whatever I was told.

But it wasn't enough. It would never be enough. I was leaving the RAF Regiment because the contradictions between what I was and what I had to be would never work.

So for me, it was the right thing to do.

In early December I interviewed for nurse training and was offered a place at North Essex Institute for Health Studies, Colchester, to train as a registered nurse. I was due to start on 28th March 1993.

A year after my darkest moment on Olympus Rock, I started a completely different chapter in my life.

Aftermath

I was way too much of an individual to have ever joined the armed forces, and I'd be the first to admit it. My friends at school, way, way back in another world, had been right, I shouldn't have done it. I'd finally worked out what people meant when they said that some things aren't for everyone, and I accept that without reservation. It wasn't for me, but it doesn't make either my experience or my opinion irrelevant.

So, having read this far, and you might disagree with me here, but I'm not actually anti-forces, I'm not anti-RAF Regiment, I'm not even anti-17 Squadron. What I'm dead set against though is all the unofficial sprog-bashing, bullying crap that the twats who call themselves old sweats think they have a right to dish out. Because you know what, as unsuited as I was to the RAF Regiment, I might, just might, have been able to make a go of it otherwise. Instead, for two and a half years I turned the other cheek for a quiet life, and I paid for it with my dignity.

I didn't do it again, and I've never been bullied since.

And if all that crap is such a good thing, why isn't it official policy? If it's such a good thing, why don't they do it on Basics? Why doesn't it happen in the hangar in full view of everyone?

Because here's the truth: it's not a good thing. It's divisive, it does nothing to make the poor bastard they're victimising feel like part of the team, and it just perpetuates a whole load of utterly sick and twisted shit.

It's also illegal. And not just military illegal. Proper, real, law of the land illegal.

Now, I'm all for an aggressive, efficient and ruthless military, but I'm really not so sure that queening, stripping and terrorising the new guys is the best way to achieve it. Especially when those new guys have already earned the right to be there by passing Basics.

And it's not like it's actually preparing you for the rigours of warfare either. Because really, when, in the entire history of humans killing humans, has one side ever advanced towards the

236

enemy stark naked and then propositioned them for sex? And when was the ultimatum 'surrender or be queened' ever dished out?

Unfortunately though, you also have to ask the question: if it's supposed to be officially frowned on and unacceptable, why has it gone on since the year dot and why is it still going on?

Because no matter what the official line is, it only takes one arsehole who gets off on that shit to be promoted, and they'll make sure it never goes away, not completely, not ever.

I'd also like to think that maybe the sweats would have developed some perspective that comes with age, but that would be a mistake. On an RAF Regiment social media site, one of them recently described 17 Squadron as a unique collection of men doing manly things when manly things were tolerated, and Saxe was one of many who actually said that 17 Squadron was good times.

Good times?

I'm sorry, but anyone who thinks eighteen months of inflicting sustained sexual harassment and assault on someone is good times *really* needs to have a word with themselves.

And you might well say that this book is set thirty years ago, so what's the relevance now? And you'd also be right. You might say that it wouldn't happen now. Well, regardless of what happens now, it shouldn't have happened then, but it bastard well did. How many other poor fuckers went through something that shouldn't have happened? And does it really not happen now?

Wishful thinking.

In March 2021, an article was run in a daily newspaper about an initiation ceremony. It involved the RAF Regiment's Support Weapons Flight and an end of course party, where some poor bastard apparently had the ball end of a mortar tube shoved up his arse.

Video footage kind of confirms that it actually happened.

How much of it was consensual, who can say? Going back to my ritual stripping, these incidents usually happen within a grey area of drunken consent, coercion and absolutely no fucking choice.

Perhaps unsurprisingly, there was a swift consensus among online Regiment bodies to say absolutely nothing about the incident.

But why?

If you think there was nothing wrong with it, shout it from the rooftops with pride, and if you don't agree with it then call it out. But playing the middle ground, sweeping it under the carpet as though it never happened will just give sickass practices like this somewhere to hide. A lot of the comments at the time from the Regiment community weren't so much critical of the incident, more that it was filmed and leaked to the press; not that it happened, but that they were caught. And all that does is give shit like this a dark space to carry on.

I wasn't even going to tell my story until that incident happened, and then I just couldn't keep it quiet.

And because the RAF in general, and the RAF Regiment in particular, did what it did best, which was pretend it didn't happen and not talk about it, it was left to Arrse, the army's unofficial web forum, to host the debate. And they were spot on, saying that when you mix immaturity, alcohol, mob mentality, sexual arousal and bullying, shit like this will never go away.

In fact, the armed forces are probably the most fertile ground for it, as the military is all about following orders, doing what you're told, smothering individual thought, going along with the crowd.

And don't think it's just an air force thing, or even just a British thing. The Americans call it hazing, and it comes with the risk of fragging. The Russians call it the Reign of the Grandfathers. Do enough digging and you'll probably find there's a name for it, and a history of it, in every armed service on the planet.

Because no matter how much the military say they'll stamp this shit out, everyone in uniform is predisposed to doing it. Sure, some things *have* changed. Now, anyone can join any branch of the military regardless of their sexuality, and that's a good thing. Now, women can join the combat arms alongside men, and that's also a good thing. But like the song says, the more things change, the more they stay the same, and the dark underside of military traditions remain.

Every now and then stories like this will appear in the media. Sometimes the army, sometimes the navy or marines, and sometimes the RAF or the Regiment. What you see on the television or read in the papers, that's just a small part of it.

There's so much more going on that you'll never see. Google military suicide and see what comes up. For sure, some of it may be down to PTSD after a tour of duty, but all of it? Dig a little deeper and see what you get. Deepcut is the most notorious incident in the UK but it sure as hell isn't, wasn't and sadly won't be, the only one.

And to say that it was all just high spirits and that no one really meant any harm, that's bollocks. Abuse in any form or description is as defined by the victim, not the perpetrator. If it wasn't, then every sick, twisted, bastard predator out there could simply say they didn't mean it, and they'd get away with it.

So, if you're thinking of joining up, you'll never get told about any of this in the recruiting office, but you need to know it exists. My advice: ask yourself if you can live with it. Even if you're lucky enough not to encounter it, don't kid yourself that it's not real. You won't be able to stop it from happening and you might even find yourself taking part. If you're okay with that, fair enough. But be aware that as much as going to war, maybe having to kill an enemy, obeying every order you're given, going wherever you're sent, this is as big a part of forces life as wearing a uniform, or saluting, or swearing.

And of course there is a counter-argument that it's actually acceptable, that if you're going to have to go into harm's way to do harm to other people, you need to be tough enough to take a bit of bullying. And anyway, it's all just part of the team building/bonding process. Personally, I think that's a bullshit argument. What I saw and what happened to me did nothing to make me feel like I was part of a team, quite the opposite in fact. I think if you subject anyone to that kind of humiliation, all you're doing is giving them the ultimate motivation to blat a round into you the first/next time you're live armed or on ops. So, if anyone is reading this and thinking about being, or actually *is*, a wanker to their troops, always remember this: the ultimate retaliation *has* happened before. Just saying.

And maybe it does get clamped down on a lot harder than it did in the past, but that's still after the event, which means it's still happening. And it's kind of too late to be doing something about it then. The damage has already been done. Believe me, I know.

But when it's all said and done, and as wrong as I was for the job, could I have done it for real?

I don't know.

I didn't come under fire, so I never really answered that defining question. I don't know how I'd have performed if I'd really faced danger, doing what soldiers have to do. I'll never really know if I had it in me. But at the same time, I'm glad I never had to take another life.

Both emotions are just different sides of the same coin. The contradictions of my mis-chosen career were too big to overcome at the time, and they follow me through my life.

And after all that, after everything, were there any positives? Well, if it hadn't rolled the way it had, I'd never have met my partner, my true soul mate. Anything else? Sure, Norwegian Army shirts are an ideal base layer when riding a motorbike. Serving in the forces also got me membership of the Victory Services Club, which is an absolute lux place to stay in London. And as a writer, it gave me the insights to create the character Sean Sawyer in my *Cold Steel* novels. For any *Cold Steel* readers with a real eye for detail, you might notice the odd reference to other characters wearing crossed rifle badges. Now you know where they came from. And if anyone's read *Cold Steel and the Underground Boneyard*, you'll now know a lot more about the origins of queening, which actually had nothing to do with the retired Spanish Mafia.

And finally, if you've got long hair and you're joining up, it's going to get cut off anyway, so do yourself a real big favour and get the job done the day before.

Dismissed

Cold Steel on the Rocks

Rick Brindle

When the pirate Blackbeard buried his treasure, he could never have imagined that it would fall to the heavy metal band, Cold Steel, to come looking for it.

Cold Steel, high-octane British rockers who came close to legendary status, until the release of their fourth album, when their excesses send them spiralling into terminal decline.

Struggling small-time band manager Johnny Faslane, in the right place at the right time, lands the dream job of managing Cold Steel, and then has the seemingly impossible mission of turning the band around.

Cold Steel's singer, Maxwell Diabolo, claims to have a treasure map that he thinks will lead him to Blackbeard's lost riches.

With the band bent on a terrifying path of self-destruction, Johnny wonders if they will even complete the tour, much less get to the Caribbean to embark on a treasure hunt.

Against all expectations, the tour ends on a high and they sail halfway around the world chasing a long-dead pirate's map. Once there, it seems as though they were safer on a decaying tour, as they face their biggest challenge.

Only the combined talents of Cold Steel and Johnny Faslane can stop a war, and save their own skins.

We Are Cold Steel

Rick Brindle

A day after their historic concert on the Caribbean island of St Clements, heavy metal band Cold Steel are heroes. Now, all they have to do is stay out of trouble and enjoy a well-earned holiday until they start work on their next album.

Except that the owner of the recording studio hates all things Cold Steel.

Except that Cold Steel's record company has blackmailed the studio into accepting them.

Except that not all reporters are as friendly as band manager Johnny Faslane's girlfriend, Rachel Shaw.

With a tight deadline, Cold Steel have to get the next album out before their tour starts. They can't afford any delays, and Johnny has his work cut out keeping the band in line.

Feral former soldiers, reporters with an agenda, cake-obsessed studio execs and international criminals all work their way into the mix as the band hurtle from one improbable incident into another. They just want to meet their deadlines, but it seems that everyone else is out to stop it happening.

Can the band get the album recorded on time? Will it ever get released? And what will happen as their upcoming tour approaches? With friends and enemies in the most unlikely places, events unfold in a way that could only ever happen to Cold Steel.

We Are Cold Steel is the explosive sequel to Rick Brindle's acclaimed novel, Cold Steel on the Rocks.

Cold Steel and the Underground Boneyard

Rick Brindle

Cold Steel are back!

Their new album has just been released. Their previously cancelled Spanish tour dates have been rearranged, with the female trio and Spain's biggest metal band, Damas Infernales, supporting.

Cold Steel's biggest asset though, is Johnny Faslane, their brutally talented manager.

But even Johnny can't fully eliminate Cold Steel's innate ability to spectacularly destroy their prospects, and even before their second concert ends, the tour is scrapped after an ill-advised trip back to the eighties, and the band are put into creative deep freeze by their record company. Only an unprecedented event and a lot of money can possibly turn their fortunes around.

Like a five hundred year old treasure hoard that a long dead pirate once offered in return for his life, treasure that has never been found.

Cold Steel find a vital clue that gives them a head start in the search for the missing treasure and they seize on their one chance to prove that even spoilt rock stars can actually do something for themselves.

At least, that's their plan, and it puts Johnny Faslane in a race against time to find Cold Steel before they engineer the mother of all musical disasters.

And it's not just the clock that Johnny has to fight. There are also two vengeful bands out for piece of Cold Steel, enraged mob family members and a reporter with a grudge.

It was never going to be easy, but now, is it even possible?

Printed in Great Britain
by Amazon

27023989R00138